experiment
CENTRAL

experiment CENTRAL

P-Z volume 6

understanding scientific principles through projects

M. Rae Nelson

Allison McNeill, Project Editor

Detroit • New York • San Diego • San Francisco • Cleveland • New Haven, Conn. • Waterville, Maine • London • Munich

Experiment Central, Volumes 5 and 6

M. Rae Nelson

Project Editor
Allison McNeill

Permissions
Margaret Chamberlain

Imaging and Multimedia
Kelly A. Quin, Christine O'Bryan

Product Design
Eric Johnson, Tracey Rowens, Cynthia Baldwin

Composition
Evi Seoud

Manufacturing
Rita Wimberley

LIBRARY OF CONGRESS CATALOGING-IN-PUBLICATION DATA

Loret, John.
Experiment central: understanding scientific principles through projects / John Loret, John T. Tanacredi.
      p. cm.
Includes bibliographical references and index.
Contents: v. 1. A-Ec – v. 2. El-L – v. 3. M-Sc – v. 4. So-Z
Summary: Demonstrates scientific concepts by means of experiments, including step-by-step instructions, lists of materials, troubleshooter's guide, and interpretation and explanation of results.
ISBN 0-7876-2892-1 (set). – ISBN 0-7876-2893-X (v. 1) – ISBN 0-7876-2894-8 (v.2)– ISBN 0-7876-2895-6 (v.3) – ISBN 0-7876-2896-4 (v. 4)
1. Science-Experiments-Juvenile literature. [1. Science-Experiments. 2. Experiments.] I. Tanacredi, John T. II. Title.
Q164 .L57 2000   199-054142
507'.8-dc2

ISBN 0-7876-7735-3 (set); ISBN 0-7876-7615-2 (volume 5); ISBN 0-7876-7622-5 (volume 6)

Printed in the United States of America
10 9 8 7 6 5 4 3 2 1

contents

Volume 5: A–O

contents

experiment
CENTRAL

Volume 6: P–Z

experiment
CENTRAL

reader's guide

Experiment Central: Understanding Scientific Principles Through Projects provides in one resource a wide variety of science experiments covering nine key science curriculum fields—Astronomy, Biology, Botany, Chemistry, Ecology, Food Science, Geology, Meteorology, and Physics—spanning the earth sciences, life sciences, and physical sciences.

Experiment Central, Volumes 5 and 6, a continuation of U•X•L's four-volume base set, presents fifty-four new experiments and projects for students in twenty-seven subject-specific chapters. Chapters, each devoted to a scientific concept, include: Air and Water Pollution, Caves, DNA, Fungi, Periodic Table, Storms, and Time. Two experiments or projects are provided in each chapter.

Entry format

Chapters are arranged alphabetically by scientific concept and are presented in a standard, easy-to-follow format. All chapters open with an explanatory overview section designed to introduce students to the scientific concept and provide the background behind a concept's discovery or important figures who helped advance the study of the field.

Each experiment is divided into eight standard sections designed to help students follow the experimental process clearly from beginning to end. Sections are:

- Purpose/Hypothesis
- Level of Difficulty
- Materials Needed
- Approximate Budget
- Timetable
- Step-by-Step Instructions
- Summary of Results
- Change the Variables

Each chapter also includes a "Design Your Own Experiment" section that allows students to apply what they have learned about a particular concept and to create their own experiments. This section is divided into:

- How to Select a Topic Relating to this Concept
- Steps in the Scientific Method
- Recording Data and Summarizing the Results
- Related Projects

Concluding all chapters is a "For More Information" section that provides students with a list of books and Web sites with further information about that particular topic.

Special Features

- A **"Words to Know"** section runs in the margin of each chapter providing definitions of terms used in that chapter. Terms in this list are bolded in the text upon first usage. A cumulative glossary collected from all "Words to Know" sections in the twenty-seven chapters is included in the beginning of each volume.

- **Experiments by Scientific Field** index categorizes experiments by scientific curriculum area. This index cumulates all 154 experiments across the six-volume series.

- **Parent's and Teacher's Guide** recommends that a responsible adult always oversees a student's experiment and provides several safety guidelines for all students to follow.

- Standard sidebar boxes accompany experiments and projects:

  "What Are the Variables?" explains the factors that may have an impact on the outcome of a particular experiment.

  "How to Experiment Safely" clearly explains any risks involved with the experiment and how to avoid them. While all experiments have been constructed with safety in mind, it is always recommended to proceed with caution and work under adult supervision while performing any experiment (please refer to the Parent's and Teacher's Guide on page xv).

  "Troubleshooter's Guide" presents problems that a student might encounter with an experiment, possible causes of the problem, and ways to remedy the problem.

- Approximately **80 photographs** enhance Volumes 5 and 6.

- Approximately **170 drawings** illustrate scientific concepts and specific steps in the experiments, helping students follow the experimental procedure.

Four indexes, which cumulate all 154 experiments across the six-volume series, conclude each volume:

- **Budget Index** categorizes experiments by approximate cost. Budgets may vary depending on what materials are readily available in the average household.
- **Level of Difficulty Index** lists experiments according to "Easy," "Moderate," "Difficult," or a combination thereof. Level of difficulty is determined by such factors as the time necessary to complete the experiment, level of adult supervision recommended, and skill level of the average student. Level of difficulty will vary depending on the student. A teacher or parent should always be consulted before any experiment is attempted.
- **Timetable Index** categorizes each experiment by the time needed to complete it, including setup and followthrough time. Times given are approximate.
- **General Subject Index** provides access to all major terms, people, places, and topics covered in *Experiment Central.*

Acknowledgments

A note of appreciation is extended to the *Experiment Central* advisors, who provided their input when this work was in its formative stages:

Teresa F. Bettac
Middle School Advanced Science Teacher
Delaware, Ohio

Linda Leuzzi
Writer, Trustee of The Science Museum of Long Island

David J. Miller
Director of Education

The Science Museum of Long Island

The author also wishes to acknowledge and thank Joyce Katz, Cindy O'Neil, and Alana Brette Nelson for their contributions to the experiments in Volumes 5 and 6, as well as science copyeditor Chris Cavette and illustrator Temah Nelson for their contributions to *Experiment Central,* Volumes 5 and 6.

Comments and Suggestions

We welcome your comments on *Experiment Central*. Please write: Editors, *Experiment Central*, U•X•L, 27500 Drake Rd., Farmington Hills, Michigan, 48331–3535; call toll free: 1–800–877–4253; fax: 248–699–8097; or send e-mail via http://www.gale.com.

parent's and teacher's guide

The experiments and projects in *Experiment Central* have been carefully constructed with issues of safety in mind, but your guidance and supervision are still required. Following the safety guidelines that accompany each experiment and project (found in the "How to Experiment Safely" sidebar box), as well as putting to work the safe practices listed below, will help your child or student avoid accidents. Oversee your child or student during experiments, and make sure he or she follows these safety guidelines:

- Always wear safety goggles if there is any possibility of sharp objects, small particles, splashes of liquid, or gas fumes getting in someone's eyes.

- Always wear protective gloves when handling materials that could irritate the skin.

- Never leave an open flame, such as a lit candle, unattended. Never wear loose clothing around an open flame.

- Follow instructions carefully when using electrical equipment, including batteries, to avoid getting shocked.

- Be cautious when handling sharp objects or glass equipment that might break. Point scissors away from you and use them carefully.

- Always ask for help in cleaning up spills, broken glass, or other hazardous materials.

- Always use protective gloves when handling hot objects. Set them down only on a protected surface that will not be damaged by heat.

parent's and teacher's guide

- Always wash your hands thoroughly after handling material that might contain harmful microorganisms, such as soil and pond water.
- Do not substitute materials in an experiment without asking a knowledgeable adult about possible reactions.
- Do not use or mix unidentified liquids or powders. The result might be an explosion or poisonous fumes.
- Never taste or eat any substances being used in an experiment.
- Always wear old clothing or a protective apron to avoid staining your clothes.

experiments by scientific field

Chapter name in brackets, followed by experiment name; *italic* type indicates volume number, followed by page number; **boldface** volume numbers indicate main entries in *Experiment Central*, Volumes 5 and 6.

Astronomy

Biology

Botany

**experiments
by scientific
field**

Ecology

experiment
CENTRAL

Food Science

Geology

Meteorology

Physics

experiments by scientific field

words to know

A

Absolute dating: The age of an object correlated to a specific fixed time, as established by some precise dating method.

Acceleration: The rate at which the velocity and/or direction of an object is changing with respect to time.

Additive: A chemical compound that is added to foods to give them some desirable quality, such as preventing them from spoiling.

Air: Gaseous mixture that envelopes Earth, composed mainly of nitrogen (about 78 percent) and oxygen (about 21 percent) with lesser amounts of argon, carbon dioxide, and other gases.

Air density: The ratio of the mass of a substance to the volume it occupies.

Air mass: A large body of air that has similar characteristics.

Air pressure: The force exerted by the weight of the atmosphere above a point on or above Earth's surface.

Alkali metals: The first group of elements in the periodic table, these metals have a single electron in the outermost shell.

Alkaline: A substance that is capable of neutralizing an acid, or basic. In soil, soil with a pH of more than 7.0, which is neutral.

Amino acids: The building blocks of proteins.

Angiosperm: A flowering plant, which has its seeds produced within an ovary.

experiment
CENTRAL

Anther: The male reproductive organs of the plant, located on the tip of a flower's stamen.

Antibiotic resistance: The ability of microorganisms to change so that they are not killed by antibiotics.

Antibiotics: A substance produced by or derived from certain fungi, bacteria, and other organisms that can destroy or inhibit the growth of other microorganisms; widely used in the prevention and treatment of infectious diseases.

Antioxidants Used as a food additive, these substances can prevent food spoilage by reducing the foods exposure to air.

Atmosphere: Layers of air that surround Earth.

Atom: The smallest unit of an element, made up of protons and neutrons in its center, surrounded by moving electrons.

Atomic mass: Also known as atomic weight, the average mass of the atoms in an element; the number that appears under the element symbol in the periodic table.

Atomic number: The number of protons (or electrons) in an atom; the number that appears over the element symbol in the periodic table.

Atomic symbol: The one- or two-letter abbreviation for a chemical element.

Axis: An imaginary straight line around which an object, like a planet, spins or turns. Earth's axis is a line that goes through the North and South Poles.

B

Bacteria: Single-celled microorganisms that live in soil, water, plants, and animals that play a key role in the decay of organic matter and the cycling of nutrients. Some are agents of disease. (Singular: bacterium.)

Barometer: An instrument for measuring atmospheric pressure, used especially in weather forecasting.

Base: Substance that when dissolved in water is capable of reacting with an acid to form salts and release hydrogen ions; has a pH of more than 7.

Base pairs: In DNA, the pairing of two nucleotides with each other: adenine (A) with thymine (T), and guanine (G) with cytosine (C).

Bedrock: Solid layer of rock lying beneath the soil and other loose material.

Biodegradable: Capable of being decomposed by biological agents.

Bioluminescence: The chemical phenomenon in which an organism can produce its own light.

Biopesticide: Pesticide produced from substances found in nature.

Blueshift: The shortening of the frequency of light waves toward the blue end of the visible light spectrum as they travel towards an observer; most commonly used to describe movement of stars towards Earth.

Boiling point: The temperature at which a substance changes from a liquid to a gas or vapor.

Bone joint: A place in the body where two or more bones are connected.

Bone marrow: The spongy center of many bones in which blood cells are manufactured.

Bone tissue: A group of similar cells in the bone with a common function.

c

Cancellous bone: Also called spongy bone, the inner layer of a bone that has cells with large spaces in between them filled with marrow.

Canning: A method of preserving food using airtight, vacuum-sealed containers and heat processing.

Carbonic acid: A weak acid that forms from the mixture of water and carbon dioxide.

Cartilage: The connective tissue that covers and protects the bones.

Cast: In paleontology, the fossil formed when a mold is later filled in by mud or mineral matter.

Cave: Also called cavern, a hollow or natural passage under or into the ground large enough for a person to enter.

Cell membrane: The layer that surrounds the cell, but is inside the cell wall, allowing some molecules to enter and keeping others out of the cell.

Cell wall: A tough outer covering that overlies the cell membrane of bacteria and plant cells.

Centrifugal force: The apparent force pushing a rotating body away from the center of rotation.

Centripetal force: A force that pushes an object inward, which causes the object to move in a circular path.

Chemosense: A sense stimulated by specific chemicals that cause the sensory cell to transmit a signal to the brain. The senses of taste and smell.

Chromatography: A method for separating mixtures into their component parts (into their "ingredients") by flowing the mixture over another substance and noting the differences in attraction between the substance and each component of the mixture.

Cilia: Hairlike structures on olfactory receptor cells that sense odor molecules.

Circumference: The distance around a circle.

Clay: Type of soil comprising the smallest soil particles.

Collagen: A protein in bone that gives the bone elasticity.

Colony: A visible growth of microorganisms, containing millions of bacterial cells.

Coma: Glowing cloud of gas surrounding the nucleus of a comet.

Comet: An icy body orbiting in the solar system, which partially vaporizes when it nears the Sun and develops a diffuse envelope of dust and gas as well as one or more tails.

Comet head: The nucleus and the coma of a comet.

Comet nucleus: The core or center of a comet. (Plural: Comet nuclei.)

Comet tail: The most distinctive feature of comets; comets can display two basic types of tails: one gaseous and the other largely composed of dust.

Compact bone: The outer, hard layer of the bone.

Concave lens: A lens that is thinner in the middle than at the edges.

Condense: When a gas or vapor changes to a liquid.

Conservation of energy: The law of physics that states that energy can be transformed from one form to another, but can be neither created nor destroyed.

Contract: To shorten, pull together.

Control experiment: A setup that is identical to the experiment, but is not affected by the variable that acts on the experimental group.

Convection current: Also called density-driven current, a cycle of warm water rising and cooler water sinking. Also a circular movement of a gas in response to alternating heating and cooling.

Convex lens: A lens that is thicker in the middle than at the edges.

Coprolites: The fossilized droppings of animals.

Coriolis force: A force that makes a moving object appear to travel in a curved path over the surface of a spinning body.

Crater: An indentation caused by an object hitting the surface of a planet or moon.

Crest: The highest point of a wave.

Cross-pollination: The process by which pollen from one plant pollinates another plant of the same species.

Crystal: Naturally occurring solid composed of atoms or molecules arranged in an orderly pattern that repeats at regular intervals.

Crystal faces: The flat, smooth surfaces of a crystal.

Crystal lattice: The regular and repeating pattern of the atoms in a crystal.

Cumulonimbus cloud: The parent cloud of a thunderstorm; a tall, vertically developed cloud capable of producing heavy rain, high winds, and lightning.

Currents: The horizontal and vertical circulation of ocean waters.

Cytoplasm: The semifluid substance inside a cell that surrounds the nucleus and other membrane-enclosed organelles.

D

Deficiency disease: A disease marked by a lack of an essential nutrient in the diet.

Degrade: Break down.

Dehydration: The removal of water from a material.

Density: The mass of a substance compared to its volume.

Deoxyribonucleic acid (DNA): (Pronounced DEE-ox-see-rye-bo-noo-klay-ick acid) Large, complex molecules found in the nuclei of cells that carry genetic information for an organism's development.

DNA replication: The process by which one DNA strand unwinds and duplicates all its information, creating two new DNA strands that are identical to each other and to the original strand.

Doppler effect: The change in wavelength and frequency (number of vibrations per second) of either light or sound as the source is moving either towards or away from the observer.

Dormant: A state of inactivity in an organism.

Double helix: The shape taken by DNA (deoxyribonucleic acid) molecules in a nucleus.

Dust tail: One of two types of tails a comet may have, it is composed mainly of dust and it points away from the Sun.

E

Effort: The force applied to move a load using a simple machine.

Elastomers: Any of various polymers having rubbery properties.

Electron: A subatomic particle with a mass of about one atomic mass unit and a single electrical charge that orbits the center of an atom.

Element: A pure substance composed of just one type of atom that cannot be broken down into anything simpler by ordinary chemical means.

Elongation: The percentage increase in length that occurs before a material breaks under tension.

Enzyme: Any of numerous complex proteins produced by living cells that act as catalysts, speeding up the rate of chemical reactions in living organisms.

Eukaryotic: Multicellular organism whose cells contain distinct nuclei, which contain the genetic material. (Pronounced yoo-KAR-ee-ah-tic)

Eutrophication: The process by which high nutrient concentrations in a body of water eventually cause the natural wildlife to die

Extremophiles: Bacteria that thrive in environments too harsh to support most life forms.

F

Family: A group of elements in the same column of the periodic table or in closely related columns of the table. A family of chemical compounds share similar structures and properties.

Fat-soluble vitamins: Vitamins such as A, D, E, and K that can be dissolved in the fat of plants and animals.

Fermentation: A chemical reaction in which enzymes break down complex organic compounds (for example, carbohydrates and sugars) into simpler ones (for example, ethyl alcohol).

Filament: In a flower, stalk of the stamen that bears the anther.

Filtration: The mechanical separation of a liquid from the undissolved particles floating in it

Fireball: Meteors that create an intense, bright light and, sometimes, an explosion.

First law of motion (Newton's): An object at rest or moving in a certain direction and speed will remain at rest or moving in the same motion and speed unless acted upon by a force.

Flagella: Whiplike structures used by some organisms for movement. (Singular: flagellum.)

Flower: The reproductive part of a flowering plant.

Focal length: The distance from the lens to the point where the light rays come together to a focus.

Force: A physical interaction (pushing or pulling) tending to change the state of motion (velocity) of an object.

Fortified: The addition of nutrients, such as vitamins or minerals, to food.

Fossil: The remains, trace, or impressions of a living organism that inhabited Earth more than ten thousand years ago.

Fossil record: The documentation of fossils placed in relationship to one another; a key source to understanding the evolution of life on Earth.

Frequency: The rate at which vibrations take place (number of times per second the motion is repeated), given in cycles per second or in hertz (Hz). Also, the number of waves that pass a given point in a given period of time.

Friction: A force that resists the motion of an object, resulting when two objects rub against one another.

Front: The area between air masses of different temperatures or densities.

Fulcrum: The point at which a lever arm pivots.

Fungi: Kingdom of various single-celled or multicellular organisms, including mushrooms, molds, yeasts, and mildews, that do not manufacture their own food.

Funnel cloud: A fully developed tornado vortex before it has touched the ground.

G

Germ theory of disease: The theory that disease is caused by microorganisms or germs, and not by spontaneous generation.

Gnomon: The perpendicular piece of the sundial that casts the shadow.

Gravity: Force of attraction between objects, the strength of which depends on the mass of each object and the distance between them.

Greenhouse effect: The warming of Earth's atmosphere due to water vapor, carbon dioxide, and other gases in the atmosphere that trap heat radiated from Earth's surface.

Greenwich Mean Time (GMT): The time at an imaginary line that runs north and south through Greenwich, England, used as the standard for time throughout the world.

Group: A vertical column of the periodic table that contains elements possessing similar chemical characteristics.

H

Heterogeneous: Different throughout; made up of different parts.

Homogenous: The same throughout; made up of similar parts.

Humus: Fragrant, spongy, nutrient-rich decayed plant or animal matter.

Hypha: Slender, cottony filaments making up the body of multicellular fungi. (Plural: hyphae)

Hypothesis: An idea in the form of a statement that can be tested by observation and/or experiment.

I

Imperfect flower: Flowers that have only the male reproductive organ (stamen) or the female reproductive organs (pistil)

Inclined plane: A simple machine with no moving parts; a slanted surface.

Inertia: The tendency of an object to continue in its state of motion.

Inorganic: Made of or coming from nonliving matter.

Insoluble: A substance that cannot be dissolved in some other substance.

Ion: An atom or groups of atoms that carries an electrical charge— either positive or negative—as a result of losing or gaining one or more electrons.

Ion tail: One of two types of tails a comet may have; it is composed mainly of charged particles and it points away from the Sun.

K

Kingdom: One of the five classifications in the widely accepted classification system that designates all living organisms into animals, plants, fungi, protists, and monerans.

L

Lava cave: A cave formed from the flow of lava streaming over solid matter.

Leaching: The movement of dissolved chemicals with water that percolates, or oozes, downward through the soil.

Ligaments: Tough, fibrous tissue connecting bones.

M

Machine: Any device that makes work easier by providing a mechanical advantage.

Macrominerals: Minerals needed in relatively large quantities.

Melting point: The temperature at which a substance changes from a solid to a liquid.

Meteor: An object from space that becomes glowing hot when it passes into Earth's atmosphere; also called shooting star.

Meteorites: A meteor that is large enough to survive its passage through the atmosphere and hit the ground.

Meteoroid: A piece of debris that is traveling in space.

Meteorologists: Professionals who study Earth's atmosphere and its phenomena, including weather and weather forecasting.

Meteor shower: A group of meteors that occurs when Earth's orbit intersects the orbit of a meteor stream.

Microvilli: The extension of each taste cell that pokes through the taste pore and first senses the chemicals.

Mineral: A nonorganic substance found in nature that originates in the ground; has a definite chemical composition and structure.

Mixture: A combination of two or more substances that are not chemically combined with each other and that can exist in any proportion.

Mold: In paleontology, the fossil formed when acidic water dissolves a shell or bone around which sand or mud has already hardened.

Molecule: The smallest particle of a substance that retains all the properties of the substance and is composed of one or more atoms.

Monomer: A small molecule that can be combined with itself many times over to make a large molecule, the polymer.

Mucus: A thick, slippery substance that serves as a protective lubricant coating in passages of the body that communicate with the air.

Muscle fibers: Stacks of long, thin cells that makeup muscle; there are three types of muscle fiber: skeletal, cardiac, and smooth.

Mycelium: In fungi, the mass of threadlike, branching hyphae.

N

Nectar: A sweet liquid found inside a flower that attracts pollinators.

Neutron: A particle that has no electrical charge and is found in the center of an atom.

Noble gases: Also known as inert or rare gases; the elements argon, helium, krypton, neon, radon, and xenon, which are unreactive gases and form few compounds with other elements.

Nucleation: The process by which crystals start growing.

experiment
CENTRAL

Nucleotide: The basic unit of a nucleic acid. It consists of a simple sugar, a phosphate group, and a nitrogen-containing base. (Pronounced noo-KLEE-uh-tide.)

Nucleus, cell: Membrane-enclosed structure within a cell that contains the cell's genetic material and controls its growth and reproduction. (Plural: nuclei.)

o

Objective lens: In a refracting telescope, the lens farthest away from the eye that collects the light.

Oceanographer: A person who studies the chemistry of the oceans, as well as their currents, marine life, and the ocean floor.

Olfactory: Relating to the sense of smell.

Olfactory bulb: The part of the brain that processes olfactory (smell) information.

Olfactory epithelium: The patch of mucous membrane at the top of the nasal cavity that contains the olfactory (smell) nerve cells.

Olfactory receptor cells: Nerve cells in the olfactory epithelium that detect odors and transmit the information to the brain.

Oort cloud: Region of space beyond Earth's solar system that theoretically contains about one trillion inactive comets.

Orbit: The path followed by a body (such as a planet) in its travel around another body (such as the Sun).

Organelle: A membrane-enclosed structure that performs a specific function within a cell.

Organic: Made of, or coming from, living matter.

Oscillation: A repeated back-and-forth movement.

Osmosis: The movement of fluids and substances dissolved in liquids across a semi-permeable membrane from an area of greater concentration to an area of lesser concentration until all substances involved reach a balance.

Ovary: In a plant, the base part of the pistil that bears ovules and develops into a fruit.

Ovule: Structure within the ovary that develops into a seed after fertilization.

P

Paleontologist: Scientist who studies the life of past geological periods as known from fossil remains.

Papillae: The raised bumps on the tongue that contain the taste buds.

Parent material: The underlying rock from which soil forms.

Particulate matter: Solid matter in the form of tiny particles in the atmosphere. (Pronounced par-TIK-you-let.)

Pasteurization: The process of slow heating that kills bacteria and other microorganisms.

Pendulum: A free-swinging weight, usually consisting of a heavy object attached to the end of a long rod or string, suspended from a fixed point.

Perfect flower: Flowers that have both male and female reproductive organs.

Period: A horizontal row in the periodic table.

Periodic table: A chart organizing elements by atomic number and chemical properties into groups and periods.

Permineralization: A form of preservation in which mineral matter has filled in the inner and outer spaces of the cell.

Pest: Any living thing that is unwanted by humans or causes injury and disease to crops and other growth.

Pesticide: Substance used to reduce the abundance of pests.

Petal: Leafy structure of a flower just inside the sepals; they are often brightly colored and have many different shapes.

Petrifaction: Process of turning organic material into rock by the replacement of that material with minerals.

pH: A measure of a solution's acidity. The pH scale ranges from 0 (most acidic) to 14 (least acidic), with 7 representing a neutral solution, such as pure water.

Photosynthesis: Chemical process by which plants containing chlorophyll use sunlight to manufacture their own food by converting carbon dioxide and water into carbohydrates, releasing oxygen as a by-product.

Pili: Short projections that assist bacteria in attaching to tissues.

Pistil: Female reproductive organ of flowers that is composed of the stigma, style, and ovary.

Plasmolysis: Occurs in walled cells in which cytoplasm, the semifluid substance inside a cell, shrivels and the membrane pulls away from the cell wall when the vacuole loses water.

Pollen: Dustlike grains or particles produced by a plant that contain male sex cells.

Pollination: Transfer of pollen from the male reproductive organs to the female reproductive organs of plants.

Pollinator: Any animal, such as an insect or bird, who transfers the pollen from one flower to another.

Pollution: The contamination of the natural environment, usually through human activity.

Polymer: Chemical compound formed of simple molecules (known as monomers) linked with themselves many times over.

Polymerization: The bonding of two or more monomers to form a polymer.

Preservative: An additive used to keep food from spoiling.

Prokaryote: A cell without a true nucleus, such as a bacterium.

Protein: A complex chemical compound consisting of many amino acids attached to each other that are essential to the structure and functioning of all living cells.

Proton: A positively charged particle in the center of an atom.

Pulley: A simple machine made of a cord wrapped around a wheel.

R

Radioisotope dating: A technique used to date fossils, based on the decay rate of known radioactive elements.

Radon: A radioactive gas located in the ground; invisible and odorless, radon is a health hazard when it accumulates to high levels inside homes and other structures where it is breathed.

Rancidity: Having the condition when food has a disagreeable odor or taste from decomposing oils or fats.

Redshift: The lengthening of the frequency of light waves toward the red end of the visible light spectrum as they travel away from an observer; most commonly used to describe movement of stars away from Earth.

Reflector telescope: A telescope that directs light from an opening at one end to a concave mirror at the far end, which reflects the light back to a smaller mirror that directs it to an eyepiece on the side of the tube.

Refractor telescope: A telescope that directs light through a glass lens, which bends the light waves and brings them to a focus at an eyepiece that acts as a magnifying glass.

Relative age: The age of an object expressed in relation to another like object, such as earlier or later.

Ribosome: A protein composed of two subunits that functions in protein synthesis (creation).

Rock: Naturally occurring solid mixture of minerals.

Root hairs: Fine, hairlike extensions from the plant's root.

Rotate: To turn around on an axis or center.

Runoff: Water not absorbed by the soil; moves downward and picks up particles along the way.

S

Salinity: A measure of the amount of dissolved salt in seawater.

Saliva: Watery mixture with chemicals in the mouth that lubricates chewed food.

Sand: Granular portion of soil composed of the largest soil particles.

Saturated: In referring to solutions, a solution that contains the maximum amount of solute for a given amount of solvent at a given temperature.

Screw: A simple machine; an inclined plane wrapped around a cylinder.

Scurvy: A disease caused by a deficiency of vitamin C, which causes a weakening of connective tissue in bone and muscle.

Sea cave: A cave in sea cliffs, formed most commonly by waves eroding the rock.

Second law of motion (Newton's): The force exerted on an object is proportional to the mass of the object times the acceleration produced by the force.

Sediment: Sand, silt, clay, rock, gravel, mud, or other matter that has been transported by flowing water.

Sedimentary rock: Rock formed from compressed and solidified layers of organic or inorganic matter.

Seed crystal: Small form of a crystalline structure that has all the facets of a complete new crystal contained in it.

Self-pollination: The process in which pollen from one part of a plant fertilizes ovules on another part of the same plant.

Sepal: The outermost part of a flower; typically leaflike and green.

Shell: A region of space around the center of the atom in which electrons are located.

Sidereal day: The system of time to measure a day based on the time it takes for a particular star to travel around and reach the same position in the sky; about four minutes shorter than the average solar day.

Silt: Medium-sized soil particles.

Simple machine: Any of the basic structures that provide a mechanical advantage and have none or few moving parts.

Smog: A form of air pollution produced when moisture in the air combines and reacts with the products of fossil fuel combustion. Smog is characterized by hazy skies and a tendency to cause respiratory problems among humans.

Soil: The upper layer of Earth that contains nutrients for plants and organisms; a mixture of mineral matter, organic matter, air, and water.

Soil horizon: An identifiable soil layer due to color, structure, and/or texture.

Soil profile: Combined soil horizons or layers.

Solar day: Called a day, the time between each arrival of the Sun at its highest point.

Solubility: The tendency of a substance to dissolve in some other substance.

Soluble: A substance that can be dissolved in some other substance.

Solute: The substance that is dissolved to make a solution and exists in the least amount in a solution, for example sugar in sugar water.

Solution: A mixture of two or more substances that appears to be uniform throughout, except on a molecular level.

Solvent: The major component of a solution or the liquid in which some other component is dissolved, for example water in sugar water.

Speleologist: One who studies caves.

Speleology: Scientific study of caves and their plant and animal life.

Spelunkers: Also called cavers, people who explore caves for a hobby.

Spoilage: The condition when food has taken on an undesirable color, odor, or texture.

Spore: A small, usually one-celled reproductive body that is capable of growing into a new organism.

Stalactite: Cylindrical or icicle-shaped mineral deposit projecting downward from the roof of a cave. (Pronounced sta-LACK-tite.)

Stalagmite: Cylindrical or icicle-shaped mineral deposit projecting upward from the floor of a cave. (Pronounced sta-LAG-mite.)

Stamen: Male reproductive organ of flowers that is composed of the anther and filament.

Stigma: Top part of the pistil upon which pollen lands and receives the male pollen grains during fertilization.

Stomata: Pores in the epidermis (surface) of leaves.

Storm: An extreme atmospheric disturbance, associated with strong damaging winds, and often by thunder and lightning.

Storm chasers: People who track and seek out storms, often tornadoes.

Stratification: Layers according to density; applies to fluids.

Style: Stalk of the pistil that connects the stigma to the ovary.

Sublime: The process of changing a solid into a vapor without passing through the liquid phase.

Sundial: A device that uses the position of the Sun to indicate time.

Supersaturated: Solution that is more highly concentrated than is normally possible under given conditions of temperature and pressure.

Supertaster: A person who is extremely sensitive to specific tastes due to a greater number of taste buds.

Supplements: A substance intended to enhance the diet.

experiment
CENTRAL

Synthesized: Prepared by humans in a laboratory; not a naturally occurring process.

Synthetic: Something that is made artificially, in a laboratory or chemical plant, but is generally not found in nature.

Synthetic crystals: Artificial or manmade crystals.

T

Taste buds: Groups of taste cells located on the papillae that recognize the different tastes.

Taste pore: The opening at the top of the taste bud from which chemicals reach the taste cells.

Telescope: A tube with lenses or mirrors that collect, transmit, and focus light.

Tendon: Tough, fibrous, connective tissue that attaches muscle to bone.

Tensile strength: The force needed to stretch a material until it breaks.

Theory of Special Relativity: Theory put forth by Albert Einstein that time is not absolute, but it is relative according to the speed of the observer's frame of reference.

Thermal inversion: A region in which the warmer air lies above the colder air; can cause smog to worsen.

Thermal pollution: The discharge of heated water from industrial processes that can kill or injure water life.

Third law of motion (Newton's): For every action there is an equal and opposite reaction.

Tides: The cyclic rise and fall of seawater.

Topsoil: Uppermost layer of soil that contains high levels of organic matter.

Tornado: A violently rotating, narrow column of air in contact with the ground and usually extending from a cumulonimbus cloud.

Toxic: Poisonous.

Trace minerals: Minerals needed in relatively small quantities.

Transpiration: Evaporation of water in the form of water vapor from the stomata on the surfaces of leaves and stems of plants.

Troglobites: An animal that lives in a cave and is unable to live outside of one.

Troglophiles: An animal that lives the majority of its life cycle in a cave but is also able to live outside of the cave.

Trogloxenes: An animal that spends only part of its life cycle in a cave and returns periodically to the cave.

Troposphere: The lowest layer of Earth's atmosphere, ranging to an altitude of about 9 miles (15 kilometers) above Earth's surface.

Trough: The lowest point of a wave. (Pronounced trawf.)

Turgor pressure: The force that is exerted on a plant's cell wall by the water within the cell.

U

Unit cell: The basic unit of the crystalline structure.

Updraft: Warm, moist air that moves away from the ground.

Upwelling: The process by which lower-level, nutrient-rich waters rise upward to the ocean's surface.

V

Vacuole: An enclosed, space-filling sac within plant cells containing mostly water and providing structural support for the cell.

Variable: Something that can affect the results of an experiment.

Velocity: The rate at which the position of an object changes with time, including both the speed and the direction.

Vitamins: Organic substance that are essential for people's good health; most of them are not manufactured in the body.

Volatilization: The process by which a liquid changes (volatilizes) to a gas.

Vortex: A rotating column of a fluid such as air or water.

W

Water clock: A device that uses the flow of water to measure time.

Water-soluble vitamins: Vitamins such as C and the B-complex vitamins that dissolve in the watery parts of plant and animal tissues.

Water vapor: The change of water from a liquid to a gas.

Wave: The rise and fall of the ocean water; also, a motion in which energy and momentum is carried away from some source; a wave repeats itself in space and time with little or no change.

Wavelength: The distance between the crest of a wave of light, heat, or energy and the next corresponding crest.

Weathered: Natural process that breaks down rocks and minerals at Earth's surface into simpler materials by physical (mechanical) or chemical means.

Wedge: A simple machine; a form of inclined plane.

Wheel and axle: A simple machine; a larger wheel(s) fastened to a smaller cylinder, an axle, so that they turn together.

Work: Force applied over a distance.

X

Xylem: Plant tissue consisting of elongated, thick-walled cells that transport water and mineral nutrients. (Pronounced ZY-lem.)

experiment
CENTRAL

chapter 15

Periodic Table

Considered one of the most important chemistry reference tools, the **periodic table** is a familiar sight around the world. The periodic table is an arrangement of the **elements** by their properties. An element is a substance in pure form, meaning that it cannot be broken down into any other substance. The smallest particle of an element is an **atom.**

With one glance, the periodic table can provide a great deal of information on both individual elements and groups of them. A person familiar with the table can extract an element's relative mass, basic properties, and how it compares with its neighbors without knowing any facts about the element itself.

Elemental developments

All matter on Earth is made up of elements. There are only a finite number of natural elements, although others are synthesized or manufactured by people. (As of 2003, there were 110 officially named elements, plus several more created in laboratories awaiting names.) The periodic table leaves spaces for unknown elements still to be discovered.

The desire to categorize elements goes back to the fifth century B.C.E. when ancient Greeks theorized that all matter falls under four elements: Earth, air, fire, and water. In 1789 French chemist Antoine Lavoisier (1743–1794) published the definition and first set of thirty-three chemical elements. Lavoisier grouped them into four categories on the basis of their chemical properties: gases, nonmetals, metals, and earths.

As more elements were discovered, many scientists worked on classifying them. The turning point came when Russian chemist Dmitri

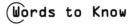
Words to Know

Alkali metals:
The first group of elements in the periodic table, these metals have a single electron in the outermost shell.

Atom:
The smallest unit of an element, made up of protons and neutrons in its center, surrounded by moving electrons.

Atomic mass:
Also known as atomic weight, the average mass of the atoms in an element; the number that appears under the element symbol in the periodic table.

Did You Know?

- Atomic weights are determined by comparing the weight of an element to that of a carbon atom, whose atomic weight is counted as 12.

- In the Middle Ages alchemists theorized that metals such as zinc, lead, and copper could be changed into gold and silver.

- The elements hydrogen and helium make up close to 80 percent and 20 percent, respectively, of all the matter in the universe.

- Elements with atomic numbers greater than 92 (uranium) have been made artificially.

- In just one year, 1898, a pair of scientists discovered three elements: krypton, neon, and xenon.

- The gas helium was discovered by astronomers analyzing light from the Sun before the gas was found on Earth. The name helium comes from the Greek word *helios*, meaning the Sun.

Words to Know

Atomic number:
The number of protons (or electrons) in an atom; the number that appears over the element symbol in the periodic table.

Atomic symbol:
The one- or two-letter abbreviation for a chemical element.

Control experiment:
A setup that is identical to the experiment, but is not affected by the variables that affects the experimental group.

Electron:
A subatomic particle with a mass of about one atomic mass unit and a single electrical charge that orbits the center of an atom.

Element:
A pure substance composed of just one type of atom that cannot be broken down into anything simpler by ordinary chemical means.

Mendeleev (1834–1907) made up cards of each of the elements and worked on arranging them in patterns. At that time there were sixty-three known elements. He found that there were repeating or periodic relationships between the properties of the elements and their atomic weights. By arranging the elements in order of increasing atomic weight, the properties of the elements were repeated periodically. The arrangement of elements in this manner was called the periodic table.

In 1869 Mendeleev published the first periodic table. In his table, rows (across) and columns (down) each shared certain properties. Mendeleev's table even left placeholders for elements that had yet to be identified. Over the next two decades, more elements were discovered, including gallium, scandium, and germanium. When these elements fit into the predicted spaces, the table gained acceptance. Over the next century the periodic table changed in several ways, yet its basic structure set down by Mendeleev remained.

Blocks of data

Each block in the periodic table contains the name and properties of that element. The letters are the abbreviation or **atomic symbol** of the chemical element. Each element has a one-or-two letter abbreviation as its symbol, often taken from the Latin word for a description, place, or name. For example, the atomic symbol for gold, Au, comes from the first two letters of the Latin word *aurum,* meaning shining dawn. Mercury's symbol, Hg, comes from the Latin *hydragyrum,* meaning

Russian chemist Dmitri Mendeleev created the basic structure of the periodic table. (Courtesy of the Library of Congress.)

liquid silver, and lead's symbol, Pb, comes from the Latin *plumbum,* meaning heavy.

Above the symbol is the **atomic number** of the element. The atomic number represents the number of **protons,** or positively charged particles, in an atom of that element. The number of protons in an atom equals the number of **electrons,** negatively charged particles, which move around the center of the atom. The number and arrangement of protons and electrons in an atom determines the chemical behavior of the element.

The number below the symbol is the **atomic mass,** the average mass of an element. Also known as atomic weight, atomic mass is given in atomic mass units (amu). An atom's atomic mass is the weight of its protons and neutrons. A **neutron** is a particle that has no charge and is located in the center of the atom.

Across and down

Each row of elements across the table is called a **period.** Rows in the periodic table are read left to right. All of the elements in a period have the same number of **shells.** A shell is the number of areas an atom needs to hold its electrons. The first shell holds two electrons, the second shell holds up to eight, and the third shell can hold up to

experiment
CENTRAL

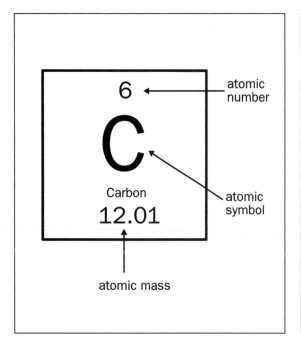

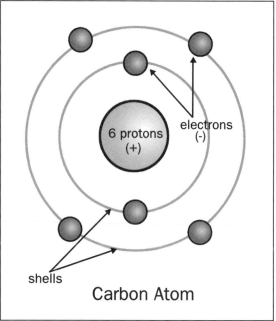

Carbon Atom

eighteen electrons. In 2003, the maximum number of shells found around any atom is seven. Thus, there are seven periods.

For example, carbon (C) atoms have six electrons: two electrons in the first shell and the remaining four are in the second shell. Hydrogen (H), which has one electron, needs only one shell. Helium (He), which has two electrons, is the only other element with one shell and the two elements share a row by themselves. Calcium (Ca) and Magnesium (Mg) each have two shells and, thus, are in the second row.

Each column of elements down the periodic table is called a **group** or **family.** Elements in a group have the same number of electrons in their outer shell. The group at the left edge of the periodic table has one electron in its outer shell. Every element in the second column has two electrons in its outer shell, and so on. Groups are numbered from left to right. There are two sets of groups: the A and B groups. The A groups run along the high columns of the table and have similar properties. The B groups in the middle section of the table are called transition elements. Transition elements have common properties; they are hard, strong metals that conduct heat and electricity well. These elements also have their electrons arranged in a complex arrangement, which is lacking in the A group.

Main–Group Elements

Transition Metals

Inner–Transition Metals

Atomic number 86 [222] **Atomic weight**
Symbol Rn
Name radon

Period

Group	1 IA	2 IIA	3 IIIB	4 IVB	5 VB	6 VIB	7 VIIB	8	9 VIIIB	10	11 IB	12 IIB	13 IIIA	14 IVA	15 VA	16 VIA	17 VIIA	18 VIIIA
1	1 1.00794 H hydrogen																	2 4.002602 He helium
2	3 6.941 Li lithium	4 9.012182 Be beryllium											5 10.811 B boron	6 12.011 C carbon	7 14.00674 N nitrogen	8 15.9994 O oxygen	9 18.9984032 F fluorine	10 20.1797 Ne neon
3	11 22.989768 Na sodium	12 24.3050 Mg magnesium											13 26.981539 Al aluminum	14 28.0855 Si silicon	15 30.973762 P phosphorus	16 32.066 S sulfur	17 35.4527 Cl chlorine	18 39.948 Ar argon
4	19 39.0983 K potassium	20 40.078 Ca calcium	21 44.955910 Sc scandium	22 47.88 Ti titanium	23 50.9415 V vanadium	24 51.9961 Cr chromium	25 54.9305 Mn manganese	26 55.847 Fe iron	27 58.93320 Co cobalt	28 58.69 Ni nickel	29 63.546 Cu copper	30 65.39 Zn zinc	31 69.723 Ga gallium	32 72.61 Ge germanium	33 74.92159 As arsenic	34 78.96 Se selenium	35 79.904 Br bromine	36 83.80 Kr krypton
5	37 85.4678 Rb rubidium	38 87.62 Sr strontium	39 88.90585 Y yttrium	40 91.224 Zr zirconium	41 92.90638 Nb niobium	42 95.94 Mo molybdenum	43 [98] Tc technetium	44 101.07 Ru ruthenium	45 102.90550 Rh rhodium	46 106.42 Pd palladium	47 107.8682 Ag silver	48 112.411 Cd cadmium	49 114.82 In indium	50 118.710 Sn tin	51 121.75 Sb antimony	52 127.60 Te tellurium	53 126.90447 I iodine	54 131.29 Xe xenon
6	55 132.90543 Cs cesium	56 137.327 Ba barium	67-70 * / 71 174.967 *Lu lutetium	72 178.49 Hf hafnium	73 180.9479 Ta tantalum	74 183.85 W tungsten	75 186.207 Re rhenium	76 190.2 Os osmium	77 192.22 Ir iridium	78 195.08 Pt platinum	79 196.96654 Au gold	80 200.59 Hg mercury	81 204.3833 Tl thallium	82 207.2 Pb lead	83 208.98037 Bi bismuth	84 [209] Po polonium	85 [210] At astatine	86 [222] Rn radon
7	87 [223] Fr francium	88 [226] Ra radium	89-102 † / 103 [262] †Lr lawrencium	104 [261] Rf rutherfordium	105 [262] Db dubnium	106 [266] Sg seaborgium	107 [264] Bh bohrium	108 [264] Hs hassium	109 [268] Mt meitnerium	110 [271] Uun ununnilium	111 [272] Uuu unununium	112 [285] Uub ununbium	113 Uut	114 [289] Uuq ununquadium	115 Uup	116 [?] Uuh ununhexium	117 Uus	118 [?] Uuo ununoctium

*Lanthanides

57 138.9055 La lanthanum	58 140.115 Ce cerium	59 140.90765 Pr praseodymium	60 144.24 Nd neodymium	61 [145] Pm promethium	62 150.36 Sm samarium	63 151.965 Eu europium	64 157.25 Gd gadolinium	65 158.92534 Tb terbium	66 162.50 Dy dysprosium	67 164.93032 Ho holmium	68 167.26 Er erbium	69 168.93421 Tm thulium	70 173.04 Yb ytterbium

† Actinides

89 [227] Ac actinium	90 232.0381 Th thorium	91 [231] Pa protactinium	92 238.0289 U uranium	93 [237] Np neptunium	94 [244] Pu plutonium	95 [243] Am americium	96 [247] Cm curium	97 [247] Bk berkelium	98 [251] Cf californium	99 [252] Es einsteinium	100 [257] Fm fermium	101 [258] Md mendelevium	102 [259] No nobelium

Periodic patterns

Both periods and groups supply information on the element's characteristics and behavior.

In a period, as the atomic mass increases from left to right the atomic size decreases. (The more electrons there are, the more they are pulled towards the center and the atom tightens.) Metals are on the left and middle sections of the periods with the most active metal in the lower left corner. Nonmetals are located on the right side. With the exception of hydrogen, the first element in a period is a solid, and the last element in a period is always a gas that does not react with other elements.

Elements that share the same number of electrons in their outer shell, the groups, share many of the same behaviors. Examples of shared characteristics include their stability, boiling point, and conductivity. For example, the elements on the far right of the table are called the **noble gases.** Noble gases are colorless gases that are all non-reactive because their outermost shell is full. When the outermost shell is full the atom is completely stable and does not react. The groups on the far left also share many properties with each other. With few electrons in their outer shells, these metals are highly reactive and react strongly with nonmetals.

Although the properties in groups are similar, they change as you move up or down the column. For example, chemical activity generally increases as you go down a metal group and decreases as you move down a nonmetal group.

Experiment 1
Metals versus Non-metals: Which areas of the periodic table have elements that conduct electricity?

Purpose/Hypothesis

Conductivity is one of the properties that relates to the position of the element in the periodic table. Conductivity relates to the electron configuration in the element's atoms. Atoms are constantly working to get a full count of atoms in their outer shell. They can do this by losing or gaining electrons. A full count gives the atom stability and,

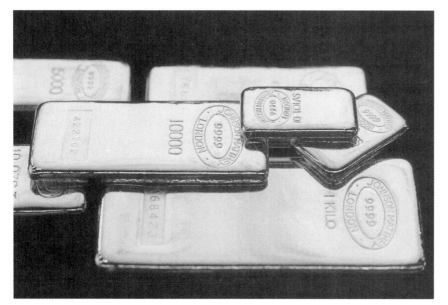

thus, it does not need to react with other atoms. Elements in the low-number groups have atoms with one or few electrons in their outer shell. This causes these atoms to lose electrons easily. Their electrons move among all the atoms in the substance. Atoms in the highest groups have a full or almost-full outer shell and usually gain electrons. Their electrons do not move about freely.

The periodic table is composed of two main groups: metals and nonmetals. Metals are on the left and middle of the table; nonmetals make up parts of groups IIIA to VIIIA. Almost all metals are solids (mercury, a liquid, is the exception). Nonmetals can be solids, liquids, or gases.

In this experiment you will determine what areas of the periodic table have elements that are electrical conductors. A conductor provides a path that allows electricity to flow from a battery's positive terminal to its negative terminal. You will test the electrical conductivity of several elements by placing each one in the path of the electricity, and connecting the path to a small light. If the light comes on, the flow of electricity is passing through the element; if the light remains off, then the element did not pass the flow of electricity. There are many elements you can test. Options are provided in the materials section.

To begin this experiment make an educated guess, or prediction, of what you think will occur based on your knowledge of the periodic

What Are the Variables?
Variables are anything that might affect the results of an experiment. Here are the main variables in this experiment:

- the element
- the battery voltage

table. This educated guess, or prediction, is your **hypothesis.** A hypothesis should explain these things:

- the topic of the experiment
- the **variable** you will change
- the variable you will measure
- what you expect to happen

A hypothesis should be brief, specific, and measurable. It must be something you can test through further investigation. Your experiment will prove or disprove whether your hypothesis is correct. Here is one possible hypothesis for this experiment: "Elements in the middle and left of the periodic table will conduct electricity, and the light will come on; elements on the right side of the table will not be good conductors, and the light will not come on."

In this experiment the variable you will change will be the element; the variable you measure will be whether electricity is conducted to the light.

Conducting a **control experiment** will help you isolate each variable and measure the changes in the dependent variable. Only one variable will change between the control and the experimental trials. The control experiment will test for a complete circuit. The positive and negative wires will carry the electric current directly to the light bulb.

Level of Difficulty
Moderate.

Materials Needed
- periodic table
- wire strippers (such as a knife)

- pliers
- scissors or wire cutters
- two 1.5-volt batteries
- battery holder, (wires should be attached to holder)
- six insulated alligator clips
- insulated copper wire (about two feet or 61 centimeters)
- small light bulb and light bulb socket, less than 3 volts
- Elements: aluminum (foil, wire); silver (jewelry, silverware, wire); gold (jewelry); zinc (penny made after 1982, which is made of 97.5 percent zinc, the remaining 2.5 percent is copper); copper (wire; penny dated 1962 to 1982, which is 95 percent copper and 5 percent zinc); carbon (lead in pencil, diamond on piece of jewelry); silicon (glass)

Approximate Budget
$12-$20.

Timetable
1 hour

Step-by-Step Instructions
1. Insert the two batteries in the battery holder so the positive and negative ends are opposite to one another.
2. Cut three pieces of wire, each 6 to 12 inches (15 to 30 centimeters) long.
3. Strip about 0.5 inch (1.3 centimeters) of the insulation off both ends of each piece of wire.
4. Insert each end of the wire through the hole in the alligator clip and twist. There should now be three pieces of wire with clips on each end.
5. Twist or press the light bulb into the base.

How to Experiment Safely
Make sure there is no water nearby as water will carry the electricity. Be careful when cutting wire. If the wire gets hot to the touch at any point, immediately disconnect the wire from the battery. Make sure the wire is fully insulated.

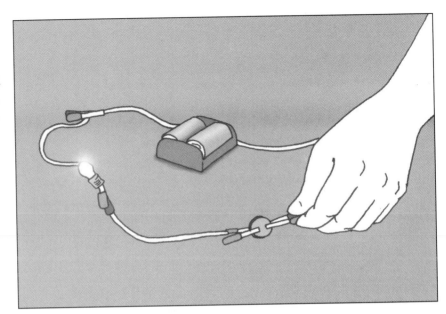

Step 8: Attach the clips to the test element and note if the current flows to the light.

6. Assemble the control experiment. With one wire, attach one clip to the exposed end of the battery wire and the clip on the other side to the light socket. Repeat with a second wire on the other side of the light socket. Note the results.

7. Remove one clip from the socket, and attach the third wire's clip in place of that clip.

8. Attach the clip of the free end of the third wire to one of the test elements. Attach the free end of the second wire to the other end of the element. When the path is complete, note whether the light glows.

9. Repeat Step 8, replacing the element with each test element one at a time. Note the results for each.

Summary of Results

Create a chart of your results, writing down whether each element was a conductor or nonconductor. Examine the results. What elements conducted electricity and where are they located in the periodic table? Air is made up of gases, mostly oxygen and nitrogen. Look at the periodic table and examine why gases do not conduct electricity. Examine the number of electrons in the elements you used. Look up how many electrons are in their outer shell. Write a brief summary of the experiment, explaining why some elements would make better conductors than others.

experiment
CENTRAL

Troubleshooter's Guide
Below are some problems that may arise during this experiment, some possible causes, and some ways to remedy the problem.

Problem: The light bulb does not light as expected.

Possible cause: The wire to the alligator clip may not be securely fastened to the element, or the alligator clip may not be touching the exposed wire. Repeat the experiment, scraping off enough plastic and checking that the exposed wires connect with each other.

Problem: The control light does not light for any element.

Possible cause: See "possible cause" above. Also, the battery may be dead and have no charge. Repeat the experiment with a fresh battery.

Change the Variables
To change the variable in this experiment, you can use a different voltage battery. You can also use a light with a different voltage.

Experiment 2
Soluble Families: How does the solubility of an element relate to where it is located on the Periodic Table?

Purpose/Hypothesis
Groups are columns running down the periodic table. In this experiment you are determining an element's solubility. Solubility is the ability of a substance to dissolve in a liquid. For example, sugar dissolves in water and is therefore called soluble in water. Chocolate chips mixed with water do not dissolve and are called insoluble in water. Solubility is one of the properties that relates to the location of the element in the periodic table.

experiment
CENTRAL

What Are the Variables?

Variables are anything that might affect the results of an experiment. Here are the main variables in this experiment:

- the type of salt
- the temperature of water
- the quantity of salt
- the size of the salt particles

In other words, the variables in this experiment are everything that might affect whether the salts are soluble in water. If you change more than one variable at the same time, you will not be able to tell which variable had the most effect on solubility.

In this experiment you will determine what areas of the periodic table have the property of being soluble in water. You will use substances made from elements in the first two families of the periodic table. The first group on the left, Group 1A, is the Alkali Metals. Group 2A is called Alkali Earth Metals. These elements will form salts when a metal combines with a nonmetal. For example, sodium and chloride combine to make table salt. By mixing these salts in water, you can then determine if either is soluble.

To begin this experiment make an educated guess, or prediction, of what you think will occur based on your knowledge of the periodic table, solubility, and groups. This educated guess, or prediction, is your **hypothesis**. A hypothesis should explain these things:

- the topic of the experiment
- the **variable** you will change
- the variable you will measure
- what you expect to happen

A hypothesis should be brief, specific, and measurable. It must be something you can test through further investigation. Your experiment will prove or disprove whether your hypothesis is correct. Here is one possible hypothesis for this experiment: "Salts made from elements in the Alkali Metals will dissolve in water more readily than salts in the Alkali Earth Metals."

experiment
CENTRAL

In this experiment the variable you will change will be the type of salt; the variable you measure will be the solubility of the salt.

Note: When making a solid-liquid solution (solid/liquid), it is standard to use weight/weight (grams/grams) or weight/volume (grams/milliliters). With water, 1 gram of water equals 1 milliliter. In this experiment, teaspoons and tablespoons are used to measure the solid.

Level of Difficulty
Easy to Moderate.

Materials Needed
- washing soda (sodium carbonate: available at many supermarkets in the detergent section)
- potassium carbonate (available at chemical supply houses: an adult must order this)
- chalk (calcium carbonate; active ingredient in many antacids)
- water
- measuring spoons
- metal spoon
- measuring cup
- plastic gloves
- three glasses
- masking tape
- marking pen

Approximate Budget
$15.

Timetable
30 minutes.

Step-by-Step Instructions
1. Pour 1 cup (about 0.25 liters or 250 milliliters) of room-tempera-

How to Experiment Safely
Be careful when working with potassium carbonate. Wear plastic gloves during this experiment. Do not ingest it or get it near your eyes. Wash your hands thoroughly after the experiment.

Step 3: Stir each of the salts in the water to determine its solubility.

ture water into each glass. Label each glass with the name of one of the salts.

2. Crush the calcium carbonate into a powder by wrapping a small piece of chalk or tablet in plastic wrap and pressing down on it with a spoon.

3. Measure out 1 teaspoon of the crushed calcium carbonate and stir it thoroughly in the water in the glass labeled "calcium carbonate" for at least 1 minute. You may need to stir for up to 2 minutes.

4. Examine the bottom of the glass for any powder residue and note the solubility.

5. Repeat Steps 4 and 5 for the other two salts using the other two glasses of water.

Summary of Results

Was your hypothesis correct? Why are the salts of Alkali Metals more soluble than Alkali Earth Metals? Determine the electron configuration of the three salts. Write up a brief description of the experiment, analyzing your conclusion.

Change the Variables

It is difficult to find pure elements as most are naturally found mixed with other elements. To change the variable in this experiment, you can try to change the water temperature. You can hypothesize what

experiment
CENTRAL

Troubleshooter's Guide

Below are some problems that may arise during this experiment, some possible causes, and some ways to remedy the problems.

Problem: The powder did not dissolve as expected.

Possible cause: The salt particles may be too large to dissolve. The particles should be a fine powder. Try repeating the experiment, crushing the chalk or tablets completely and stirring thoroughly.

Problem: The salt does not completely dissolve where it theoretically should dissolve.

Possible cause: See "possible cause" above. The metallic element you used may not be pure. Make sure you are not using colored chalk. You can also try purchasing real chalk or use another antacid tablet.

the combination of other salts would be and then conduct research to verify your hypothesis.

Design Your Own Experiment

How to Select a Topic Relating to this Concept

There are many ways to categorize and group the elements in the periodic table. All matter is made up of elements, yet it is difficult to find elements in their pure form. When experimenting with the properties of elements, look for the active ingredient on major products.

Check the For More Information section and talk with your science teacher to learn more about the periodic table and the elements.

Steps in the Scientific Method

To conduct an original experiment, you need to plan carefully and think things through. Otherwise, you might not be sure what question you are answering, what you are or should be measuring, or what your findings prove or disprove.

Here are the steps in designing an experiment:

- State the purpose of—and the underlying question behind—the experiment you propose to do.
- Recognize the variables involved and select one that will help you answer the question at hand.
- State your hypothesis, an educated guess about the answer to your question.
- Decide how to change the variable you selected.
- Decide how to measure your results.

Recording Data and Summarizing the Results

Your data should include charts and graphs such as the one you did for these experiments. They should be clearly labeled and easy to read. You may also want to include photographs and drawings of your experimental setup and results, which will help other people visualize the steps in the experiment.

If you are preparing an exhibit, you may want to display your results, such as any experimental setup you designed. If you have completed a nonexperimental project, explain clearly what your research question was and illustrate your findings.

Related Projects

For projects related on the periodic table, you can compare a variety of metals with one another to determine their differences and similarities. Some properties you can look at are the metal's relative softness, conductivity, and how it is affected by oxygen. Because elements are difficult to come across in their pure form, you can theorize on the properties of other metals and then conduct research. Certain groups of elements also react with bases, such as baking soda. If you order elements from a lab supply house, make sure you follow all the necessary safety precautions. Scientists are continuing to discover elements in the laboratory. For a research project you could look at the history of the periodic table and the story of the discoveries.

For More Information

"Elements." *Chem4Kids.* http://www.chem4kids.com/files/elem_intro.html (accessed on August 26, 2003). ❖ Detailed information about the periodic table, elements, metals, and other subjects for intermediate and advanced students.

Emsley, Dr. John. "The Development of the Periodic Table." *Chem. Soc: the ASC's Chemical Science Network.* http://www.chemsoc.org/viselements/pages/history.html

(accessed on August 26, 2003). ❖ The history of the development of the periodic table.

Heiserman, David L. *Exploring Chemical Elements and their Compounds.* Blue Ridge Summit, PA: Tab Books, 1992. ❖ A basic introduction to chemical elements.

PeriodicTable.com http://periodictable.com/ (accessed on August 26, 2003). ❖ Information about the periodic table suited to different audiences.

"The Periodic Table of Comic Books." *Department of Chemistry, University of Kentucky.* http://www.uky.edu/Projects/Chemcomics (accessed on August 26, 2003). ❖ An informative and amusing collection of information about various chemical elements and their properties as found in the pages of comic books.

"Periodic Table: Date of Discovery." *Chemical Elements.com* http://www.chemical elements.com/show/dateofdiscovery.html (accessed on August 26, 2003). ❖ An interactive periodic table, with history and background.

Sacks, Oliver. *Uncle Tungsten: Memories of a Chemical Boyhood.* New York: Vintage Books, 2002. ❖ Autobiography of Sacks tells of early chemistry experiments and learning about the elements.

chapter 16

Pesticides

A **pesticide** is any substance that prevents, repels, or kills pests. The definition of a pest is a relative one. A **pest** is an organism that is unwanted by humans at a specific time or in a specific place. Pests can range from cockroaches and mice, to fungi and plants. In modern day, pesticides are an integral part of food production and household use.

The use of pesticides has a long history. There is evidence that ancient Romans and Chinese, for example, used various minerals and plant extracts as pesticides. Manufactured chemical pesticides began in the 1930s and dramatically increased after World War II (1939–45). The widespread use of chemical pesticides led to an increased concern for how pesticides were affecting the environment, animals, and people. Over the years, pesticides have undergone much advancement, including the development of natural substances and improvements on the traditional.

Pest control

Pesticides are categorized according to what type of pests they affect. Some common types of pesticides include insecticides for insects, herbicides for weeds, fungicides for fungi, and rodenticides for rodents.

A pesticide can be a natural or a chemically **synthesized** substance. Chemical pesticides are **toxic,** meaning they contain poisons. Natural pesticides do not use poisons to affect pests. Both types of pesticides have positives and negatives. These pesticides control pests by physically, chemically, or biologically disrupting a pest's life cycle or behavior.

There are hundreds of different **synthetic** chemicals used in pesticides. How each pesticide works depends on its active ingredient(s).

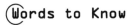

Words to Know

Biopesticide:
Pesticide produced from substances found in nature.

Control experiment:
A setup that is identical to the experiment, but is not affected by the variables that affects the experimental group.

Degrade:
Break down.

Deoxyribonucleic acid (DNA):
Large, complex molecules in cells that carries genetic information for an organism's development.

Did You Know?

- Total pesticide use in the United States is estimated at about 1 billion pounds per year; agriculture accounts for about 70 to 80 percent of pesticide use.

- At any time, it is estimated that there are about 10 quintillion (10,000,000,000,000,000,000) insects alive.

- The first pesticide-related law was passed in California in 1901—it regulated the quality of a single compound, an arsenic-based chemical that was commonly used as an insecticide.

- Organic farms, which are not allowed to use synthetic pesticides, became one of the fastest-growing segments of agriculture in the United States during the 1990s. Despite this growth, their number is still small: Only about 0.3 percent of all U.S. farmland was certified organic in 2001, according to the U.S. Research Service of the U.S. Department of Agriculture.

Words to Know

Hypothesis:
An idea in the form of a statement that can be tested by observation and/or experiment.

Leaching:
The movement of dissolved chemicals with water that is percolating, or oozing, downward through the soil.

Pest:
Any living thing that is unwanted by humans or causes injury and disease to crops and other growth.

Pesticide:
Substance used to reduce the abundance of pests.

Runoff:
Water not absorbed by the soil; moves downward and picks up particles along the way.

Synthesized:
Prepared by humans in a laboratory; not a naturally occurring process.

Some pesticides have similar properties based on their chemical structure. There are several groups of synthetic chemical pesticides that interrupt a pest's nerves from communicating with each other and from activating certain muscles. Organophosphates, for example, are a group of long-lasting pesticides that affect the central nervous system (brain) and peripheral nervous system (nerves found outside of the brain or spinal cord). In one pesticide, for example, the organophosphates prevent the nerves from signaling to the muscles that control the pest's breathing, resulting in suffocation and death.

The possible health effects for humans associated with an excess of chemical pesticide exposure include headaches, dizziness, muscle twitching, nausea, and damage to the central nervous system and kidneys.

Biopesticides are pesticides produced from substances found in nature; these do not use poison to affect pests. There are three main categories of biopesticides. One category includes those in which the active ingredient occurs in nature. For example, pheromones are

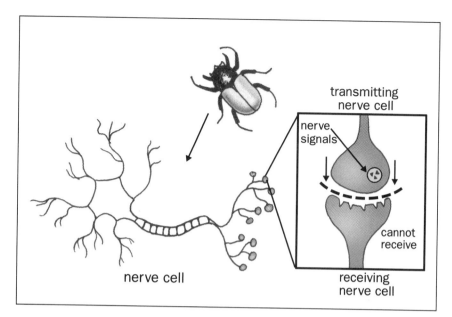

transmitting
nerve cell

nerve
signals

cannot
receive

nerve cell

receiving
nerve cell

Organophosphates, one type of synthetic pesticide, prevent the nerves from signaling to the muscles that control the pest's breathing, resulting in suffocation and death.

chemical scents animals use to communicate, attract mates, and mark territory. If a pheromone-based pesticide is released into the air at a time when insects are looking for each other to mate, the insects will become confused. Less mating and far fewer offspring will result. Other types of this biopesticide are garlic, mint, and red peppers.

The active ingredient in another type of biopesticide is microorganisms or microbes, such as bacteria and fungi. Microbes produce substances that destroy a range of other microbes. For example, there are fungi that control weeds, and other fungi that kill specific insects. The most widely used microbial insecticide is the soil-dwelling bacterium *Bacillus thuringiensis,* also known as Bt. When certain insects ingest the bacteria during the larvae stage, the bacteria interfere with the insect's digestion and cause the insect to starve.

One of the fastest-growing categories of biopesticides includes pesticide products that are genetically engineered or modified. Developed in the 1970s, genetic engineering is based on the understanding that genes are responsible for a species' characteristics. Genes are segments of deoxyribonucleic acid (DNA), a molecule in every organism's cell that carries genetic information for its development. Many organisms have genes that are responsible for producing substances that kill or prevent the growth of other organisms. This technique inserts the gene of one species into the DNA of the same or another

Words to Know

Synthetic:
A substance that is synthesized, or manufactured, in a laboratory; not naturally occurring.

Toxic:
Poisonous.

Variable:
Something that can affect the results of an experiment.

Volatilization:
The process by which a liquid changes (volatilizes) to a gas.

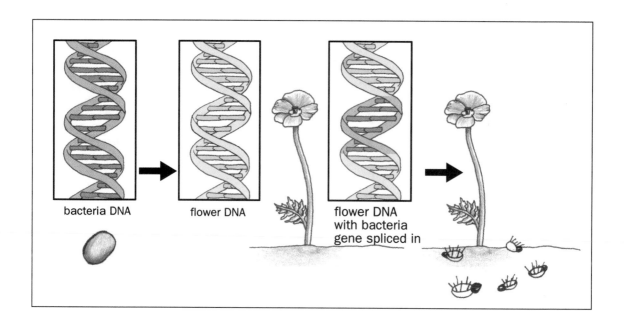

bacteria DNA

flower DNA

flower DNA
with bacteria
gene spliced in

By splicing bacteria DNA into the plant's DNA, scientists can create a genetically engineered plant that destroys specific pests.

species. The genetically modified organism then produces a desired trait. For example, scientists have taken the pest-fighting gene out of the Bt bacteria and inserted it into a corn plant's genetic material. The Bt corn then manufactures the substance that destroys the corn borer or another hungry insect.

The good, the bad, and the pesty

Pesticides both directly and indirectly hold many benefits for people. They increase agricultural yields by eliminating pests and weeds, providing more food and income for people around the world. They protect crops from disease that can devastate food supplies. In the mid-1800s, for example, a fungus spread quickly through Ireland's potato crops, resulting in the starvation of more than a million people and causing mass emigration. Shielding plants from disease also lessens disease in plant-eating livestock and, ultimately, in humans who would eat that plant or livestock. For the nonfarmer, the use of pesticides has become commonplace. Insect repellents, flea and tick pet collars, weed killers, and mildew cleaners are just a few of the household products that contain pesticides.

Yet because pesticides are designed to control living organisms, some affect organisms they are not targeted to control, called nontarget organisms. The result can harm humans, animals, and the environment. The pesticide dichlorodiphenyltrichloroethane (DDT) is the classic example of how pesticides can cause unintended effects. DDT was discovered to be an effective insecticide in 1939 and within a few years it became one of the most widely used pesticidal chemicals in the United States. Farmers used it on their crops, and the government used it to protect people against disease-carrying insects, such as mosquitoes that carried malaria.

A cotton farmer in India points to genetically modified Bt cotton infected with bollworms, January 2003. Bt cotton has failed to prevent bollworm attacks, for which it was designed. (Reproduced by permission of AP/Wide World.)

For years scientists warned about the possible harmful effects of DDT; then in 1962 Rachel Carson's book *Silent Spring* was published. Her book mapped out how DDT was harming wildlife, the environment, and people. In one scenario, DDT sprayed on plants was eaten by small animals, which were then consumed by birds. The pesticide harmed both the adult birds and their eggs. The eggs' shells were so thin they were often crushed when the mother sat on them during their incubation period. Eggs that were not crushed often did not hatch. The book stimulated widespread public concern, and in 1973 the chemical was banned in the United States (it is still used in other countries).

A balancing act

The danger of pesticides to humans and the environment depends upon the pesticide and its mechanism for pest control. Some factors that determine a pesticide's potential harm are its toxicity, specificity

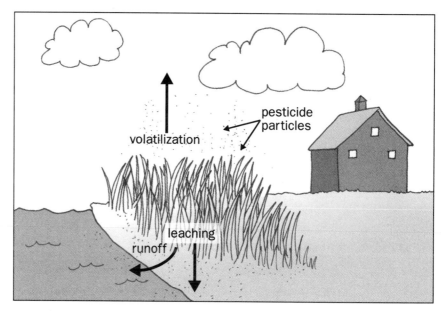

Pesticides can spread through the environment through volatilization, runoff, and leaching.

in its targets, and how long it remains in the environment before it breaks down or **degrades.**

Pesticides can enter nontarget plants, insects, and other organisms in several ways. Pesticides do not always stay where they are put down. Wind or rain can carry the pesticide into bodies of water. There, it can affect sea life and contaminate water. It can move through or **leach** into the soil. Leaching is the movement of dissolved chemicals with water downward through the soil. Water not absorbed into the soil also causes pesticides to travel. When this water moves over a sloping surface it is called **runoff;** the runoff picks up and carries the pesticides. Leaching and runoff cause pesticides to travel into unintended locations, sometimes winding up in groundwater, lakes, oceans, or neighboring areas. In a process called **volatilization,** some pesticides convert into a gas and move in the air. These pesticides can travel long distances before they settle down into waters or on land.

One of the most important factors that affects the risk of pesticide leaching is the amount of time it takes for the pesticide to degrade. Pesticides degrade into substances that are usually less toxic. Pesticides can attach to soil particles and remain in effect long after the manufacturers intended. The longer a pesticide lasts, the greater the chance it will accumulate in an unintended area or nontarget organism. DDT was an example of a long-lasting pesticide.

experiment
CENTRAL

The advantage of biopesticides is that they have a low danger level (toxicity) to organisms they are not targeted for and to humans. Low toxicity means less risk to water supplies and life. Many of these biopesticides also degrade relatively rapidly.

The drawback to biopesticides is that they are not as powerful as conventional chemical pesticides. Because these pesticides degrade quickly, they have only a short time period where they can be used. In addition, certain microbial pesticides can become inactive if exposed to extreme environmental conditions, such as too much heat or dryness. Some environmental and citizens groups are also concerned about genetically modified organisms. They say that these plants may produce unintended consequences to people, the environment, and animals.

The U.S. federal government evaluates and regulates pesticide use. Regulations on pesticides applied to foods have especially strict safety standards. Pesticides are labeled as to their level of toxicity. Washing and cooking foods are ways that people can reduce pesticide residue.

A swarm of locusts surrounds a Filipino farmer. A locust infestation of rice and sugar farms in Tarlac, Philippines, in 1994 caused major crop and financial losses for farmers. (© Reuters NewMedia/CORBIS. Reproduced by permission.)

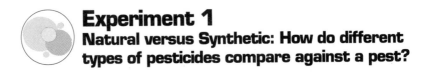

Experiment 1
Natural versus Synthetic: How do different types of pesticides compare against a pest?

Purpose/Hypothesis

Many plants produce substances that prevent or harm pests. Some of these substances kill their insect predators and others repel them. For example, a plant can emit an odor that prevents pests from approaching. Yet while biopesticides are generally safer to the environment and carry fewer risks to people, chemicals remain the pesticide of choice for the vast majority of professionals. Because pesticides are so important to society, people are continuously searching for the most effective substance that will cause the least harm.

In this experiment you will examine how biopesticides compare to a synthetic pesticide. The two natural pesticides are a spray made from chili peppers and one made from garlic. These are commonly used among gardeners as repellents. With chili, it is the hot chilies that make the most effective repellent. Garlic's strong odor can also act as a repellent. With the synthetic insecticides, look for one that works against general pests, such as aphids, caterpillars, beetles. Evidence of these pests can be seen in the holes they bore or bits of leaves that they have munched. Aphids will leave a sticky residue on the leaves.

Once you have made a spray of the natural substances, you can apply all the pesticides to the same type of plant and set outside. To measure the effective of each pesticide you can examine the plant's general health, count holes in the leaves and pests on the plant, and feel the leaves.

Before you begin, make an educated guess about the outcome of this experiment based on your knowledge of synthetic pesticides and biopesticides. This educated guess, or prediction, is your **hypothesis.** A hypothesis should explain these things:

- the topic of the experiment
- the **variable** you will change
- the variable you will measure
- what you expect to happen

A hypothesis should be brief, specific, and measurable. It must be something you can test through further investigation. Your experi-

experiment
CENTRAL

What Are the Variables?

Variables are anything that might affect the results of an experiment. Here are the main variables in this experiment:

- the type of plant
- the pests in the environment
- the type of pesticide
- the climate

In other words, the variables in this experiment are everything that might affect the amount of pests that are attracted to the plant. If you change more than one variable at the same time, you will not be able to tell which variable had the most effect on the pesticide's effectiveness.

ment will prove or disprove whether your hypothesis is correct. Here is one possible hypothesis for this experiment: "The synthetic pesticide product will better prevent pests from harming the plants than the biopesticides."

In this case, the variable you will change is the type of pesticide sprayed on the plant. The variable you will measure is the amount of damage to the plant caused by pests.

Conducting a control experiment will help you isolate each variable and measure the changes in the dependent variable. Only one variable will change between the control and your experiment. For your control in this experiment you will not apply any pesticide to a plant. At the end of the experiment you can compare the control plant to the experimental plants.

Level of Difficulty

Moderate.

Materials Needed

- four small plants of the same type, preferably broad leafed (coleus works well)
- one hot chili pepper (habañeros work well)

- one garlic bulb (five cloves) or crushed garlic
- spray bottle
- chemical pesticide (available from hardware store, drugstore, or greenhouse)
- outside area
- water
- two bowls
- marking pen
- chopping knife
- cheesecloth
- funnel
- rubber gloves
- several nice days

Approximate Budget
$15.

Timetable
45 minutes set-up; overnight waiting; 10 minutes every 3 days for about 2 weeks.

Step-by-Step Instructions
1. Label the plant containers: "Pepper," "Garlic," "Chemical," and "Control."
2. Prepare the chili pepper spray: Chop one chili and place the pieces in a bowl. Boil 1 cup (about 240 milliliters) of water and pour over the chopped peppers. Set aside overnight.

How to Experiment Safely
Have an adult present for this experiment. Be careful when working with hot water and chili peppers. The pepper's seeds and juices can burn, so wear rubber gloves and avoid touching your face; never directly ingest the peppers or touch your eyes. Make sure you apply the chemical pesticide outside and follow the directions and warnings carefully. Wear a long-sleeved shirt and long pants when applying and wash your hands afterwards.

Materials needed to compare different pesticides in Experiment 1.

3. The next day, prepare the garlic spray: Finely chop about five cloves of garlic and add 1 cup (about 240 milliliters) of hot water. Set aside for 2 hours until cool.

4. When the solutions are ready, use the cheesecloth to strain out the garlic and the peppers. Use the funnel to pour one of the solutions into the spray bottle.

5. In an open area outside, spray the first solution on the plant labeled for that pesticide. (See Troubleshooter's Guide.) After each application, set the plant in a distant area to keep each pesticide isolated from the other plants. Make sure to wash out the spray bottle thoroughly between the pepper and garlic spray (save each solution in a covered and labeled container). Repeat with the other two solutions. Do not spray anything on the control.

6. Set the four plants outside in the same general area, leaving enough room between the plants so they do not touch one another.

Troubleshooter's Guide

Below are some problems that may arise during this experiment, some possible causes, and some ways to remedy the problems.

Problem: The natural sprays did not stick to the plant leaves.

Possible cause: The mixtures adhere to the leaves of some plants more than others. Try adding a drop of nondetergent dishwashing soap and mixing well, then reapply.

Problem: None of the plants had much evidence of pests.

Possible cause: This experiment works best when there are many insects around, often during the spring and summer months. Try to set your plants down in a wooded area or one that has a large quantity of plants and then continue your observations.

7. Every 3 days for the next 15 days observe the plants and note any pests or effects of pests. Reapply the sprays if it rains. If you reapply, again make sure to isolate each plant when you spray.

Summary of Results

Was your hypothesis correct? Look at your data and determine how the pesticides compared to one another. Was there one type of pest that was on one plant more than another? Some types of insects, such as aphids, gather on the underside of leaves. Note the relative amount of any different type of pests on each plant. How did the control plant compare to the experimental plants?

Change the Variables

In this experiment you can change the variables in several ways.

- change the type of plant
- use the same pesticide and set the plants down in different environments, such as near lush plant growth or in an open space
- apply different types of synthetic pesticides
- make up and apply different natural pesticides, such as pesticides made from onions, soaps, neem oil, and molasses.

- use the same pesticide and see how close you need to apply it to the plant for it to be effective.

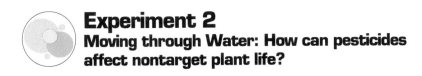

Experiment 2
Moving through Water: How can pesticides affect nontarget plant life?

Purpose/Hypothesis

Leaching and runoff can cause pesticides to move away from their target location. When pesticides mix with rain or irrigation water, they can seep into the soil and travel to another area where they can affect the plant, animals, and environment. In this experiment, you will examine the effects of pesticides on new growth. You will plant a lettuce seed and nurture it with water that has insecticide in it. Planting three sets of seeds, you will add two varying amounts of insecticide to the water and compare them to lettuce grown in unaltered water.

Before you begin, make an educated guess about the outcome of this experiment based on your knowledge of leaching, runoff, and pesticides. This educated guess, or prediction, is your **hypothesis.** A hypothesis should explain these things:

- the topic of the experiment
- the **variable** you will change
- the variable you will measure
- what you expect to happen

A hypothesis should be brief, specific, and measurable. It must be something you can test through further investigation. Your experiment will prove or disprove whether your hypothesis is correct. Here is one possible hypothesis for this experiment: "Water with the greatest amount of pesticide will result in stunted or no plant growth."

In this case, the variable you will change is the amount of insecticide in the water. The variable you will measure is the plant health.

Conducting a **control experiment** will help you isolate each variable and measure the changes in the dependent variable. Only one variable will change between the control and your experiment. For the control in this experiment you will give the lettuce plant plain water. At the end of the experiment, you can compare the results from the control experiment with the experimental plants.

experiment
CENTRAL

What Are the Variables?

Variables are anything that might affect the results of an experiment. Here are the main variables in this experiment:

- the type of plant
- the environment
- the amount of pesticide
- the type of pesticide

In other words, the variables in this experiment are anything that might affect the growth of the plant. If you change more than one variable at the same time, you will not be able to tell which variable had the most effect on the plant's health.

Level of Difficulty

Easy to Moderate.

Materials Needed

- 15 lettuce seeds
- peat pots, with moist to dry soil (available at garden stores)
- water
- liquid synthetic insecticide
- marking pen
- masking tape
- ruler
- area with light
- paper towels
- plastic wrap
- two rubber bands
- plastic teaspoon
- measuring cup
- three disposable plastic cups

Approximate Budget

$7.

Timetable

20 minutes setup; about 5 minutes daily for 8 to 12 days (longer if desired).

How to Experiment Safely

Have an adult present for this experiment. Be careful when working with the pesticide. Measure the pesticide outside or in a sink. Follow the warnings carefully and wash your hands afterwards. Make sure you throw away the disposable cups and spoons that come into contact with the pesticide. Keep younger children away from the cups containing the pesticide mixtures.

Step-by-Step Instructions

1. Label the disposable cups: "Low Pesticide," "High Pesticide," and "Control." Label each peat pot "Low," "High," and "Control." The dirt should be dry to moist.

2. In the Low Pesticide cup, use the plastic spoon to place 2 teaspoons (about 10 milliliters) of the pesticide in the cup.

3. In the High Pesticide cup, use the plastic spoon to place 5 teaspoons (about 25 milliliters) of the pesticide in the cup.

4. Measure and pour 0.5 cup (about 125 milliliters) of water into each of the cups. The Control cup should have plain water. Use plastic spoons to stir the High and Low cups, making sure to throw the spoons away when you have finished.

5. In each peat pot, plant five lettuce seeds per the instructions on the package.

6. Working over a sink or paper towels, pour the High pesticide water into the peat pot labeled High. Pour enough water to saturate the lettuce seeds. Water will start to drip out the bottom when you have poured enough.

7. Repeat with the Low water, and the Control water. Set the plants on a plastic container or holder to catch the water dripping out the bottom.

8. To seal in the water, tightly cover the disposable cups (not the peat pots) with plastic wrap and wrap a rubber band around the plastic. Place the water cups aside near the plants and make sure labeling is clearly visible.

9. After the seeds sprout (about 5 days), start daily observations of the plants. Count how many sprouts there are in each pot and measure the height. Make your measurements at the same time every day.

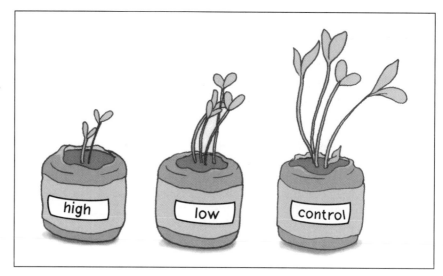

Step 9: Note the number of sprouts in each pot and measure the height of the plants.

10. When the seeds need more water, use the water from its designated cup until the water is gone. (You may need to restir.)

Summary of Results

Examine the height and number of sprouts from each peat pot. Average the heights of each group and graph the results. Is there a difference between the experimental trials and the control? Are there any other physical characteristics that are different among the groups of lettuce sprouts? Write up a brief summary of the experiment.

Change the Variables

You can change the variables in this experiment in several ways:

- Change the brand of insecticide; try to find one with different main ingredients than the one you used
- Alter the type of pesticide, to a herbicide or fungicide
- Compare different types of plants, such as peas, tomatoes, and a flower

 # Design Your Own Experiment

How to Select a Topic Relating to this Concept

Pesticides are a continuously evolving groups of products, which have a significant impact on society. Organic food products are not treated

Troubleshooter's Guide

Below are some problems that may arise during this experiment, some possible causes, and some ways to remedy the problem.

Problem: None of the plants grew.

Possible cause: Make sure you are following instructions as to the amount of light and warmth the seeds need. You may also have bought defective seeds. Try the experiment again with a new packet, making sure to follow the instructions.

Problem: There was not much difference between the two groups of seeds watered with the pesticides.

Possible cause: All the pesticide water may not have soaked into the plants. Make sure you stir the water thoroughly before applying it to the seeds, and repeat the experiment.

with chemical-based pesticides. You can compare organic fruits and vegetables to chemically treated foods. You can also look at the impact pesticides have had on food production throughout the world.

When experimenting with pesticides, always make sure to work in an open area and take proper safety precautions. Check the For More Information section and talk with your science teacher to learn more about pesticides. You could also speak with a professional at a local greenhouse or nursery, or any knowledgeable gardener.

Steps in the Scientific Method

To conduct an original experiment, you need to plan carefully and think things through. Otherwise, you might not be sure what question you are answering, what you are or should be measuring, or what your findings prove or disprove.

Here are the steps in designing an experiment:

- State the purpose of—and the underlying question behind—the experiment you propose to do.

- Recognize the variables involved and select one that will help you answer the question at hand.
- State your hypothesis, an educated guess about the answer to your question.
- Decide how to change the variable you selected.
- Decide how to measure your results.

Recording Data and Summarizing the Results

Your data should include charts and graphs such as the one you did for these experiments. They should be clearly labeled and easy to read. You may also want to include photographs and drawings of your experimental setup and results, which will help other people visualize the steps in the experiment.

If you are preparing an exhibit, you may want to display your results, such as any experimental setup you designed. If you have completed a nonexperimental project, explain clearly what your research question was and illustrate your findings.

Related Projects

With so many pesticide options, there are many possible project ideas. You can explore the biology of how pesticides work on insects. Choose one or two groups of chemical pesticides, then compare the effect of these to the substances that plants produce to ward off insects. How do herbicides affect plants? The amount of time pesticides remain in the soil and on plants is another area of study. An experiment can look at how often a pesticide needs to be reapplied for effectiveness.

You can also conduct a project that looks at how different pesticides move through the soil. Determining if a pesticide is on soil or in water is usually determined through chemical analysis. One home technique to find out where pesticides are would be to compare the test samples against a standard. Measure the standard by setting a pesticide-sprayed plant outside for a certain length of time and noting the results. You can then spray the water with possible pesticide in it and compare the results to the standard.

For a research project, you can explore the use of pesticides on food products, how pesticides have changed over the years, and the precautions that are taken on the foods. How do organic products compare in size and yield? Compare the United States to other countries' use of pesticides.

For More Information

"About Pesticides." *U.S. Environmental Protection Agency.* http://www.epa.gov/pesticides/about (accessed on August 26, 2003). ❖ Provides answers to frequently asked questions about pesticides.

"50 Ways Farmers Can Protect Their Groundwater: 24. Determine the Soil–Pesticide Interaction Rating." *University of Illinois Extension: College of Agricultural, Consumer, and Environmental Sciences.* http://www.thisland.uiuc.edu/50ways/50ways_24.html (accessed on August 26, 2003). ❖ This site is intended primarily for farmers, but offers good explanations of how pesticides get into soil and their effects.

Nancarrow, Loren, and Janet Hogan Taylor. *Dead Snails Leave No Trails.* Berkeley, CA: Ten Speed Press, 1996. ❖ Natural pest control information and recipes.

"Pesticides As Water Pollutants." *Food and Agriculture Organization.* http://www.fao.org/docrep/W2598E/w2598e07.htm#historical%20development%20of%20pesticides (accessed on August 26, 2003). ❖ Information on how pesticides can pollute groundwater.

chapter 17

Plants and Water

Plants are a diverse group of organisms that include over 250,000 species. They live in a range of environmental conditions, from mountaintops to the ocean floor. They can claim the world's largest organism, a redwood tree that can stretch to a height of 364 feet (110 meters), and the world's oldest organism, the 4,700-year-old bristlecone pine tree.

Without plants, life on Earth as it is now could not exist. Plants make their own food by **photosynthesis,** a process that uses the energy of the Sun to make sugar and oxygen. Humans and other organisms use the oxygen released by photosynthesis to survive. Plants are also used for food, shelter, and protection by organisms in every known environment.

Plants depend on water for several essential functions. Water is needed for photosynthesis and to help transport nutrients through a plant's system. Most growing plants contain about 90 percent water. This water maintains the plant's internal temperature and provides it structure. Without water or with too much water, a plant dies. How plants take in water and what they do with it is essential for their survival.

Rooting water flow

Water enters a plant through the plant's **root hairs,** hundreds of fine hairs that extend out from the root. These hairs suck in the water that lies between the soil particles. Most of the nutrients that a plant needs are dissolved in this water. The root hairs absorb the water through a process called **osmosis.** Osmosis is the movement of water from an area where there is a high concentration of water to an area of low

Words to Know

Cell membrane:
The layer that surrounds the cell, but is inside the cell wall, allowing some molecules to enter and keeping others out of the cell.

Cell wall:
A tough outer covering over the cell membrane of bacteria and plant cells.

Dormant:
A state of inactivity in an organism.

Words to Know

Control experiment:
A setup that is identical to the experiment, but is not affected by the variable that acts on the experimental group.

Hypothesis:
An idea in the form of a statement that can be tested by observation and/or experiment.

Osmosis:
The movement of fluids and substances dissolved in liquids across a semi-permeable membrane from an area of greater concentration to an area of lesser concentration until all substances involved reach a balance.

Photosynthesis:
Chemical process by which plants containing chlorophyll use sunlight to manufacture their own food by converting carbon dioxide and water into carbohydrates, releasing oxygen as a by-product.

water concentration through the **cell membrane,** the layer that encircles and holds the parts of a cell together. The cell's membrane is semipermeable, meaning it allows some things to pass through the membrane and prevents others from passing.

Once inside the root hair, the plant uses osmosis to move the water into the **xylem** (pronounced ZY-lem). The xylem are long tubes or vessels made up of bundles of dead cells with tough cell walls. Xylem vessels transport water to all parts of the plant, from the root to the leaves. Water in the xylem is mainly drawn upwards through osmosis because there is a continual need for water in the outer leaves of a plant. Water in leaves is constantly evaporating or turning into water vapor. Water vapor is water in its gas state. The low concentration of water in the leaves pulls the water upwards.

In plants, this loss of water is called **transpiration.** For most plants transpiration occurs primarily on the leaves. A leaf's surface has tiny pores called **stomata** that open and close regularly to exchange gases, such as oxygen and carbon dioxide. When stomata are open, the plant loses water or transpires.

Like evaporation, transpiration occurs more rapidly in hot, dry weather. In most plants there are more stomata located on the under-

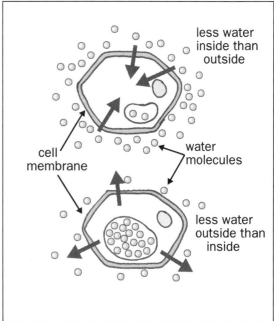

side of the leaves. This ensures the plant will not lose too much water since it is transpiring on the side facing away from the sun. Some plants have tiny hairs that protect them from transpiring too much. Other plants are protected from excess water loss by a waxy film covering the outer layer of the leaves. Desert plants have thorns in place of leaves to avoid losing too much water.

Standing up straight

Aside from providing a plant's basic food and water requirements, water maintains a plant cell's structure and shape. The visible sign that a plant has taken in enough water is when it stands up straight and shows no sign of limpness.

In a plant cell the membrane is surrounded by a rigid **cell wall.** Inside the cell wall in the center of the plant cell there is a large, liquid compartment called a **vacuole** (pronounced VAK-yoo-ole). Vacuoles transport and store nutrients, waste products, and other molecules. A vacuole is also the area in the cell where water collects. When water enters the vacuole, it causes pressure to build inside the cell. The pressure of the vacuole pushing outwards on the cells is called **turgor pressure.** The strong cell walls keep the buildup of water from bursting the cell, which results in increased pressure.

LEFT:
Water enters a plant through the plant's root hairs. The root hairs absorb the water through a process called osmosis. (Copyright © Kelly A. Quin. Reproduced by permission of Kelly A. Quin.)

RIGHT:
Osmosis is the movement of water through the cell membrane from an area of high water concentration to an area of low water concentration.

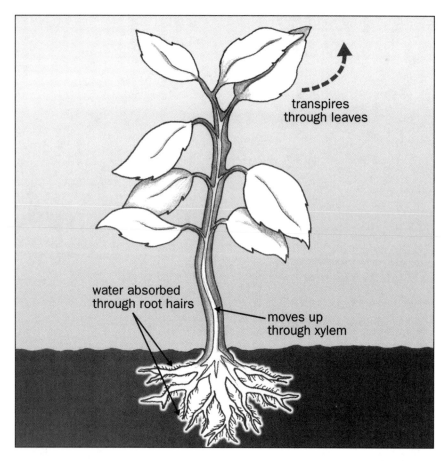

The plant uses osmosis to move the water into the xylem. Xylem vessels transport water to all parts of the plant, from the roots to the leaves.

transpires
through leaves

water absorbed
through root hairs

moves up
through xylem

Turgor pressure of all the neighboring cells is what allows a plant to stand upright. If a plant does not have enough water in its cells there is nothing pressing against the cell walls. This phenomenon causes **plasmolysis,** meaning when a cell has lost its water, and wilting results. Plasmolysis frequently occurs in plants left in hot sunny windows and not given enough water. As long as the cells are still living the turgor pressure can be increased. Watering the plant will cause the cells to take in water and the vacuoles again press against the wall to straighten the plant.

Turgor pressure also impacts transpiration as it affects whether the stomata (singular: stoma) open. A stoma is surrounded by two guard cells. When water enters these surrounding cells, the turgor pressure causes them to swell and creates an opening between them, which is the stoma. When the turgor pressure decreases, the cells relax and the stomata close.

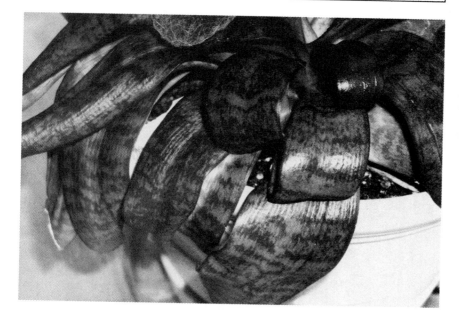

vacuole

turgor pressure

cell wall

not enough water
causes the cell
to deflate

increased water
causes vacuole to push
against cell wall

Turgor pressure is what allows a plant to stand upright.

A wilting plant is a sure sign of plasmolysis, meaning the plant is in need of water. (Copyright © Kelly A. Quin. Reproduced by permission of Kelly A. Quin.)

Adapting to dry environments

In places where water is a rare resource, such as deserts, plants have had to adapt to survive in the dry, hot environment. These plants usually have special methods of storing and conserving water. The desert cacti, for example, have few or no leaves, which reduces transpiration. Some desert plants have deep roots to pull up water deep in the sand. Other plants have shallow roots that

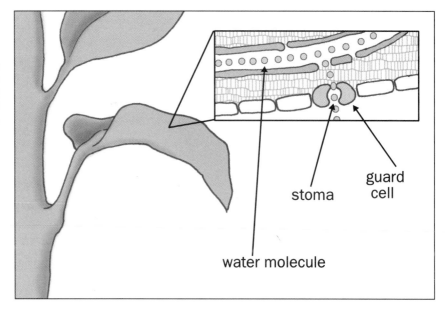

Turgor pressure causes guard cells to open the stoma, causing transpiration to occur.

stoma

guard cell

water molecule

thread out extensively so they can quickly suck up water close to the surface.

Desert plants can store water in their stems, leaves, or thick roots. For example, the old man cactus has a layer of hair that helps it to store water. This hair can also keep it from losing water by lessening the drying effects of the wind.

Desert plants, such as the organ pipe cactus, have developed special methods of storing and conserving water to survive in the dry, hot environment. (Reproduced by permission of Field Mark Publications.)

Some desert plants are **dormant,** not active, during dry periods, and then spring to life when it rains. To avoid the heat of the Sun, many plants move into action during the night hours. For example, the Sonoran Desert's saguaro only opens its white flowers at night.

Some desert plants have adapted by having smaller or no leaves. On others, leaves will have a thick covering that is coated with a waxy substance to reduce water loss. Hair on the leaves of plants helps to reduce the evaporation of moisture from the surface of leaves by reflecting sunlight.

Experiment 1
Water Flow: How do varying solutions of water affect the amount of water a plant takes in and its turgor pressure?

Purpose/Hypothesis

To maintain a stable environment, plants move water in and out of their cells until the concentration of water molecules is equal on both sides of the cell membrane. Osmosis causes the water to flow from a region of high concentration to a region of low concentration. As the plant cells takes in more water, the turgor pressure increases; when the plant cells take in less water, the turgor pressure decreases.

Changing the concentration of the particles, or solutes, dissolved in water will change the amount of water present. Adding salt to water, for example, makes the water have a high concentration of solutes, which is called a hypertonic solution. A low-solute concentration is called a hypotonic solution. In osmosis, cells will try to equalize the concentration of the solute molecules. A cell placed in a hypotonic solution will draw water into its cells to equalize the solute molecules. A cell in a hypertonic solution will move water out of the cell to make the solutes more equal.

In this experiment, you will examine the movement of water in a plant. This experiment will investigate how varying concentrations of salt water affect the amount of water that enters or leaves a plant's cells. You will place a flower in three colored-water solutions, two of which contain different concentrations of salt. You will measure the movement of water in three ways: observing the plant's turgor pressure, observing the water movement in the plant, and weighing the flowers before and after they are placed in the water.

Before you begin, make an educated guess about the outcome of this experiment based on your knowledge of plant cells and turgor

(W)ords to Know

Transpiration:
Evaporation of water in the form of water vapor from the stomata on the surfaces of leaves and stems of plants.

Turgor pressure:
The force that is exerted on a plant's cell wall by the water within the cell.

Vacuole:
An enclosed, space-filling sac within plant cells containing mostly water and providing structural support for the cell.

Variable:
Something that can affect the results of an experiment.

Xylem:
Plant tissue consisting of elongated, thick-walled cells that transport water and mineral nutrients. (Pronounced ZY-lem.)

What Are the Variables?

Variables are anything that might affect the results of an experiment. Here are the main variables in this experiment:

- the amount of salt
- the type of plant
- the water
- time of experiment
- environmental conditions

In other words, the variables in this experiment are everything that might affect the amount of water the plant draws in or out of its cells. If you change more than one variable, you will not be able to tell which variable impacted the water uptake.

pressure. This educated guess, or prediction, is your **hypothesis.** A hypothesis should explain these things:

- the topic of the experiment
- the **variable** you will change
- the variable you will measure
- what you expect to happen

A hypothesis should be brief, specific, and measurable. It must be something you can test through further investigation. Your experiment will prove or disprove whether your hypothesis is correct. Here is one possible hypothesis for this experiment: "Water with a low concentration of salt will flow into a plant's cells and cause an increase in turgor pressure and weight; water with a high concentration of salt will flow out of a plant's cells and cause a decrease in turgor pressure and weight."

In this case, the variable you will change is the amount of salt in the water. The variable you will measure is how much water the plant has drawn into its cells.

Conducting a **control experiment** will help you isolate each variable and measure the changes in the dependent variable. Only one variable will change between the control and the experimental plants, and that is the amount of salt. For the control, you will place the flower in plain water. At the end of the experiment you will compare this plant with each of the others.

Note: When making a solid-liquid solution (solid/liquid), it is standard to use weight/weight (grams/grams) or weight/volume (grams/milliliters). With water, 1 gram of water equals 1 milliliter. In this experiment, teaspoons and tablespoons are used to measure the solid.

Level of Difficulty
Easy to Moderate.

Materials Needed
- four clear plastic cups
- three white carnation flowers
- blue food coloring, concentrated
- salt
- measuring spoons
- scale
- sharp knife or plant shears
- marking pen

Approximate Budget
$7.

Timetable
45 minutes for setup and followup; 8 to 12 hours waiting.

Step-by-Step Instructions
1. Make a 40 percent weight/weight (gram/gram) solution of salt water. One gram of water equals 1 milliliter of water. Add 7 tablespoons (96 grams) of salt to 1 cup (240 milliliters or 240 grams) of warm water. If you have a gram scale you can measure 40 grams

How to Experiment Safely
Handle the knife or scissors carefully when cutting the stems.

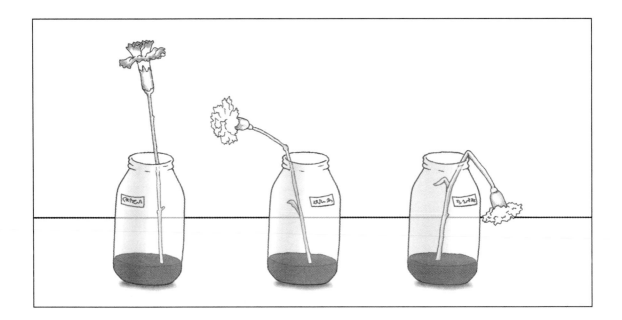

Step 9: Leave the flowers undisturbed eight to twelve hours.

of salt and add that with 100 grams of warm water. Add the salt slowly and stir after each addition. The salt should be completely dissolved in the water. Label the cup "40 percent."

2. To make a 20 percent solution of salt water, add 3.5 table-spoons (46 grams) of salt to 1 cup (240 milliliters or 240 grams) of warm water. If you have a gram scale you can measure 20 grams of salt and add that to 100 grams of water. Label the cup "20 percent."

3. Allow the water to cool to room temperature.

4. Fill up a cup with plain water. Label the cup "Control."

5. Stir several drops of blue dye into each cup for a strong blue color.

6. Carefully cut each carnation's stem under cool running water.

7. Dry off the stems and weigh each flower.

8. Place one carnation in each of the cups of water.

9. Leave the flowers undisturbed 8 to 12 hours.

10. In a chart, describe the turgor pressure of each flower relative to the 20 percent salt concentration. Weigh each flower and note in the chart. Examine the blue water's movement and note whether the water has entered each flower.

Summary of Results

Examine the chart. Has the water entered some flower or flowers more than others? If the blue water is not visible in the white flower of

experiment
CENTRAL

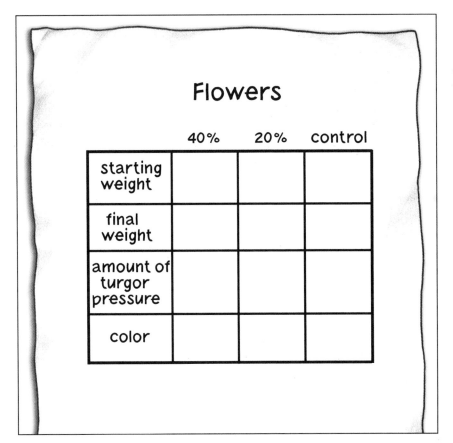

Step 10: Data chart for Experiment 1.

the carnation, you may want to carefully cut the bottom part of the stem to see if the water has entered the flower. Observe the stem's bottom of each flower and the petals of the carnations. Look at the before and after weights of each flower. How do the test flowers compare to the control flowers? In any flower that took up the water, describe how the water entered the petals. Write a paragraph describing your results and explanations of what occurred.

Change the Variables

You can vary this experiment several ways.

- Change the type of flower or plant you use. Celery stalks, with leaves, and white-colored flowers with large stems work well.
- Alter the solute you put in the water to another substance, such as sugar.
- Decrease or increase the amount of time the plant is sitting in the solution.

Troubleshooter's Guide

Below are some problems that may arise during this experiment, some possible causes, and some ways to remedy the problem.

Problem: The water did not go move at all or barely moved into any of the carnations.

Possible cause: You may have started out with a flower that was dead. Purchase another flower and repeat the experiment.

Possible cause: You may have crushed the stem when you cut it. Try the experiment again, making sure to cut the stem under cool water. Cutting under water prevents the flowers from taking in air instead of water.

Problem: The flower was heavier and the turgor pressure increased but water did not go appear to enter the plant.

Possible cause: The water may have moved into the plant but you were not able to see it because the color was not strong enough. Make sure you are using a non-sweetened concentrated dye. Blue ink works well also. Repeat the experiment, making sure the water is a rich blue color.

- Change the environmental conditions of the plant by placing one flower under a heat lamp or out in the sun, and another in a cool, dark place.

Experiment 2
Transpiration: How do different environmental conditions affect plants' rates of transpiration?

Purpose/Hypothesis

All plants transpire. The rate of transpiration depends on a plant's physical properties and its environmental conditions. As transpiration occurs mainly on the leaf, a general rule is that plants with larger leaves will transpire more than plants with smaller leaves.

In this experiment, you will examine the environmental factors that affect a plant's transpiration rate. Using the same type and size plants, you will vary the amount of heat and wind each plant receives. You will place one plant in a warm environment, a second plant in a windy environment, and a third plant in a cool, calm environment.

Before you begin, make an educated guess about the outcome of this experiment based on your knowledge of plants and transpiration. This educated guess, or prediction, is your **hypothesis.** A hypothesis should explain these things:

- the topic of the experiment
- the **variable** you will change
- the variable you will measure
- what you expect to happen

A hypothesis should be brief, specific, and measurable. It must be something you can test through further investigation. Your experiment will prove or disprove whether your hypothesis is correct. Here is one possible hypothesis for this experiment: "Plants that receive more heat and wind will transpire at a greater rate than plants in a cool, calm environment."

In this case, the variable you will change is the environment of the plant. The variable you will measure is the amount of water the plant transpires.

Conducting a **control experiment** will help you isolate each variable and measure the changes in the dependent variable. Only one variable will change between the control and the experimental plants, and that is the change to its environment. For the control, you will place the plant in a standard indoor environment. At the end of the experiment you will compare this plant with each of the others.

Level of Difficulty
Moderate.

Materials Needed
- four potted plants with large leaves; make sure the leaves are not waxy or hairy: geraniums, caladiums, coleus, and philodendrons work well
- four plastic sandwich bags
- wire ties
- small fan

What Are the Variables?

Variables are anything that might affect the results of an experiment. Here are the main variables in this experiment:

- environmental conditions, temperature and wind
- time given for experiment
- type of plant
- leaf size
- leaf shape
- soil content

    In other words, the variables in this experiment are everything that might affect the amount of water that the plant transpires. If you change more than one variable at the same time, you will not be able to tell which variable impacted the plant's rate of transpiration.

- four small dry sponges
- scale

Approximate Budget
$15.

Timetable
1 hour preparation time; 24 hours waiting.

Step-by-Step Instructions
1. Assign each plant a number. On each plant, place a sandwich bag over a group of three to four leaves. Choose leaves that are of equal dimensions.
2. Fasten each bag securely on the stem with a wire tie.
3. Place one plant in the direct sunlight or under a heat lamp. Place one plant in a dark, covered area. Place the third plant in front of the fan and turn the fan on low. Leave the control plant indoors and set it aside.
4. After 24 hours note the results of any water in the bags.

How to Experiment Safely

This experiment poses no safety hazards. For the plants' health, when you have completed the experiment remove the plastic bags and care for the plant as directed.

5. Weigh a dry sponge and record the weight.
6. Carefully, soak up all the water in the bag with the sponge. Reweigh the sponge and record the weight.
7. Repeat Steps 5 and 6 for every plant, using a new sponge each time.

Summary of Results

Create a data table to record your observations. Subtract the weight of the dry sponge from the final weight of the wet sponge to calculate

Step 3: Place each plant in a different environmental condition.

the weight of the water each plant transpired. Was your hypothesis correct? For additional information, you could determine the area of each of the leaves and calculate the rate of transpiration for the entire plant. Hypothesize what adaptations outside plants could make to transpire less, compared to the characteristics of indoor plants.

Change the Variables

There are several ways that you can change this experiment. One variable you can change is the type of plant. Choose another plant with a broader leaf. With a larger bag, you can also conduct the transpiration experiment on trees. You can lengthen the amount of time the plants transpire. You can also alter the environmental conditions, such as producing a humid environment or a dry environment.

Design Your Own Experiment

How to Select a Topic Relating to this Concept

You come into contact with plants every day through your diet and environment. Observe the plants that are around you as you prepare to design an experiment. You could also visit a greenhouse and examine the different species of plants available.

Check the For More Information section and talk with your science teacher to learn more about plants and water. You could also talk with a botanist in your area or a professional who works with plants.

Steps in the Scientific Method

To conduct an original experiment, you need to plan carefully and think things through. Otherwise, you might not be sure what question you are answering, what you are or should be measuring, or what your findings prove or disprove.

Here are the steps in designing an experiment:

- State the purpose of—and the underlying question behind—the experiment you propose to do.
- Recognize the variables involved and select one that will help you answer the question at hand.
- State your hypothesis, an educated guess about the answer to your question.
- Decide how to change the variable you selected.
- Decide how to measure your results.

Recording Data and Summarizing the Results

Your data should include charts and graphs such as the one you did for these experiments. They should be clearly labeled and easy to read. You may also want to include photographs and drawings of your experimental setup and results, which will help other people visualize the steps in the experiment.

If you are preparing an exhibit, you may want to display your results, such as any experimental setup you designed. If you have completed a nonexperimental project, explain clearly what your research question was and illustrate your findings.

Related Projects

You can take advantage of the many species of plants to conduct an experiment with plants and water. For example, you could compare the characteristics and behavior of a desert plant, such as a cactus, with a water plant. How does transpiration differ in the two species of plants? You could study the adaptations related to transpiration in a variety of plant species. Covering one side of a leaf with petroleum jelly will allow you to determine where transpiration occurs in a plant's leaves. You could also investigate in more detail how water flows into a plant by examining parts of a plant's stem, leaves, roots, and cells under a powerful microscope.

Another related project could focus on how water allows a plant to acquire its essential nutrients. Plants will usually get their nutrients from the soil, once the nutrients dissolve in water and are pulled into the plant. Some plants do not need soil to get their nutrients. Hydroponics is the technique of growing plants in water that contains dissolved nutrients. A hydroponics experiment could vary the nutrients in the water or the plants.

For More Information

Black, David, and Anthony Huxley. *Plants*. New York: Facts on File, 1985. ❖ Readable scientific introduction to plants.

Bruce, Anne. "Water movement through a plant." *Microscopy–UK*. http://www.microscopy-uk.org.uk/mag/artmar00/watermvt.html (accessed on August 26, 2003). ❖ Explains how water moves through plants; includes informative pictures.

"Cell Expansion and Differentiation." *Ohio State University: Horticulture and Crop Science in Virtual Perspective*. http://www.hcs.ohio-state.edu/hcs300/cell3.htm (accessed on August 26, 2003). ❖ Illustrations on turgor pressure and the cell wall.

"Desert Plant Survival." *Desert USA*. http://www.desertusa.com/du_plantsurv.html (accessed on August 26, 2003.) ❖ Describes ways animals and plants survive in the desert.

"Plasmolysis." *7th Grade Life Sciences: American Community School*. http://www.acsamman.edu.jo/~ms/science/7/plas.html (accessed on August 26, 2003). ❖ Middle school page has plasmolysis animation and facts on plant structure.

chapter 18

Polymers

Polymers are everywhere, both inside us and around us. The word comes from the Greek words *poly,* meaning "many," and *meros,* meaning "parts." A **polymer** is a material composed of long string of repeating molecular units. They can contain a chain of hundreds to thousands of these units, in the shape of a single straight chain or multiple branching chains. The type and number of the repeating units, along with how the polymer connects to other polymers, determine the physical properties of that polymer.

Polymers are valuable in both nature and industry because they can have great strength and durability, yet be lightweight. There are both natural and **synthetic,** or manmade, polymers. Proteins, silk, and starches are polymers found in nature. Understanding how polymers function in the natural world has led not only to advancements in biology, but also to the development of synthetic polymers that have revolutionized numerous products and fields. Space science depends on synthetic polymers for their space vehicles and equipment. In medicine polymers are used in heart valves, artificial skin, and organ replacements. Plastic bags, nylon, rugs, and fabrics are examples of synthetic polymers that people commonly use.

Chain properties

One of the first polymers created was due to the popular sport of billiards in the late 1800s. At that time, billiard balls were made of ivory, a material in short supply even then. An American inventor won a contest to find a material to replace the ivory. He took the basic structural material that makes up plant cell walls and treated it with chemicals. The result

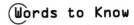

Words to Know

Biodegradable:
Capable of being decomposed by biological agents.

Control experiment:
A setup that is identical to the experiment, but is not affected by the variable that acts on the experimental group.

Elastomers:
Any of various polymers having rubbery properties.

Elongation:
The percentage increase in length that occurs before a material breaks under tension.

Did You Know?

- The polymer nylon was introduced as a substitute for silk stockings in 1937.

- In the 1970s researchers boosted the conductivity of a plastic polymer by a factor of 10 million so that it could conduct electricity as easily as a metal.

- Silly Putty is a polymer invented in the 1940s by an engineer trying to invent a synthetic rubber compound. It had no real advantage as a rubber compound, but was wildly successful as a toy!

- Artificial limbs, teeth, bones, and joints are made of polymers.

- The Statue of Liberty and other monuments are protected from corrosion by a polymer coating that was originally designed to protect space vehicles' launch pads.

Words to Know

Hypothesis:
An idea in the form of a statement that can be tested by observation and/or experiment.

Monomer:
A small molecule that can be combined with itself many times over to make a large molecule, the polymer.

Polymer:
Chemical compound formed of simple molecules (known as monomers) linked with themselves many times over.

Polymerization:
The bonding of two or more monomers to form a polymer.

Synthetic:
Something that is made artificially, in a laboratory or chemical plant, but is generally not found in nature.

Tensile strength:
The force needed to stretch a material until it breaks.

Variable:
Something that can affect the results of an experiment.

was the polymer celluloid—a shiny, hard material that could be molded when hot. This type of plastic became commonly used in X-ray film and motion picture film. In the early 1900s the first synthetic polymer from a non-natural substance was developed. That was soon followed by the first synthetic fiber, rayon. Companies began to get involved in developing polymers, and the study of polymers began in earnest.

Polymers start off from tiny units called **monomers.** To make a polymer, monomers are strung together like beads to form a long polymer chain. A polymer can be made up of billions or trillions of monomers. The chemical reaction that makes polymers from monomers is called **polymerization.**

Each bead on the chain is the basic unit. In many cases, the chain links on a polymer are made up of only carbon atoms. The carbon-carbon bond is a strong one and this gives these polymers strength. In other cases, the chain units are made of nitrogen, oxygen, and/or silicon.

Many classes of polymers are made of just carbon and hydrogen. In these polymers, carbon makes up the basic links in the chain, and hydro-

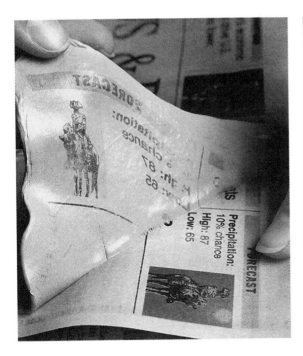

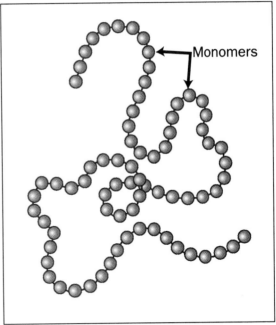

Monomers

gen atoms are bonded along the carbon backbone. For example, the common plastic polyethylene, which is found in grocery bags, juice containers, and bottles, is one such polymer. Composed of the monomer ethylene, polyethylene is composed of a chain of carbon atoms bonded together, with each carbon atom attached to two hydrogen atoms.

What kind is it?

Because there are so many different kinds of polymers, there are also many different ways to classify them, depending on their properties. There are some polymers that are flexible and others are that are hard. **Elastomers** are polymers that have an elastic or rubbery behavior. They can be stretched or bent, but spring back to their original shape. Other polymers, such as a fishing line, are hard and difficult to stretch. Some polymers can be heated and reheated repeatedly. Others will undergo a permanent chemical change if they are heated, which will alter their properties.

One way polymers are differentiated is according to their mechanical properties, such as **tensile strength.** A polymer's tensile strength is the force needed to stretch a material until it breaks. **Elongation** is another mechanical property. A polymer's elongation is the percentage increase in length that occurs before it breaks under tension.

experiment
CENTRAL

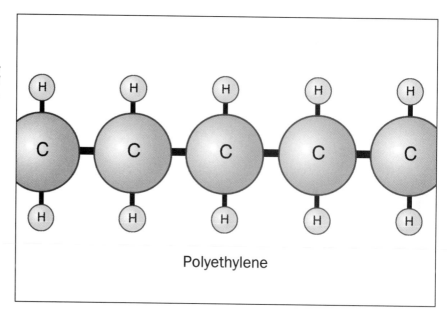

Many polymers are made of hydrogen atoms bonded along a carbon backbone.

Polyethylene

Plastic wrap, food containers, and bags are synthetic polymers commonly used in the average household. (Copyright © Kelly A. Quin. Reproduced by permission of Kelly A. Quin.)

Physical properties of polymers are another way to group them. The chain length of a polymer plays a major role in the polymer's physical properties and behavior. One factor that affects tensile strength is the chain length or the molecular weight. As a general rule, polymers with a higher molecular weight produce stiffer, stronger, and denser materials. The greater the molecular weight, the higher the tensile strength.

How the chains are arranged also affects the physical properties of a polymer. The chains in a polymer can tangle up with each other, like a plate of spaghetti. This makes many polymers incredibly durable. The chains can be either linear (straight), branched, or cross-linked.

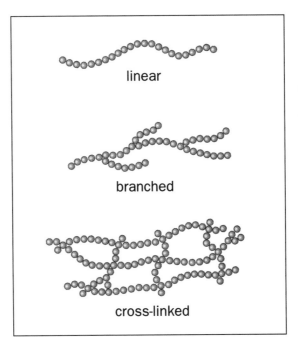

linear

branched

cross-linked

The arrangement of a polymer chain has an impact on its physical properties.

Getting rid of polymers

The positive qualities in polymers—their durability, strength, and lightness—bring with them the challenge of how to get rid of many of these products. Enormous quantities of disposable, synthetic polymers are produced every year in the United States alone. The production of these materials is causing concerns for the environment.

Many of the products are plastics and are not **biodegradable,** meaning that they do not break down naturally and quickly into the raw materials of nature. Plastic soda can rings, for example, can take an estimated four hundred years to break down!

Recycling these plastics will help reduce the amount of garbage in the environment. When plastics are recycled they are reprocessed and made into new products. Yet different methods are used to recycle different materials, and there can be multiple polymers in a person's garbage. Most plastics and bottles are made from six polymers. The plastics industry has developed a chart to distinguish the six polymers from each other: A specific number is written in a three-arrow triangle that is imprinted on most plastic products. Polymers' physical properties, such as density, are also used to separate the different types. People are encouraged to recycle and separate their plastic containers. In the meantime, researchers are working to develop polymers with improved biodegradability.

A mound of plastic products awaits reprocessing at a Des Moines, Iowa, recycling facility. (Reproduced by permission of AP/Wide World.)

Experiment 1

Polymer Strength: What are the tensile properties of certain polymers that make them more durable than others?

Purpose/Hypothesis

Tensile strength is one key test that researchers conduct on polymers. A polymer's tensile strength depends on what molecules make up the polymer, as well as the orientation of the polymers. Polymers align themselves as long chains. These chains are aligned parallel to each other and tangle together in many synthetic polymers. When pulled lengthwise, these chains can stretch a great distance before breaking. However, widthwise it is only the entanglements that hold the polymers together. In this direction the polymer will break much more easily. Companies make many synthetic polymers by manufacturing the long chains of polymers parallel to each other along the length of the product. This results in a strong bond lengthwise, from top to bottom, and a weak bond widthwise, from left to right.

In this experiment you will test in what direction the orientation of the polymer is strongest: lengthwise or widthwise. The polymer you will use will be any plastic bag. Most plastic bags are made of the polymer polyethylene. To test a polymer's tensile strength, one end of the polymer is held stationary while a force is applied to the other end until the sample breaks. Before the sample breaks it elongates, or lengthens.

Tensile testing is usually done on samples shaped like a "dogbone." The size of the sample can vary, but the shape is important. Almost all the elongation will occur in the narrow section of the dogbone. Elongation occurs in the thinnest section because it is the weakest.

You will test plastic samples in both directions by taping one end of the samples to a stationary object and attaching a weight to the opposite end. You will increase the weight incrementally, measuring the plastic's elongation after each addition of the weight, until the plastic breaks. Samples should always break in the thinnest section, the middle of the dogbone. For increased accuracy, you will conduct three trials for both the lengthwise and widthwise direction.

To begin this experiment make an educated guess, or prediction, of what you think will occur based on your knowledge of polymer strength and orientation. This educated guess, or prediction, is your **hypothesis.** A hypothesis should explain these things:

- the topic of the experiment
- the **variable** you will change
- the variable you will measure
- what you expect to happen

A hypothesis should be brief, specific, and measurable. It must be something you can test through further investigation. Your experiment will prove or disprove whether your hypothesis is correct. Here

What Are the Variables?

Variables are anything that might affect the results of an experiment. Here are the main variables in this experiment:

- The type of plastic bag (polymer) used
- The amount of weight
- The direction the polymer is cut
- The size of the cut polymer
- The shape of the cut polymer

In other words, variables in this experiment are everything that might affect the amount of weight the polymer can hold. If you change more than one variable, you will not be able to tell which variable impacted the polymer's strength.

is one possible hypothesis for this experiment: "The plastic bag cut in the lengthwise direction will support far more weight than the sample cut widthwise."

In this experiment the variable you will change will be the orientation of the polymer chains, and the variable you will measure will be the amount of weight the polymer can hold before it breaks.

Level of Difficulty
Difficult.

Materials Needed
- bar to hold the clothes hanger or plastic sample (clothing rod works well).
- sturdy clothes hanger with a stiff, straight section across the bottom (wood or very stiff metal)
- two plastic garbage bags (white or light color)
- scissors
- wide duct tape
- a 2-liter empty plastic bottle
- string
- wastebasket or bucket to catch plastic bottle

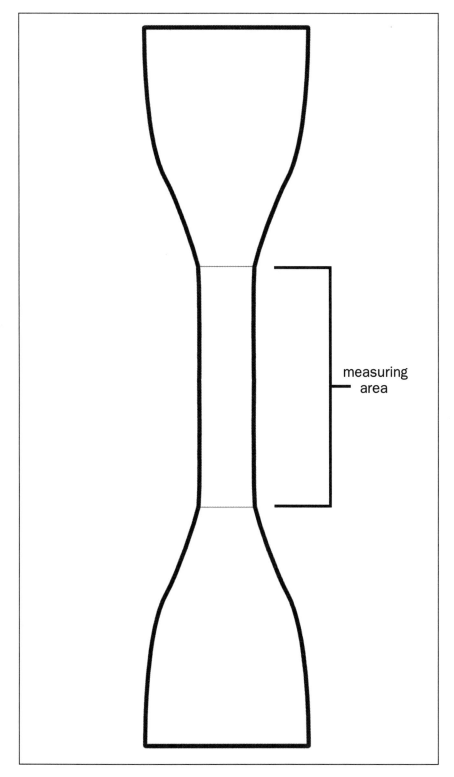

Step 1: The dogbone template.

measuring area

- water
- funnel
- measuring cup
- piece of 8.5-inch by 11-inch (216-millimeter by 280-millimeter) paper
- marking pen

Approximate Budget
$8.

Timetable
1 hour

Step-by-Step Instructions
1. Trace the template of the dogbone on the paper and cut out the paper. (See figure on page 335.)
2. To determine the lengthwise direction of the bag, stretch the bag gently in each direction and determine which way has the least pull. This is the lengthwise direction. It is not always the top-to-bottom direction of the bag. Mark the "top" and the "bottom" with the marking pen.
3. Lay the plastic bag in the lengthwise, top-to-bottom, direction and place the paper template over the bag. Cut out the plastic bag, making sure the cuts are smooth.
4. Repeat Step 3 two more times so that you have three dogbone-shaped pieces of plastic. Mark each piece with an "L" for lengthwise.
5. Repeat Steps 2 and 3 in the crosswise direction. Mark each piece with a "C" for crosswise.
6. On each of your samples draw a line across the beginning and end of the mid-section of the bone. This will be the area you will measure.
7. Attach one end of a plastic sample to the hanger with duct tape, wrapping the tape firmly around the hanger.

How to Experiment Safely
Be careful when using the scissors.

experiment
CENTRAL

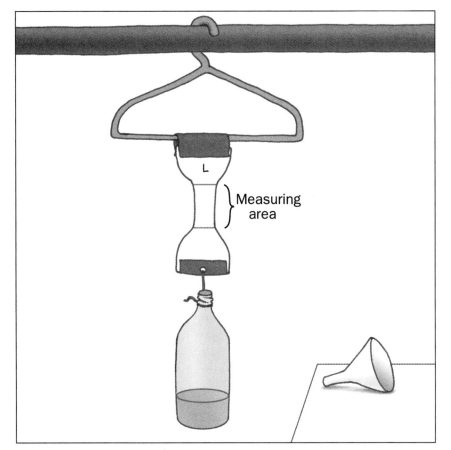

8. Attach another piece of duct tape to the bottom of the plastic. In the center of this bottom piece of duct tape make a small hole. Put a string around the neck of the 2-liter bottle and attach the other end of the string through the hole. Tie with a double knot.

9. Measure the length between the top and bottom marks on the bag and write it down.

10. Place the wastebasket or bucket on the floor directly under the bottle. Carefully pour 1/4 cup of water (60 milliliters) into the bottle using a funnel. Measure the length between the top and bottom marks on the bag again and write it down.

11. Continue adding 1/4 cup (60 milliliters) of water, measuring the stretch or elongation of the sample after every water addition until the sample breaks. Note your results.

12. Repeat Steps 7 through 11 for each of the remaining five sample bags.

Troubleshooter's Guide

Below are some problems that may arise during this experiment, some possible causes, and some ways to remedy the problem.

Problem: The plastics break at the top or bottom.

Possible Cause: There could be a slight tear or cut in the plastic. If it breaks anywhere but the middle you will need to repeat the experiment.

Problem: The widthwise-labeled dogbone was stronger.

Possible Cause: You may have mislabeled the plastics when you first stretched the bag to determine the lengthwise direction. Repeat the experiment, making sure to pull gently on the bag to determine which direction pulls the least amount.

Problem: The elongation for the three trials varied greatly.

Possible Cause: You may have changed more than one variable. Make sure you used the same sturdy hanger for each trial. Was one a thin metal hanger that bent? Could you have mismeasured the water or spilled some as you were pouring? Repeat the experiment, making sure all the variables are equal.

Summary of Results

Average the three trials of elongation for both the lengthwise and crosswise polymer orientations. Construct a chart where Column 1 is the weight of the water, Column 2 is the length of the sample, and Column 3 is the percent elongation. The percent elongation is the length of the end sample minus the original length of the sample divided by the original length of sample. Multiply that number times 100 to get the percent. Percent elongation = [(finished sample length – original sample length) divided by original sample length] x 100.

Plot a graph of the results with the amount of water on the y-axis and the percent elongation on the x-axis. Did the samples break at different weights? Clearly label your graph. Did the samples break at different weights? Did the lengthwise or crosswise sample break first? Write a brief explanation of your results.

Change the Variables

You can vary this experiment in several ways. Try using different types of plastic, such as a food wrapper compared to a thick plastic garbage bag. You could experiment with cutting the bag in the diagonal direction. Cut out different sizes of the dogbone, using the same direction and plastic. Does this impact the plastic's elongation?

Experiment 2
Polymer Slime: How will adding more of a polymer change the properties of a polymer "slime"?

Purpose/Hypothesis

The objective of this experiment is to create a cross-linked polymer and observe the physical properties of adding increased polymer chains. Guar gum is used as a thickening agent in foods. The guar contains a polymer called polysaccharide. Polysaccharide is a large molecule composed of carbon, oxygen, and hydrogen atoms joined together in long chains, which makes it long and flexible. Because it is a linear polymer that is not cross-linked, guar gum pours like a thick solution.

In order to form a "slime" the linear polysaccharide must be cross-linked to form a three-dimensional network. This creates stronger bonds between the separate chains. Borax has sodium borate as the active ingredient. Sodium borate is the cross-linking agent, meaning that it creates the interconnecting bonds between the carbon and oxygen atoms that link the linear polymer chains together.

In this experiment you will determine how the amount of a polymer alters the properties of a mixture. You will make three different polymer slimes with varying amounts of polysaccharide. The borax will cross-link the polysaccharides. After you have made the three different slimes, you will conduct tests to compare the firmness and elasticity of the slimes.

Before you begin, make an educated guess about the outcome of this experiment based on your knowledge of polymers and their prop-

What Are the Variables?

Variables are anything that might affect the results of an experiment. Here are the main variables in this experiment:

- the amount of borax used
- the amount of guar gum
- the amount of water used
- the temperature of the mixture
- any added food coloring

In other words, the variables in this experiment are everything that might affect the properties of the slime. If you change more than one variable at the same time, you will not be able to tell which variable had the most effect on the slime's physical properties.

erties. This educated guess, or prediction, is your **hypothesis.** A hypothesis should explain these things:

- the topic of the experiment
- the **variable** you will change
- the variable you will measure
- what you expect to happen

A hypothesis should be brief, specific, and measurable. It must be something you can test through further investigation. Your experiment will prove or disprove whether your hypothesis is correct. Here is one possible hypothesis for this experiment: "Increasing the amount of polymer in the slime will give the polymer greater firmness and elasticity."

In this case, the variable you will change is the amount of polymer you add to your slime. The variables you will measure are the slime's firmness and elasticity.

When making a solid-liquid solution (solid/liquid), it is standard to use weight/weight (grams/grams) or weight/volume (grams/milliliters). With water, 1 gram of water equals 1 milliliter. In this experiment, teaspoons and tablespoons are used to measure the solid.

Level of Difficulty
Moderate.

Materials Needed
- borax (found in supermarkets in the laundry section)
- guar gum (a thickener agent; found in health food stores)
- water
- four stirring rods or spoons
- measuring spoons
- scale or measuring cup
- resealable bags
- food coloring (optional)
- four clear mixing bowls [to see if the materials dissolved]
- marking pen
- masking tape
- latex gloves

Approximate Budget
$10.

Timetable
45 minutes.

Step-by-Step Instructions
1. Pour one-half of a cup (120 milliliters or 120 grams) of water into a bowl.
2. Add 1 teaspoon of borax (sodium borate) to the water and stir until completely dissolved. The solution should be clear.
3. Label the solution "Borax."
4. Measure out one-third of a cup (80 milliliters or 80 grams) of water into a second bowl or measuring cup.

How to Experiment Safely
Borax is a weak bleaching agent. Avoid contact with your eyes and face. Use latex gloves when handling the slime as a precaution. Do not ingest any of the slimes. Wash all the bowls, spoons, and other utensils afterwards.

	Firmness		Elasticity	
	Diameter	Description	Length	Breaks Apart
1/4 tsp. guar				
1/2 tsp. guar				
3/4 tsp. guar				

TOP:
Step 10: When finished making the three slimes, lay each on the counter; one at a time, determine its firmness by measuring its diameter.

BOTTOM:
Data chart for Experiment 2.

5. Add 1/4 teaspoon of guar gum to the solution while stirring. Continue stirring until completely dissolved. The guar gum will suspend in the liquid so this solution will not be clear.

6. Label the solution on the tape: "1/4 teaspoon Guar gum."

7. If you want to make colored slime, add a specific amount of the desired color to the solution. You will need to add this exact color and amount to each of the mixtures.

8. Add 1 teaspoon of the borax solution to the guar gum solution. Stir for one minute and then let sit for at least two minutes.

9. Repeat the previous steps to make two more mixtures, replacing the1/4 teaspoon guar gum with 1/2 teaspoon and 3/4 teaspoon guar gum respectively. Label the two mixtures accordingly.

10 When finished making the three slimes, lay each on the counter; one at a time, determine its firmness by measuring its diameter. Note your results in a chart.

11 Hold each in your hand and describe the slime's firmness, using the "1/4 guar gum" as the standard of comparison.

12 Hold one of the slimes to an edge and let it hang down. Time one minute; determine its elasticity by measuring its length, or if it breaks apart. Note your results. Repeat for two other slimes.

Summary of Results

Examine the chart of your data and observations. Which amount of guar gum made the polymer the most firm? How do the physical properties of the slimes with the lowest and highest amount of guar gum compare with each other? What does measuring the diameter show? What can you conclude about the slime if it had a longer stretch than the others? What if it broke during the stretch? If you want to display the results of your slime experiment, the slime can be

Troubleshooter's Guide

Below are some problems that may arise during this experiment, some possible causes, and ways to remedy the problems.

Problem: The slime is not a uniform consistency.

Possible causes: The borax is not dissolved well. When mixing the borax make sure to stir continuously until the mixture is clear. Mix the guar gum continuously.

Problem: The slime is too firm or loose.

Possible causes: You may have mixed up the stirring spoons between the borax and guar gum. Make sure to use separate spoons or rinse thoroughly between measurements.

stored in a resealable bag. You can demonstrate the slime's firmness by having people feel it and experiment with it themselves.

Change the Variables

There are many ways to vary this experiment. Here are some suggestions:

- Keep the amount of guar gum equal and vary the amount of borax.
- Keep the amount of guar gum and borax equal and vary the amount of water used. Does using more or less water give the slime added bounce?
- Place the slime in different temperature environments after you have made three mixtures that use the same measurements. Put one in the refrigerator, one at room temperature, and one in a hot-water bath.

 Design Your Own Experiment

How to Select a Topic Relating to this Concept

Polymers are everywhere. They are in your kitchen, clothes, and many disposable products that you purchase. You could examine how polymers have changed over history or how they impact people's lives.

Check the For More Information section and talk with your science teacher to learn more about polymers. Because polymers are so diverse, there are many different types of polymer chemists. Ask family, teachers, and friends if they know a polymer chemist you can talk with.

Steps in the Scientific Method

To do an original experiment, you need to plan carefully and think things through. Otherwise, you might not be sure what question you are answering, what you are or should be measuring, or what your findings prove or disprove.

Here are the steps in designing an experiment:

- State the purpose of—and the underlying question behind—the experiment you propose to do.

- Recognize the variables involved and select one that will help you answer the question at hand.
- State your hypothesis, an educated guess about the answer to your question.
- Decide how to change the variable you selected.
- Decide how to measure your results.

Recording Data and Summarizing the Results

Your data should include charts and graphs such as the one you did for these experiments. They should be clearly labeled and easy to read. You may also want to include photographs and drawings of your experimental setup and results, which will help other people visualize the steps in the experiment.

If you are preparing an exhibit, you may want to display your results, such as any experimental setup you designed. If you have completed a nonexperimental project, explain clearly what your research question was and illustrate your findings.

Related Projects

You can use the many different physical and mechanical properties of polymers for further experiments and projects. For example, you could investigate the biodegradability of plastics by composting a number of materials. You could first compare the biodegradability of the six different types of polymers. You probably have several different types of plastic products (as determined by the number in the three-arrow triangle printed on a product) in your house already. You could then compare the breakdown of a specific plastic and determine how it relates to both other plastics and nonpolymer materials, such as an organic material like a food item or dead insect.

You could compare synthetic polymers' properties to synthetic nonpolymer materials, such as aluminum foil or specific fabrics. To determine the specific polymer in the product you can look at the ingredients listed on the packaging or call the toll-free number. You could also look at polymers in a specific industry, such as the medical or space field, and explore how polymers have impacted the industry, everyday life, and products related to that field.

For More Information

American Plastics Council. http://www.americanplasticscouncil.org (accessed on August 26, 2003). ❖ This industry page has loads of basic information and news on plastics.

Leutwyler, Kristin. "Therapeutic Plastics." *Scientific American.com,* April 3, 2000. http://www.sciam.com/article.cfm?articleID=0005B91E-4BFD-1C75-9B81809EC 588EF21 (accessed on August 26, 2003). ❖ A report on some of the latest biological and medical uses for polymers.

The MacroGalleria. http://www.psrc.usm.edu/macrog/index.htm (accessed on August 26, 2003). ❖ Detailed site on all aspects of polymers, from studying them to everyday applications.

"Polymer recipes for thickening." *Response Online.* http://www.responseonline.com/ tech/polym.htm (accessed on August 26, 2003). ❖ Technical article that looks at synthetic polymers and their properties.

Polymers. http://www.calpoly.edu/~drjones/smartpoly/polymers.html (accessed on August 26, 2003). ❖ Professor at California Polytechnic State University presents pictures and information on polymers.

Worldwise. http://www.worldwise.com/biodegradable.html (accessed on August 26, 2003). ❖ Article on biodegradable products.

chapter 19

Rotation and Orbits

Earth, like all the planets in our solar system, is in constant motion. All of the planets revolve or **orbit** around the Sun. An orbit is when one object in the universe goes round another one without touching it. For Earth, it takes about 365 days to complete one orbit around the Sun. Without Earth's rotation and orbit, the world would be a far different place. The rotation gives Earth its night and day. That allows the many life forms on Earth to remain at a comfortable temperature, warming during the sunlight hours and cooling down at the night. It affects the direction of wind and the ocean's daily tides. The orbit and tilt of rotation also give Earth its four seasons.

All the planets in the solar system also **rotate,** or spin, as they orbit the Sun. On average, Earth rotates once every 24 hours—or more precisely, 23 hours, 56 minutes, 4.091 seconds. The complete rotation of an object with respect to the stars is called a **sidereal** (pronounced sy-DEER-ee-awl) **day.**

Renaissance rules

Today's knowledge of planets' rotations and orbits evolved during the sixteenth and seventeenth centuries in what is known as the Renaissance age. Scientists at that time were building telescopes and were able to observe how celestial objects behaved in detail for the first time. In 1543 Polish astronomer Nicolaus Copernicus (1473–1543) published his theory that Earth spins on its axis once daily and revolves around the sun annually. The widespread belief at that time was that the Sun and other planets revolved around Earth. Copernicus' theory caused great controversy and most people did not accept it.

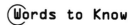

Words to Know

Axis:
An imaginary straight line around which an object, like a planet, spins or turns. Earth's axis is a line that goes through the North and South Poles.

Centrifugal force:
The apparent force pushing a rotating body away from the center of rotation.

Circumference:
The distance around a circle.

Did You Know?

- Earth revolves in its orbit around the Sun at a speed of nearly 19 miles (30 kilometers) per second, or about 68,000 miles (108,000 kilometers) per hour.

- Jupiter rotates on its axis the fastest (once every 11 hours), while Venus rotates the slowest (once every 243 days).

- Earth's time of rotation is not constant. Every day it varies by a few thousandths of a second.

- Some planets have such an elliptical orbit that it can change the planet's order from the Sun. For example, during about 220 years of Pluto's orbit it is the farthest planet from the Sun. Because of its elliptical orbit, however, for about 20 years Pluto is actually closer to the Sun than Neptune.

- Long-range artillery calculations and missile guidance systems are designed to correct for the Coriolis effect.

All of the planets in the solar system revolve, or orbit, around the Sun; the planets also rotate, or spin, as they orbit the Sun.

*Earth time		Period of revolution*	Period of rotation
	Mercury	88 days	59 days
	Venus	225 days	243 days
	Earth	365 days	24 hours
	Mars	687 days	25 hours
	Jupiter	12 years	10 hours
	Saturn	29 years	10 hours
	Uranus	84 years	18 hours
	Neptune	165 years	18 hours
	Pluto	248 years	6.4 days

Some scientists did believe Copernicus however, including German astronomer Johannes Kepler (1571–1630). In the early 1600s Kepler worked out three laws that applied to planetary motion. One of the laws stated that Earth orbits the Sun in an elliptical path. With this knowledge, astronomers could predict

experiment
CENTRAL

the movement of other planets through observations and mathematical calculations.

Around and around

There are many orbits in the solar system. Planets and other objects orbit around the Sun. Moons orbit around their planets. The main reason why objects orbit around another object is due to **gravity.** Gravity is the force pulling all matter together.

In the seventeenth century, English scientist Isaac Newton (1642–1727) realized the revolutionary idea of gravity when he was just twenty-three years old. Newton explained that the force of gravitation makes every pair of bodies attract and applies to all objects in the universe. This gravitational force relates to why objects fall to Earth as well as the motion of the moon and the planets in orbit. (For further information on gravity, see the Force chapter.)

The pull of gravity is stronger from heavier objects, and so lighter objects orbit the heavier one. The Sun is the heaviest object in the solar

Each planet revolves as it orbits the Sun.

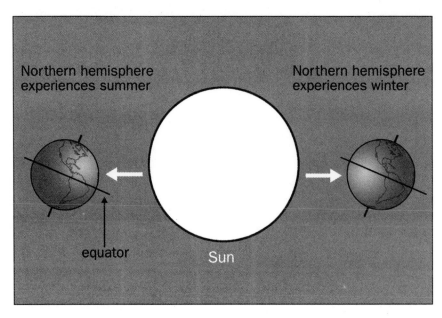

The tilt of the Earth on its axis, and its rotation, causes the four seasons.

Northern hemisphere experiences summer

Northern hemisphere experiences winter

equator

Sun

system. It is about a thousand times heavier than the largest planet, Jupiter, and more than 300 thousand times heavier than Earth. The gravity of the Sun keeps Earth and all the planets in their orbits. The gravity of Earth pulls our Moon into its orbit around Earth.

Why we spin

All the planets in the solar system rotate on their **axis.** A planet's axis is an imaginary line drawn through its center from the North to South Pole. The Earth's axis is tilted at a 23.45° angle from vertical. Other planets rotate at different angles. Except for Venus and Uranus, all planets rotate in the same direction that they orbit the Sun—from west to east.

Earth's continuous rotation began as the planet was formed, an estimated 4.6 billion years ago. The solar system formed from clouds of dust and gases that were spinning around the Sun. When these materials collapsed together they formed a larger and larger object that eventually formed a planet. Since these materials were already spinning, they began to spin faster as they collapsed inwards. This phenomenon is similar to an ice skater spinning. When the ice skater brings his or her arms closer to the body, he or she will spin faster.

Astronomers theorize that a large object collided with the newly formed planet, setting Earth spinning at a faster rate. The collision

ⓦords to Know

Control experiment:
A setup that is identical to the experiment, but is not affected by the variable that acts on the experimental group.

Coriolis force:
A force that makes a moving object appear to travel in a curved path over the surface of a spinning body.

Gravity:
Force of attraction between objects, the strength of which depends on the mass of each object and the distance between them.

Hypothesis:
An idea in the form of a statement that can be tested by observation and/or experiment.

also may have tilted Earth's axis to its 23.45° angle. The seasons are caused by this angle of rotation. Since the axis is tilted, different parts of the planet are oriented towards the Sun at different times of the year. For example when Earth is at a certain place in its orbit, the northern hemisphere (the half of the planet north of the equator, including the United States) is tilted toward the Sun. During this portion of Earth's orbit, the northern hemisphere experiences the summer season. Six months later Earth is on the opposite side of the Sun. The northern hemisphere is tilted away from the Sun and experiences the winter season.

Leaves fall from the trees in autumn as a prelude to the coming winter season. (Reproduced by permission of Field Mark Publications.)

The Earth spins continuously because there is no force in space to make it stop. One of the laws of motion states that a force is required to slow or stop a moving object. For example, when you roll a ball along the ground it will eventually stop due to the friction with the ground and the force of the air pushing against the ball. For Earth rotating on its axis, there is no force to counteract the rotation. That means it does not require any energy to keep it rotating.

Rotation's moving effects

Earth's daily tides are caused both by gravity and our planet's spinning movements. Both the Sun and Moon produce a gravitational pull on

Words to Know

Orbit:
The path followed by a body (such as a planet) in its travel around another body (such as the Sun).

Rotate:
To turn around on an axis or center.

Sidereal day:
The system of time to measure a day based on the motion of the stars.

Variable:
Something that can affect the results of an experiment.

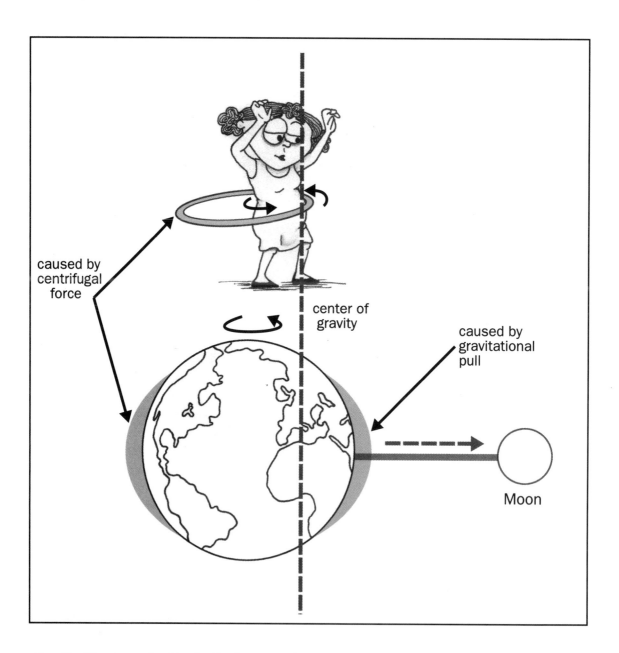

caused by
centrifugal
force

center of
gravity

caused by
gravitational
pull

Moon

Centrifugal force is caused by an object's tendency to keep moving in a straight line. This outward-pull effect occurs in all rotating objects.

Earth. Yet because the Moon is closer to Earth than the Sun, it has about double the gravitational force as that of the Sun, which means it has about double the influence on the tides.

As the Moon revolves around Earth, the Earth and Moon are revolving together, like one unit, around a common point located within the Earth. This point is called the center of gravity or the center of mass. At this center of gravity, the gravitational forces of the

experiment
CENTRAL

Earth and the Moon pull out on each other equally. As the two objects rotate as one system, everything in and on Earth experiences **centrifugal force.** (While centrifugal force actually acts on all matter, only the water is free to move about.)

Centrifugal force is actually not a force, but the absence of a force. A force is a push or pull. Centrifugal force is caused by an object's tendency to keep moving in a straight line. This outward-pull effect occurs in all rotating objects. For example, when a car turns sharply the passenger will seem to be pushed to the outside of the curve. The centrifugal force that the rider is experiencing is not due to an actual push: The passenger's body is trying to keep moving forward in the same direction. Centrifugal force causes Earth's water to be pulled away from the center of the spin.

On the side of the Earth closest to the Moon, the Moon's gravity is strong enough to overcome the centrifugal force. The total or net gravitational force is in the direction of the Moon and causes a bulge or tide that is pulled towards the Moon. (For further information on tides, see the Ocean chapter.)

On the side of the Earth opposite the Moon, the Moon's gravity is not strong enough to overcome the centrifugal force. The net gravitational force is away from the Earth, causing a second bulge or tide to occur on the opposite side of the Moon. At any one time there are two bulges of water of roughly equal size, one towards and one away from the Moon. Low tides are created in areas about halfway between these two high-tide bulges when the water withdraws.

Curving around

Another effect caused by Earth's rotation causes large moving bodies on or above Earth's surface to curve instead of moving in a straight path. Called the **Coriolis force,** this bending

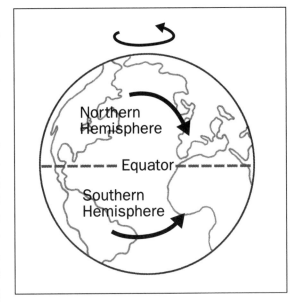

The rotation of the Earth causes the Coriolis force.

The first picture of the Earth and Moon in a single frame, taken September 18, 1977, by Voyager 1. (Courtesy of the National Aeronautics and Space Administration.)

movement is named after French mathematician Gustave-Gaspard Coriolis. In 1835, he explained mathematically that this phenomenon is due to the object's course relative to the rotation of Earth.

The direction the object will curve depends on whether it is located north or south of the equator. In the northern hemisphere an object will turn to the right of its direction of movement; in the southern hemisphere, to the left. At the equator moving objects do not turn at all.

The **circumference** or distance around Earth at the equator is larger than it is at the poles. Since the whole Earth rotates once every twenty-four hours, the surface of the earth at the equator moves faster than it does at the poles. People living at the equator might not feel it, but they are rotating at a rate of about 1,000 miles per hour (1,609 kilometers per hour). As the equator moves more quickly to the east than other points on Earth, objects traveling away from the equator are deflected to the east.

The Coriolis force is a relatively weak one for most objects and is not noticeable. In large objects that move over a length of time, the Coriolis force can have a significant effect. For example, winds naturally move in ways that equalizes their warmth. Warm winds located at the equator move towards cold air at the poles; cold air at the poles moves toward the equator. The Coriolis force causes these winds to follow a curved path as they move.

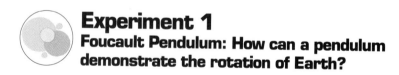

Experiment 1
Foucault Pendulum: How can a pendulum demonstrate the rotation of Earth?

Purpose/Hypothesis
In 1851, French physicist Jean-Bernard-Leon Foucault (1819–1868) proved that Earth rotates on its axis through a demonstration with a pendulum. A pendulum consists of a free-swinging cord set at a fixed point with a weight hanging from it. A pendulum swings at a constant rate and direction if there is no force moving against it.

Foucault hung a pendulum from a high ceiling and noted that the path of the pendulum's swing slowing changed its direction of swing. Since there was no force acting on the pendulum, he concluded that Earth had to be rotating beneath it.

What Are the Variables?

Variables are anything that might affect the results of an experiment. Here are the main variables in this experiment:

- the length of the pendulum's cord
- the amount of time the pendulum swings
- wind

In other words, the variables in this experiment are everything that might affect the pendulum's swing. If you change more than one variable at the same time, you will not be able to tell which variable had the most effect on the pendulum's swing.

In this experiment you will make a simple Foucault pendulum. When a pendulum is moving freely in air, the air resistance causes the pendulum to slow down and eventually stop. A heavy weight and tall pendulum will reduce the effect of friction. (Foucault's original pendulum consisted of a 62-pound (28-kilogram) iron ball suspended on a 220-foot (67-meter) steel wire.)

You will use a bag of sand as the pendulum's weight, and then note how the sand moves as it trickles from the bag. To observe results from the pendulum it should swing for at least thirty to sixty minutes. After that time, note the apparent change in the direction in which the pendulum is swinging.

To begin this experiment, make an educated guess about the outcome of the experiment based on your knowledge of Earth's rotation. This educated guess, or prediction, is your **hypothesis.** A hypothesis should explain these things:

- the topic of the experiment
- the **variable** you will change
- the variable you will measure
- what you expect to happen

A hypothesis should be brief, specific, and measurable. It must be something you can test through further investigation. Your experiment will prove or disprove whether your hypothesis is correct. Here is one possible hypothesis for this experiment: "The lines of sand falling from the Foucault pendulum will shift slightly over time as Earth is continuously rotating."

In this experiment, the variable you will change is time. The variable you will measure will be the appearance of the pendulum's swing.

Level of Difficulty

Moderate to Difficult (because of the difficulty in keeping the swing straight).

Materials Needed

- 13 feet (4 meters) of nylon cord or strong string
- cloth or canvas sack
- ladder at least 12 to 15 feet (3.5 to 4.5 meters) high, high swing set, or other tall stable outdoor structure
- fine, dry sand (available at hardware stores or greenhouses)
- calm, nonwindy day
- large garbage bag
- watch or timer
- tape
- sharp nail
- chair

Approximate Budget

$8.

Timetable

75 minutes.

Step-by-Step Instructions

1. Fill the sack with sand. Make sure there are no leaks in the bag by holding it over a clean surface and moving it gently.
2. Tie the open end of the sack together with the cord or string, and stand on a chair to hang the bag from the top of the ladder or other stand. You may need an adult's help with this.
3. Use the nail to punch a small hole in the bottom of the sand bag. The hole should be slightly larger than the tip of a pen, to allow the sand to fall out slowly. Hold the bag up to make sure that sand drops out at a visible rate. When it is flowing properly, seal the hole with a piece of tape.

How to Experiment Safely

Make sure the pendulum stand you are using is securely attached to the ground and will not tip over. Be careful when handling the sharp nail. Also, be careful when you are attaching the string to the tall structure. Ask an adult to either help you balance or attach the string for you.

4. Lay out the garbage bag on the ground under and around the pendulum.

5. Make sure the bag of sand hangs straight down and is not tilted. If it is, adjust either the sack or the cord.

6. Keep the cord tight and pull the bag straight back about 4 feet (1.2 meters) high. Remove the tape and carefully set the pendulum in motion. Make sure you swing in a straight line and do not have an elliptical swing.

Step 6: Carefully release the sack so that the pendulum moves in a straight line.

7. Over the next 45 to 60 minutes, carefully give the cord an extra swing when it slows down. Try to keep the pendulum swinging for 60 minutes. Make sure you simply push the swing in the direction it is moving and do not shift the cord at all. This experiment may take more than one attempt.

Summary of Results

Draw the pattern of the sand. Explain the results, including how the Coriolis force influences the direction of the sand lines. For example, a Foucault pendulum set in motion in the northern hemisphere traces out a line that is always shifted toward the right.

How many degrees the pendulum shifts depends on where it is geographically located or its latitude. Latitude identifies the north-to-south position of a point on Earth The equator is 0° latitude; the north and south poles are each 90° latitude. At the equator the pendulum would not shift at all. At either of the poles the pendulum's swing would complete a circle in about twenty-four hours. You can

Troubleshooter's Guide

Below are some problems that may arise during this experiment, some possible causes, and some ways to remedy the problem.

Problem: The bag is moving in a circular, elliptical path.

Possible cause: You may not have pushed the bag in a straight line for the first push or any subsequent pushes. Try practicing a straight-line push with the tape on the bag, and then repeat the experiment.

Problem: There was no shift in the lines of sand.

Possible cause: You may have set the cord slightly off-kilter during one of your pushes, or the pendulum may not have swung long enough. Try practicing a straight-line push with the tape on the bag, and then repeat the experiment, making sure to keep the pendulum swinging for at least sixty minutes.

figure out the rate of rotation where you live by finding your latitude and figuring out the following equation through longhand or a calculator. Mathematically, the pendulum's rate of shift is equal to the rate of rotation of Earth multiplied by the sine of the number of degrees of latitude: n = 360 degrees x sine (latitude), where n equals the number of degrees of rotation. The sine of latitude represents the angular distance of a place from the equator.

Change the Variables

By increasing the time you keep the pendulum swinging, the more the sand lines will shift and the better you will be able to observe Earth's rotation. You can attempt to find an even taller structure from which to hang your pendulum. Keeping the pendulum swinging manually is challenging because of any inadvertent shifting of the swing's direction. One way to increase the swing time of a Foucault pendulum is to build a mechanical device that automatically pushes the cord back and forth. There are several such designs available. See the For More Information section, talk to your teacher, or research the topic independently.

Experiment 2
Spinning Effects: How does the speed of a rotating object affect the way centrifugal force can overcome gravity?

Purpose/Hypothesis

The term centrifugal force comes from the Latin meaning "center-fleeing" or "away from the center," which explains the outward movement of an object experiencing centrifugal force. Centrifugal force can overcome the effects of gravity. One of the factors that affect centrifugal force depends on the speed of rotation or an object's velocity. The greater the speed of the object, the greater the force.

In this experiment you will observe centrifugal force occurring with different velocities, and see how each overcomes the effects of gravity. You will measure the outward pull of water in a small container that is revolving. The faster you spin the container, the higher its velocity. You will spin the container at two different speeds, each for the same length of time.

experiment
CENTRAL

What Are the Variables?

Variables are anything that might affect the results of an experiment. Here are the main variables in this experiment:

- length of string

- speed of rotation

- shape of container

- mass of spinning object

In other words, the variables in this experiment are everything that might affect the way the water moves. If you change more than one variable at the same time, you will not be able to tell which variable had the most effect on centrifugal force.

Before you begin, make an educated guess about the outcome of this experiment based on your knowledge of centrifugal force and gravity. This educated guess, or prediction, is your **hypothesis.** A hypothesis should explain these things:

- the topic of the experiment
- the **variable** you will change
- the variable you will measure
- what you expect to happen

A hypothesis should be brief, specific, and measurable. It must be something you can test through further investigation. Your experiment will prove or disprove whether your hypothesis is correct. Here is one possible hypothesis for this experiment: "At higher speeds, the water will be pushed further outwards."

In this case, the variable you will change is the velocity of a spinning object. The variable you will measure is the distance the water was pushed outwards.

Conducting a control experiment will help you isolate each variable and measure the changes in the dependent variable. Only one variable will change between the control and the experimental trials. Your control experiment will use no centrifugal force and, thus, will only have the effects of gravity. At the end of the experiment you can compare your observations from the control with the experimental trials.

Level of Difficulty

Easy.

Materials Needed

- 5 feet (1.5 meters) of string
- shallow Styrofoam or thin plastic cup
- single hole puncher
- clear area outside
- tape measure
- small cloth rag
- water
- watch with second hand
- partner

Approximate Budget

$5.

Timetable

20 minutes.

Step-by-Step Instructions

1. Punch two holes on opposite sides of the plastic cup and thread the string through the holes.
2. Punch holes all around the sides of the container.
3. Stand in an open area outside and use an object to mark where you are standing.
4. Wet the rag with water until it is dripping wet, and place it in the cup. This is the control. Wait a few seconds and note your observations of what happens to the water.
5. Wet the rag again and replace it the container. Slowly swing the container in an arc until you get a slow circular motion over your head.

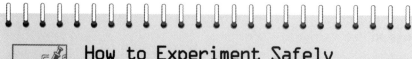

How to Experiment Safely

Be careful that your partner or anyone else is not too close when you are swinging the cup. You may get wet so wear the appropriate clothes.

6. Have your partner time you and count the number of complete revolutions you make in 10 seconds.

7. Increase the speed of the revolutions and again count the number of revolutions you make in 10 seconds.

8. Find the midpoint of where the water landed in the circle for the first set of revolutions. Measure from that point to the mark where you were standing.

9. Repeat the measurement at the midpoint of where the water landed for the first higher-speed revolutions.

Step 5: Swing the container overhead.

Summary of Results

Construct a chart with your results and graph the data. Examine how the outward force of the water changes with the velocity of the spinning object. How does gravity affect the control experiment? The

Troubleshooter's Guide

Below is a problem that may arise during this experiment, a possible cause, and a way to remedy the problem.

Problem: The water stopped coming out of the container before the revolutions stopped.

Possible cause: The rag may not have been wet enough. Try pouring a little water in the container to a point below where the holes start. Dump the rag in water, place it in the container, and repeat the experiment.

experimental setups? What does the velocity of the revolving container illustrate about the speed of rotation and planets?

Change the Variables

To change the variables in this experiment you can alter the weight of the revolving object. Fill up a container with different amounts of water and weigh each object before you start spinning. You can also change the spinning object to a solid material, such as a marble or a rock. Another variable that you can change is the length of the string.

 # Design Your Own Experiment

How to Select a Topic Relating to this Concept

The movements of celestial objects have fascinated people long before there were any astronomical gadgets. For projects related to rotation and orbits, you can think about how the movements of the Sun and Moon have an effect on Earth. You can also visit a local planetarium to view how objects in our solar system move. Check the For More Information section and talk with your science teacher to learn more about rotations and orbits of celestial objects. Remember that if you conduct a project where you observe celestial objects, never look directly at the Sun to avoid damage to your eyes.

Steps in the Scientific Method

To conduct an original experiment, you need to plan carefully and think things through. Otherwise, you might not be sure what question you are answering, what you are or should be measuring, or what your findings prove or disprove.

Here are the steps in designing an experiment:

- State the purpose of—and the underlying question behind—the experiment you propose to do.
- Recognize the variables involved and select one that will help you answer the question at hand.
- State your hypothesis, an educated guess about the answer to your question.
- Decide how to change the variable you selected.
- Decide how to measure your results.

Recording Data and Summarizing the Results

Your data should include charts and drawings such as the one you did for the experiments in this chapter. They should be clearly labeled and easy to read. You may also want to include photographs and drawings of the experimental setup, models of any celestial setup, and the results, which will help other people visualize the experiment.

If you are preparing an exhibit, you may want to display your results, such as any experimental setup you designed. If you have completed a nonexperimental project, explain clearly what your research question was and illustrate your findings.

At any one time there are two bulges of water (or high tide) of roughly equal size, one towards and one away from the Moon. Low tides are created in areas about halfway between these two high-tide bulges. Here, boats docked near the shore are beached during low tide. (© Nik Wheeler/CORBIS. Reproduced by permission.)

Related Projects

There are multiple projects related to the orbits and rotations of celestial bodies. You can focus on the Moon's orbit through the sky, recording its phases throughout a month and its effect on Earth. There are certain celestial bodies that are held together by mutual gravitational attraction, such as the Earth and the Moon. You can examine other planet-moon systems, determine the point at which the bodies orbit around, and map out the orbit of each body. Another factor relating to orbits is the relationship between the time it takes a planet to complete one orbit and its distance from the Sun. You can explore how mass and distance affect a celestial body's orbit.

Another project could be to focus on the basic shapes of planetary orbits. Each planet has its own unique orbital path; some are close to circular and others are far more elliptical. You can map out the paths of the orbits on paper or construct a model. To further explore tides, you could examine how the Sun impacts tides and map the high and low tides in your area. Ocean tides are not exactly twelve hours apart. Another possible project is to explore what causes the time between tides, look up tidal information in a certain area, and then predict the high and low tides for the next month. Scientists have found that a planet's rotation affects its shape. You can explore this principle on Earth and other celestial bodies. For a research project, you can look at the many people and discoveries that led to the understanding that the Earth orbits and rotates around the Sun.

For More Information

Fraser, Alistair B. *Bad Coriolis FAQ.* http://www.ems.psu.edu/~fraser/Bad/BadFAQ/BadCoriolisFAQ.html (accessed on August 26, 2003). ❖ Answers to common misperceptions about the Coriolis force and other phenomena.

"Coriolis Force." *Department of Atmospheric Sciences at the University of Illinois at Urbana-Champaign.* http://ww2010.atmos.uiuc.edu/(Gh)/guides/mtr/fw/crls.rxml (accessed on August 26, 2003). ❖ Brief explanation of the Coriolis force with a video.

Curious about Astronomy. http://curious.astro.cornell.edu/index.php (accessed on August 26, 2003). ❖ Clear answers to many astronomy questions.

Groleau, Rick. "What Causes the Tides?" *PBS: Nova.* http://www.pbs.org/wgbh/nova/venice/tide_nf.html (accessed on August 26, 2003). ❖ PBS's *Nova* site illustrates the centrifugal force that causes tides.

Holloway, Marguerite. "Follies and Foucault's Pendulum." *Scientific American.com,* March 2003. http://www.sciam.com/article.cfm?articleID=00016A7C-5064-1E40-89E0809EC588EEDF (accessed on August 26, 2003). ❖ Story of a new science museum that features science history.

NASA Observatorium. http://observe.arc.nasa.gov/nasa/space/centrifugal/centrifugal_index.html (accessed on August 26, 2003). ❖ Detailed explanation of centrifugal force.

Scagell, Robin. *Space Explained: A Beginner's Guide to the Universe.* New York: Henry Holt & Company, 1996. ❖ Look at how the universe was created; includes lots of illustrations.

Simon, Seymour. *Our Solar System.* New York: William Morrow & Co., 1992. ❖ Simple description of the origins, characteristics, and future of the solar system, with lots of illustrations.

The Space Place. http://spaceplace.jpl.nasa.gov/phonedrmarc (accessed on August 26, 2003). ❖ Answers to space-related questions, activities, and clear space science explanations.

chapter 20

Separation and Identification

Most natural and manufactured materials are **mixtures,** not pure substances. In a mixture, each of the substances has its own chemical properties. Salt water, gravel, and cookies are a few examples of mixtures. People can use physical means to separate mixtures into their component parts. Separating mixtures is important because it allows people to identify the substances that make up the mixture.

Separating the components in a substance is usually one of the first steps in identifying its components. All mixtures can be separated and identified by the distinguishing chemical or physical properties of the components. The separation technique chosen depends on the type of mixture and its characteristics. After a mixture is separated, one or all of its components can be identified. Researchers can match the properties of the unknown substance to those properties of a known substance. Appearance and the way the unknown substance reacts with other substances are ways to identify a substance.

Separation and identification techniques are used for all types of different purposes. If there are pollutants in the water, scientists first separate and identify the pollutants to clean the water. Forensic scientists, people who work in criminal investigations, use the techniques to identify evidence, such as fabrics or blood. Research scientists will separate unknown biological samples to identify the molecules in the sample. In blood tests doctors may need to identify and then separate iron or another component out of the blood.

Words to Know

Boiling point:
The temperature at which a substance changes from a liquid to a gas or vapor.

Chromatography:
A method for separating mixtures into their component parts (into their "ingredients") by flowing the mixture over another substance and noting the differences in attraction between the substance and each component of the mixture.

Mixing it up

Anything a person can combine is a mixture. Mixtures with varying compositions are called **heterogeneous,** meaning that they have different appearance and properties at different points in the mixture.

When mixed together, oil and water form a heterogeneous mixture. Here, a layer of olive oil floats atop a layer of water. (Copyright © Kelly A. Quin. Reproduced by permission of Kelly A. Quin.)

For example, a mixture of oil and water is a heterogeneous mixture. The two substances form layers because of their different chemical properties, and one part of the mixture will have a higher concentration of oil, while another part of the mixture will have a higher concentration of water.

Solutions are a type of mixture in which all the sub-

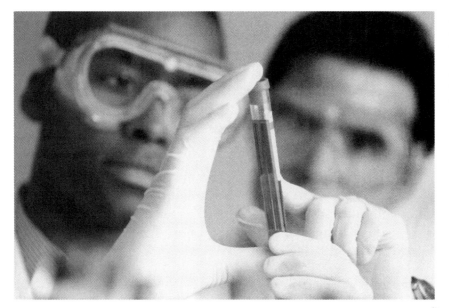

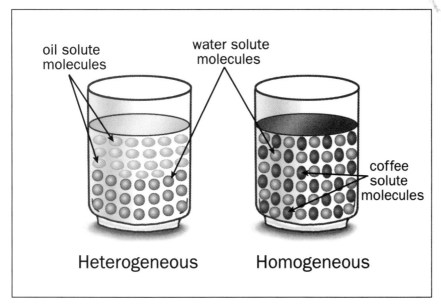

oil solute molecules

water solute molecules

coffee solute molecules

Heterogeneous   Homogeneous

In a homogenous mixture, solute molecules are evenly distributed; in a heterogeneous mixture, molecules are unevenly distributed and can be visually distinguished from one another.

stances are evenly distributed, or **homogeneous.** A solution has the same appearance and properties throughout the entire mixture. When sugar is mixed into a cup of hot tea, for example, the sugar molecules dissolve and are spread evenly throughout the cup. The sugar-tea mixture is a solution. The sugar molecules are called the **solute molecules.** The substance it dissolved in, the tea water, is called the **solvent.**

Separating by size

Size is one method used to separate many simple mixtures. If the parts of a heterogeneous mixture are large enough, the mixture can be separated by hand or by a sieve. A sieve has holes in it that are small enough for some of the solid substance or substances to pass through and the larger particles will remain above the holes. Soil, for example, is sifted through a sieve to separate out the chunks of rock and gravel from the fine soil particles.

Filtration is a commonly used separation technique similar to a sieve except it separates undissolved solid particles from a liquid. In filtration, a mixture passes through a filter, a material with spaces in it that holds back the particles. Filters are used frequently to clean water, make coffee, and purify air.

Other simple separation techniques include settling and evaporation. Settling is when the larger, heavier components will sink or settle to form distinct layers. When muddy water sits for a period of time, for example, the dirt will sink to the bottom. In evaporation, the liquid is heated until it becomes a gas and leaves behind the solid particles.

Separating by speed

One widely used method that scientists use to identify the parts in a solution is known as **chromatography.** Chromatography is a technique that separates components based on the rate each moves over a specific material. Each component has properties that determine its movement. Chromatography has many uses. It is commonly used in laboratories to isolate new compounds, analyze differences between environmental samples, and identify drugs from urine or blood samples.

In chromatography, a gas or liquid mixture travels over an unmoving substance. The unmoving substance chosen depends on the type of mixture. Paper chromatography is one of several types of chromatography that are all based on the same principles. In paper chromatography the unmoving substance is paper. The components in the mixture move at different rates over the paper based on their attraction to the paper. Some large-sized components may stick to the paper and hobble along; other small-sized components may glide over the paper and travel quickly. For example, to separate the colors in a dye, the dye is made into a preparation. A spot of the dye preparation is placed on the end of a piece of chromatography paper. Different colors that make up the dye then travel at varying rates along the paper.

(Words to Know

Control experiment:
A setup that is identical to the experiment, but is not affected by the variable that acts on the experimental group.

Filtration:
The mechanical separation of a liquid from the undissolved particles floating in it.

Heterogeneous:
Different throughout.

Homogenous:
The same throughout.

Hypothesis:
An idea in the form of a statement that can be tested by observation and/or experiment.

Insoluble:
A substance that cannot be dissolved in some other substance.

Melting point:
The temperature at which a substance changes from a solid to a liquid.

experiment
CENTRAL

Paper chromatography is one of the most basic types of chromatography. Other types include gas chromatography and liquid chromatography. Gas chromatography has a gaseous mixture while liquid chromatography uses liquids. Each is used in many ways including detecting explosive materials, analyzing fibers and blood, and testing water for pollutants.

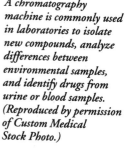

A chromatography machine is commonly used in laboratories to isolate new compounds, analyze differences between environmental samples, and identify drugs from urine or blood samples. (Reproduced by permission of Custom Medical Stock Photo.)

What is it?

Over the years scientists have gathered and compiled the many properties of individual substances. To identify an unknown substance in a mixture, scientists try to match the properties of the unknown substance to those of known substances. While there are numerous properties used in identification, there are some routine techniques that test for common properties.

A substance's shape and color is one of the first pieces of evidence scientists note. Its **solubility** or its ability to dissolve in another substance is another first step in identification. Because water is a common and known substance, it is the standard for many tests. A substance that dissolves in water is called **soluble** in water, and one that does not is called **insoluble** in water. Another common method used to identify a liquid is to determine its **pH,** or the measure of its acidity. The pH scale goes from 0 to 14. The lower the pH, the more acidic the solution. For example, lemons are acidic and so would have

Words to Know

Mixture:
A combination of two or more substances that are not chemically combined with each other and that can exist in any proportion.

pH:
A measure of a solution's acidity. The pH scale ranges from 0 (most acidic) to 14 (least acidic), with 7 representing a neutral solution, such as pure water.

Solubility:
The tendency of a substance to dissolve in some other substance.

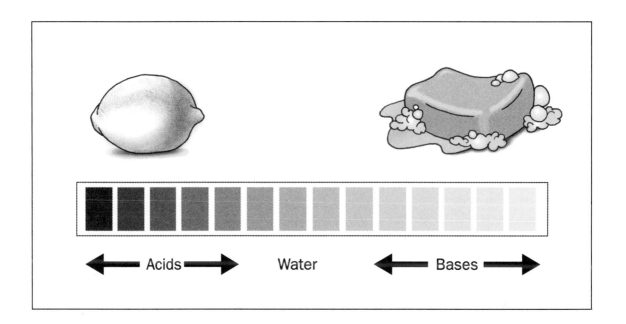

Acids ➡   Water   ⬅ Bases ➡

A pH scale ranges from 0 to 14 and is used to determine a solution's acidity. With 7 being neutral, a pH of 0 is the highest acid value and a pH of 14 is the highest base value.

a lower pH than soaps, which are basic. At the midway point, where the pH is 7, the substance is neutral. Water is an example of a neutral substance.

The effect of heating a substance can also provide several pieces of information. The temperature where a solid substance turns into a liquid is called its **melting point.** The temperature where a liquid turns into a gas is called its **boiling point.** Different substances also give off unique colors when placed in a flame. Potassium, for example, gives off a violet flame when heated in a flame; sodium emits a yellow-colored flame.

In the following two experiments, you will use separation and identification techniques to identify a mixture.

Experiment 1
Chromatography: Can you identify a pen from the way its colors separate?

Purpose/Hypothesis
Chromatography is a common technique used to identify substances, from drugs in blood samples to a type of pen used in a crime. The

What Are the Variables?

Variables are anything that might affect the results of an experiment. Here are the main variables in this experiment:

- type of paper

- time allowed for separation

- concentration of alcohol and water

- type of ink used in the pens

In other words, the variables in this experiment are everything that might affect the ink colors moving over the paper. If you change more than one variable at the same time, you will not be able to tell which variable had the most effect on color separation.

word chromatography comes from the Greek word *chromato,* which means color.

In this experiment, you will use paper chromatography to separate the colors out of four different types of black ink. The color black is a mixture of several colors. Different types of pens mix together varying amounts of colored inks to produce black ink. Once the colors are separated you will have a partner select one of the black pens as the unknown. You will then identify the unknown pen based on the pattern of the colors.

Paper chromatography identifies the parts of a mixture by first treating the paper with a solvent, a liquid that can dissolve other substances, and then observing how those substances travel different distances over the paper. How far each substance travels depends on the attraction it has for the paper.

Before you begin, make an educated guess about the outcome of this experiment based on your knowledge of chromatography and separation. This educated guess, or prediction, is your **hypothesis.** A hypothesis should explain these things:

- the topic of the experiment
- the **variable** you will change

Words to Know

Solute:
The substance that is dissolved to make a solution and exists in the least amount in a solution; for example, sugar in sugar water.

Solution:
A mixture of two or more substances that appears to be uniform throughout except on a molecular level.

Soluble:
A substance that can be dissolved in some other substance.

Solvent:
The major component of a solution or the liquid in which some other component is dissolved; for example, water in sugar water.

Variable:
Something that can affect the results of an experiment.

- the variable you will measure
- what you expect to happen

A hypothesis should be brief, specific, and measurable. It must be something you can test through further investigation. Your experiment will prove or disprove whether your hypothesis is correct. Here is one possible hypothesis for this experiment: "Different colors will separate out from each other by traveling different distances on the stationary phase. The pattern of the separated colors can then be used for identification."

In this case, the variable you will change is the type of black ink. The variable you will measure is the pattern of how the ink's colors separate.

Conducting a control experiment will help you isolate each variable and measure the changes in the dependent variable. Only one variable will change between the control and the experimental trials. Your control experiment will use an ink of one color, either red or blue.

Level of Difficulty
Moderate to Difficult.

Materials Needed
- four paper coffee filters
- pencil
- four different kinds of black pens, permanent ink
- red or blue pen (control)
- 91 percent isopropyl alcohol
- water
- ruler
- measuring cups
- two small glasses about 4 inches (10 centimeters) tall
- three paperclips
- scissors
- marking pen

Approximate Budget
$10.

Timetable
2 hours.

How to Experiment Safely
Be careful when handling alcohol; do not ingest it and keep it away from your face.

Step-by-Step Instructions

1. Cut the coffee filter paper into four strips measuring 2 inches by 4 inches (5 centimeters by 10 centimeters). One paper will hold the control ink, one the unknown ink, one the two black inks, and one the other two black inks.

2. Assign each of the four black pens a number, 1 through 4.

3. On each strip of paper, draw a line about 0.75 inches (2 centimeters) from the end of the paper with a pencil (NOT a pen). This end will be the bottom of the strip.

4. To separate the four unknown pen inks: Take two of the strips of filter paper. On the pencil line, about 0.5 inches (1.3 centimeters) in from the edge of the paper, make a large dot with Pen 1. The dot should be about the size of an eraser on a pencil. On the same pencil line on the opposite edge of the paper make a dot with Pen 2. Use the pencil to label each dot below the line (between the line and the bottom of the strip) with the pen number. (For example, the dot made with pen number 1 should be labeled "1.") On a fresh strip of filter paper, repeat this process for Pen 3 and Pen 4.

5. To separate the control ink: On the pencil line in the middle of a fresh strip of paper, make a large dot with the control ink. The control is a single color ink of red or blue. Label the dot "Control."

6. Stir together 1/4 cup (60 milliliters) of the alcohol with 1/4 cup (60 milliliters) of water. Pour this mixture into each of the two glasses so that the liquid sits below the 2-centimeter line. It should be about halfway to the line.

7. Straighten the two paperclips. Push one paperclip carefully through the top (the end without the dots) of two labeled strips of paper, and push the second paperclip through the top of the third strip of paper.

8. Rest each straightened paper clip across the top of one glass, with the bottom of the paper strips hanging down into the liquid. There will be two strips of paper in one glass and a third strip of

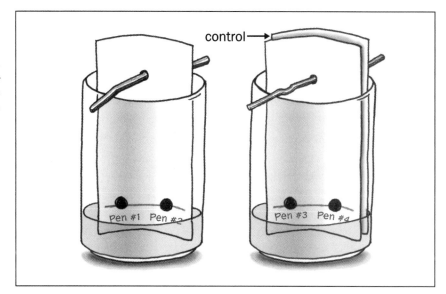

Step 8: Experiment 1 set-up. Make sure the ink dots are not submerged in the liquid.

control →

Pen #1 Pen #2   Pen #3 Pen #4

paper in the second glass. The ink dots should be close to the surface of the liquid, but NOT submerged in it.

9. Wait 30 minutes.

10. While you are waiting, turn away and have a partner select one of the four pens tested. This will be the "Unknown" ink.

11. To separate the unknown ink: On the pencil line in the middle of a fresh strip of paper make a large dot with the unknown pen. Label the dot "Unknown." Push a straightened paperclip carefully through the top.

12. Remove the first three strips of paper after the 30 minutes, and rest the paperclip holding the "Unknown" pen along the top of one of the glasses. This strip should also sit in the liquid 30 minutes.

Step 14: Different types of pens mix together varying amounts of colored inks to produce black ink. Measure from the top of every new color to the pencil line to determine how far the separate colors traveled up the strip

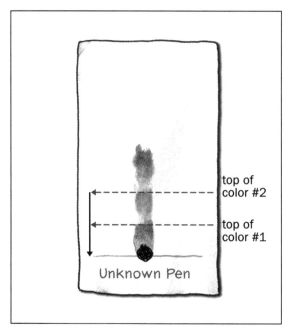

top of color #2

top of color #1

Unknown Pen

experiment
CENTRAL

Troubleshooter's Guide

Below are some problems that may arise during this experiment, some possible causes, and some ways to remedy the problem.

Problem: The spot disappeared off of the paper.

Possible cause: The liquid level is too high and is over the line. The ink dot could have dissolved into the liquid. Repeat the experiment with less liquid in the glass, making sure the dots are not submerged in the liquid.

Problem: The ink spot does not spread.

Possible cause: The ink is not soluble in the liquid. Repeat the experiment using a different type of ink.

Problem: The black ink did not separate into its different components.

Possible cause: The paper may not be able to separate all the components. Repeat the experiment using a filter paper of a finer grade or of a different weave. You can also purchase chromatography paper from a lab supply house.

Problem: The unknown ink did not match any of the inks already separated.

Possible cause: There may have been a problem during the experiment for any of the reasons above, or you may have changed more than one variable, which is the unknown pen. Check that the mixture preparation was given the same amount of time to move up the paper. Make sure the paper was the same. If you prepared a different mixture preparation, that could also have altered the results. Repeat the experiment, making sure that all the other variables are equal.

13. Allow the first three strips of paper to dry (about 30 minutes). When the unknown ink has been submerged for 30 minutes, remove and let dry.

14. For each of the known inks, measure from the top of every new color to the pencil line to determine how far the separate colors traveled up the strip. Write your results in a table, noting the description and measurement for the four pens.
15. Repeat the measurements for the separated colors of the unknown ink. Identify the unknown pen by comparing its measurements and pattern to the four black pens.

Summary of Results

Examine the results of the table compared to that of the unknown pen. How closely does the unknown pen match the pattern of one of the inks? Scribble a few lines with each of the black pens and label the scribble with the associated pen number. Compare each of the pen's patterns with its associated color black. Can you see a difference between the shades of each black pen? Look at the color of each black pen again and re-examine the table. Evaluate whether the black inks that appear more similar also have a greater likeness in their patterns.

Change the Variables

Changing some of the variables may lead to interesting results. Try changing the type of paper you are using to a coffee filter paper or a finer grade of white paper. You could also change the mobile phase. Try using water without adding alcohol or alcohol without adding water. Mix the two in different amounts and record what your results. You can also change the color and types of pen you use.

Experiment 2
Identifying a Mixture: How can determining basic properties of a substance allow you to identify the substances in a mixture?

Purpose/Hypothesis

Because the components in a mixture keep their own chemical properties, scientists can identify the substances in a mixture by knowing the properties of its components. In order to identify a substance, its components are isolated and tested.

In this experiment, you will determine different properties of several substances that are similar in appearance. You will then have a partner create a mixture with two of the substances. Using the proper-

What Are the Variables?

Variables are anything that might affect the results of an experiment. Here are the main variables in this experiment:

- the substance

- the solvent

- the quantity of each component in the mixture

- the temperature of the solvent

- the pH indicator

In other words, variables in this experiment are anything that might affect the identification of the components in the mixture. If you change more than one variable, you will not be able to tell which variable impacted the determination of the substance's properties and, thus, the mixture's composition.

ties of the substances that you determined, you will identify the composition of the mixture.

The substances you will use are three household items: flour, sugar, and baking soda. The properties you will determine for each substance are its appearance, solubility in water, solubility in vinegar, and pH.

To determine pH you will use red cabbage. The chemicals that give red cabbage its red/purplish color also can act as a pH indicator. The red cabbage pH indicator does not determine an exact pH number, but it can distinguish between acid (pH of 0 to 6), neutral (pH near 7), and base (pH of 8 to 14). When the juice of red cabbage is added to an acid, such as vinegar or lemon juice, it will become pink to red; when it is added to a base, it will turn blue or green. If the solution turns purple, it indicates that the substance is neutral, neither an acid nor a base.

To begin this experiment make an educated guess about what you think will occur based on your knowledge of mixtures. This educated guess, or prediction, is your **hypothesis.** A hypothesis should explain these things:

- the topic of the experiment
- the **variable** you will change
- the variable you will measure
- what you expect to happen

A hypothesis should be brief, specific, and measurable. It must be something you can test through further investigation. Your experiment will prove or disprove whether your hypothesis is correct. Here is one possible hypothesis for this experiment: "A mixture can be identified by determining the properties of the individual substances in the mixture."

In this experiment the variable you will change will be the substances that might possibly make up the mixture. The variable you will measure will be the mixture's properties.

Level of Difficulty

Moderate.

Materials Needed

- clear plastic cups (at least six, as many as twenty)
- water
- vinegar
- white flour (about a cup)
- white sugar (about a cup)
- baking soda (about a cup)
- measuring spoons
- measuring cups
- mixing spoons
- red cabbage
- sealable sandwich bag
- knife
- measuring cups
- marking pen

Approximate Budget

$12.

Timetable

2 hours.

How to Experiment Safely

Be careful when handling alcohol; do not ingest it and keep it away from your face. Handle the knife carefully when cutting. Even though you are working with food products, never ingest any of the experimental solutions because one might contain alcohol. Throw away each solution in the sink and clean the cups thoroughly if you are going to reuse them.

Step-by-Step Instructions

1. Prepare a chart with four columns down and four rows across. Label the columns with the headings of "Flour," "Sugar," "Baking Soda," and "Unknown." Label the rows: "Appearance," "Soluble with water," "Soluble with vinegar," and "Acid/Base/Neutral."

2. Label one clear plastic cup "Flour," a second "Sugar," and a third "Baking Soda." The cups may be reused throughout the experiment by rinsing them thoroughly with water and drying.

3. Put 1 teaspoon of each of the three substances in the appropriate plastic cup.

Step 1: Prepare a chart to record the results of Experiment 2.

	Flour	Sugar	Baking Soda	Unknown
Appearance				
Soluble with Water				
Soluble with Vinegar				
Acid, Base, or Neutral				

Step 5: Stir completely before you note if the mixture is soluble or not soluble

4. Record the color and description of the substance's appearance on the chart (for example, powder, grainy, etc.)

5. Add 1/4 cup (about 60 milliliters) of water to each of the cups and stir vigorously for 30 to 60 seconds. Allow the mixtures to stand for 15 minutes, then record whether each substance is soluble in water. If the solvent is clear it is soluble; if the solvent is cloudy and most of the substance remains at the bottom of the cup, it is insoluble.

6. In a clean cup, repeat Step 4 and Step 5, using vinegar in place of water.

7. Prepare a pH indicator: Chop red cabbage into small pieces and measure 1/2 cup of the pieces. Put the pieces into a sealable sandwich bag. Add 1/2 cup (about 120 milliliters) of very warm water to the cabbage. Close the bag and mix gently by squeezing. Let the water and cabbage sit for 5 minutes, mixing occasionally. Pour the purple water into a separate plastic cup.

8. In a clean cup, add 1 teaspoon of each of the substances into the appropriate cup.

9. Place 2 teaspoons (10 milliliters) of the purple pH indicator into each of the three cups and stir. Note whether the substance is an acid (solution turns pink to red), a base (solution turns blue or green), or neutral (solution remains purple).

Troubleshooter's Guide

Below are some problems that may arise during this experiment, some possible causes, and some ways to remedy the problem.

Problem: Some of the substance will not dissolve.

Possible cause: The mixture may need to be stirred further, or more solvent should be added to the substance. Repeat the test, stirring the solution thoroughly.

Problem: The solvent has turned a slight color.

Probable cause: The substance you are using may not be pure and some small part of the substance may be soluble in the solvent. Make sure you are using pure white flour and white sugar, and repeat the test.

Probable cause: You may not have rinsed the cups thoroughly. Repeat the test, washing the cup again or using a fresh plastic cup.

10. Turn away and have a partner mix two of the three substances together, using 2 tablespoons of each of the substances into a clean cup. Have your partner write down the two substances he or she selected.

11. Follow the procedures in Steps 4 through 9 to test the mixture for the properties defined in the chart. (You can use the same pH indicator made in Step 7.) For example, after recording the appearance of the mixture, add vinegar and stir the mixture to determine if it is soluble in water, and so on. Remove 1 teaspoon of the mixture each time you test for a specific property.

Summary of Results

Use the data you have collected for each property to identify which of the substances made up the unknown mixture. When you have reached a conclusion check with your partner. How did each of the properties enable you to narrow down the identification of the mixture? Hypothesize how a mixture of another two substances would have reacted. Record your results and list the steps you took to identify your mixture.

Change the Variables

There are numerous ways you can change the variables in this experiment. You can use different food substances that have the same powdery appearance as the ones given. Cream of tartar, powdered sugar, and cornstarch are some examples. You can change the look of the materials completely and use any substances that appear similar. You can also examine how other liquids react with these substances. Make sure you change only one variable at a time for each test, and keep careful records of your results.

 # Design Your Own Experiment

How to Select a Topic Relating to this Concept

Separation techniques and identification are used in many professions for a variety of reasons. Wherever there is a mixture, there is some way to separate it.

Check the For More Information section and talk with your science teacher to learn more about separation and identification. You can examine the *CRC Handbook of Chemistry and Physics,* listed in For More Information, which provides detailed tables of chemicals' behaviors and characteristics. Using this book as a guide could provide ideas on how to separate and identify substances. If you construct a project that uses heat or flames, make sure you have adult supervision.

Steps in the Scientific Method

To conduct an original experiment, you need to plan carefully and think things through. Otherwise, you might not be sure what question you are answering, what you are or should be measuring, or what your findings prove or disprove.

Here are the steps in designing an experiment:

- State the purpose of—and the underlying question behind—the experiment you propose to do.
- Recognize the variables involved and select one that will help you answer the question at hand.

- State your hypothesis, an educated guess about the answer to your question.

- Decide how to change the variable you selected.

- Decide how to measure your results.

Recording Data and Summarizing the Results

Your data should include charts and graphs such as the one you did for these experiments. They should be clearly labeled and easy to read. You may also want to include photographs and drawings of your experimental setup and results, which will help other people visualize the steps in the experiment.

If you are preparing an exhibit, you may want to display your results, such as any experimental setup you designed. For any unknown substance you may want to have a sample out so that people can note the characteristics of the substance. If you have completed a nonexperimental project, explain clearly what your research question was and illustrate your findings.

Related Projects

Separation and identification is a broad topic that can branch out to many projects. You can use paper chromatography to analyze the makeup of other liquid mixtures, such as candy or the pigments in vegetables. To identify the makeup of solid substances, you can examine rocks and minerals. Rocks are made of minerals and minerals each have specific properties. Certain minerals will dissolve in an acid like vinegar, for example, and others will not.

You can also explore how different fields of study use separation and identification techniques, and what techniques they use. You can select one profession to focus and conduct an experiment related to that area of study. Or you can research the many techniques and uses used by a range of professions. For example, the biotechnology field performs separation techniques on many biological substances to identify the molecules. Astronomers use separation and identification techniques to analyze any chunks of rocks or other materials that have landed on Earth from space. Examples of other professions you can explore include art conservators, archaeologists, and food scientists.

For More Information

Kurtus, Ron. "Mixtures." *School for Champions.* http://www.school-for-champions. com/science/chemixtures.htm (accessed on August 26, 2003). ❖ Basics of mixtures versus compounds.

Lide, David R, ed. *CRC Handbook of Chemistry and Physics, 83rd edition.* Boca Raton, FL: CRC Press, 2002. ❖ This authoritative reference provides properties of chemical substances.

"Separating and Purifying." *Journal of Chemical Education.* http://jchemed.chem. wisc.edu/JCESoft/CCA/CCA6/MAIN/1ChemLabMenu/Separating/MENU.HTM (accessed on August 26, 2003). ❖ Somewhat technical description of separation techniques.

Volland, Walt. "Separation of Mixtures: Physical Changes versus Chemical." *Bellevue Community College.* http://scidiv.bcc.ctc.edu/wv/e3/e3.html (accessed on August 26, 2003). ❖ Simple animation and explanation of chromatography techniques.

chapter 21

Simple Machines

When most people envision machines, the image probably does not include a simple screwdriver or pencil sharpener. Yet these devices are also machines. A **machine** is any object that makes work easier by altering the way in which the work is accomplished. Put another way, a machine can use a smaller force to overcome a larger force. In physics, **work** is defined as force applied over a distance. For example, a person does work when pushing a shopping cart down an aisle, yet does no work when pushing against a closed door.

Simple machines have few moving parts, or sometimes none at all. They are the building blocks for machines of all levels of complexity and all mechanical devices. People have been using simple machines for thousands of years. Zippers, staplers, nails, and scissors are just a few examples of common modern-day machines.

Machines can enlarge and change the direction of a force, yet all machines must follow the principles of **the conservation of energy.** This principle states that the work or amount of energy coming out of a machine is equal to the amount of energy put into the machine. Work is made up of the amount of force applied and the distance over which the force is maintained. **Effort** is the force applied. In mathematical terms, work equals force times distance *(w=fd)*. Put another way, a machine that uses half the force to lift an object must then double the distance it applies the force.

Simple machines include the inclined plane, wedge, screw, lever, pulley, and wheel and axle.

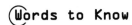

(W)ords to Know

Conservation of energy:
The law of physics that states that energy can be transformed from one form to another, but can be neither created nor destroyed.

Control experiment:
A setup that is identical to the experiment, but is not affected by the variables that affects the experimental group.

Effort:
The force applied to move a load using a simple machine.

Did You Know?

- Ancient Greek scientist Archimedes (287–212 B.C.E.) invented the water screw, a machine for raising water, that people still use today. He is also credited with coming up with the idea of the lever.

- Scissors have been found in ancient Egyptian ruins dating back to roughly 1500 B.C.E., yet they were not in common use until about 1500 C.E..

- Italian artist Leonardo da Vinci (1452–1519) had a fascination with machines that led him to write one of the first explanations of how machines work and how simple machines can be combined. He designed numerous machines that were revolutionary in his time, including a modern-style tank, an early helicopter, a crane, and a one-person elevator.

Incline at work

In a ramp or inclined plane, the greater the distance, the less effort.

An **inclined plane,** also called a **ramp,** decreases the amount of force needed to lift a load or weight by increasing the distance the load travels. For example, an inclined plane that covers twice the distance of

distance of ramp determines amount of effort

Full Effort

Slides of all kinds are examples of inclined planes. (© Kelly–Mooney Photography/CORBIS. Reproduced by permission.)

the vertical side will need half the amount of effort to lift a weight than if the weight was lifted straight up. The amount of work remains the same.

Historians theorize that ancient Egyptians used long, shallow ramps to help them carry five-ton stones up pyramids that soared hundreds of feet tall. Driveways, slides, and car ramps are modern-day examples of machines that make use of inclined planes.

A **wedge** looks like an inclined plane, yet it does work by moving (an inclined plane always remains still). A wedge changes the direction of a force. When a wedge comes into contact with an object, the wedge changes the direction of the force and causes it to move at a right angle. Wedges are often used to push things apart. The force needed for the wedge depends upon the size of the wedge angle. The smaller the angle of the wedge, the less force is needed yet the greater the distance it must be pushed. The pointed end of the nail is an example of a wedge. As the nail is pounded down with a force, the wood is pushed apart sideways. A narrow nail with a small angle must be moved more distance than that of a thick nail with a larger angle. Less force is needed for the thin nail yet it must move a greater distance. Doorstops, the tines on a fork, and knives are other examples of wedges.

A **screw** is basically an inclined plane wrapped around a cylinder. The length of the screw is the height of the plane, and the distance traveled is determined by the amount of threads on the screw. While turning, a screw converts a rotary motion into a forward or backward motion. The spiral ridges, or threads, around the screw cause the screw to turn many times to move forward a short distance. This is similar to moving an object up an inclined plane or ramp.

The width between the threads, or pitch, is similar to the angle of the inclined plane. The closer together the threads are around the screw, the more it needs to turn to move the same distance, making it less effort to turn. Screws with threads spaced farther apart travel less distance and take more force to turn. The screw's spiral threads act like wedges. Each thread produces a force at right angles to its rotation.

Pulley power

A pulley consists of a rope or other cord pulled over a steadied wheel. At one end of the rope is the object or **load** to be lifted; the other end is where the force is applied.

Words to Know

Friction:
A force that resists the motion of an object, resulting when two objects rub against one another.

Fulcrum:
The point at which a lever arm pivots.

Hypothesis:
An idea in the form of a statement that can be tested by observation and/or experiment.

Inclined plane:
A simple machine with no moving parts; a slanted surface.

Machine:
Any device that makes work easier by providing a mechanical advantage.

Pulley:
A simple machine made of a cord wrapped around a wheel.

Screw:
A simple machine; an inclined plane wrapped around a cylinder.

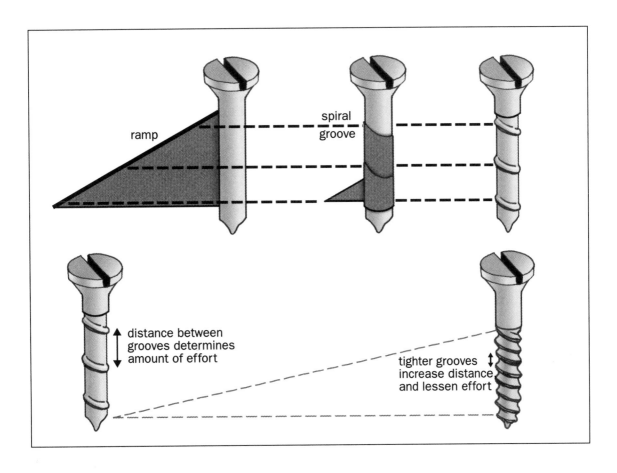

ramp

spiral
groove

distance between
grooves determines
amount of effort

tighter grooves
increase distance
and lessen effort

A single, fixed pulley changes the direction of a force. The force needed to lift the load still equals the weight of the load, yet it can feel easier if a person is pulling down instead of pushing up. Using two or more pulleys connected together can decrease the amount of effort needed to lift the same load. If using two pulleys, the rope leading to each individual pulley can hold half as much weight. With the load weighing half as much, a person need apply only half the force. The tradeoff is that the rope needs to be pulled twice the distance. The force is cut in half but the distance the rope must be pulled has doubled.

Screws are examples of simple machines. The closer together the threads are around the screw, the more it needs to turn to move the same distance, making it less effort to turn. Screws with threads spaced farther apart travel less distance and take more force to turn.

Lever lifts

A lever is any bar-type object free to move or pivot about at a fixed point. The point at which the lever pivots is called the **fulcrum.** A downward motion at one end results in an upward motion on the opposite side.

In a lever, the fulcrum's relationship to its load and the force applied, or effort, determines the work of the lever. Levers are catego-

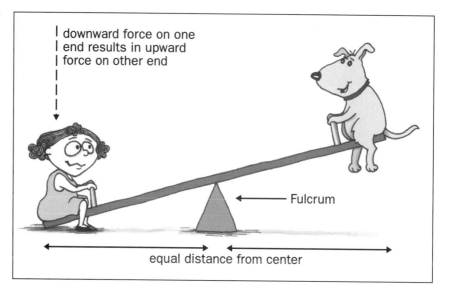

A seesaw is an example of a lever where the fulcrum is equally centered between load and effort.

downward force on one
end results in upward
force on other end

Fulcrum

equal distance from center

A wheelbarrow is an example of a lever where the fulcrum (in this case, the wheel) is at one end with the load (the bucket) in the middle and the effort (person lifting the handles) at the far end. (Copyright © Kelly A. Quin. Reproduced by permission of Kelly A. Quin.)

rized by where the fulcrum is located in relation to the load and effort. There are three basic types of levers. A first-class lever has its fulcrum placed between its load and the effort. One end is forced down and the other end moves up. When the fulcrum is in the center of the lever, the amount of effort pushed down on one side equals the amount of load lifted on the other side. If the distance from the effort to the fulcrum increases by two, then only half as much pushing effort is needed to raise the same load. If the load doubles, then the distance from the fulcrum to the load must also double in order for the same effort to move it. Pliers, a person's jaw, and a seesaw are examples of this type of lever.

A fulcrum at one end with the load in the middle and the effort at the far end is a second-class lever. This type of lever, such as a wheelbarrow, increases the force needed to lift the load, but decreases the distance it has to move. A third-class lever has the fulcrum at one end, the effort in the middle, and the load at the far end. Tweezers and fishing rods are examples of this type of lever.

A **wheel and axle** machine rotates around a fixed point and works in a similar way to a revolving lever. The **axle** is the object that attaches to the wheel. The wheel moves the axle. When the wheel revolves it moves a greater distance than the axle. The larger the diameter of the wheel, the less effort needed to turn it, but the greater distance needed for the same work. In reverse, a greater force applied to the axle will turn the wheel a greater distance. Doorknobs, pencil sharpeners, screwdriver handles, and steering wheels all use a wheel and axle.

Experiment 1
Wheel and Axle: How can changing the size of the wheel affect the amount of work it takes to lift a load?

Purpose/Hypothesis
A wheel and axle can be used to do work using less force. In a wheel and axle, both parts move together. In this experiment you will con-

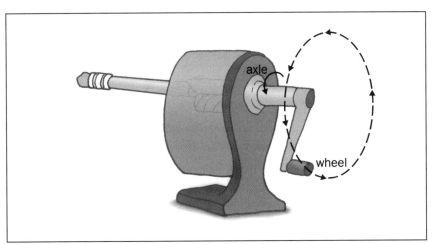

In a pencil sharpener, the wheel turns the axle, which is attached to a blade. The more turns you have to make, the less effort it takes.

struct a wheel and axle that also incorporates the pulley. You will join two spools together, one the wheel and the other the axle. The axle will hold a load and you will apply force to the wheel. Washers will be the load and also apply the force. This experiment will use three wheels of different diameters. By changing the diameter of the wheel, you will find out how the relationship in size between the wheel and the axle determines how easy it is to lift the load.

Before you begin, make an educated guess about the outcome of this experiment based on your knowledge of work and machines. This educated guess, or prediction, is your **hypothesis.** A hypothesis should explain these things:

- the topic of the experiment
- the **variable** you will change
- the variable you will measure
- what you expect to happen

A hypothesis should be brief, specific, and measurable. It must be something you can test through further investigation. Your experiment will prove or disprove whether your hypothesis is correct. Here is one possible hypothesis for this experiment: "Given that the axle stays constant, the larger the wheel, the less force will be needed to lift the load."

In this case, the variable you will change is the diameter of the wheel. The variable you will measure is the amount of force needed to lift the load.

Conducting a **control experiment** will help you isolate each variable and measure the changes in the dependent variable. Only one variable will change between the control and the experimental setup, and that is the diameter of the wheel. For the control, you will use a wheel that is of equal size to the axle. At the end of the experiment you can compare the results of the control to the experimental trials.

Level of Difficulty
Easy to Moderate.

Materials Needed
- two small paper or plastic cups
- metal washers all of equal size, at least 20
- dowel (should fit through spools to allow spools to spin)
- masking tape

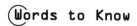

Words to Know

Simple machine:
Any of the basic structures that provide a mechanical advantage and have no or few moving parts.

Variable:
Something that can affect the results of an experiment.

Wedge:
A simple machine; a form of inclined plane.

Wheel and axle:
A simple machine; a larger wheel(s) fastened to a smaller cylinder, an axle, so that they turn together.

Work:
Force applied over a distance.

What Are the Variables?

Variables are anything that might affect the results of an experiment. Here are the main variables in this experiment:

- the diameter of the wheel
- the weight of the cups
- the diameter of the axle
- the load

In other words, the variables in this experiment are everything that might affect the amount of force needed. If you change more than one variable at the same time, you will not be able to tell which variable had the most effect on getting the work done.

- ruler
- hole puncher
- marking pen
- string (optional)
- two full thread spools of equal size (wheel and axle)
- three cylindrical objects of varying sizes: (full thread spools or ribbon spools work well). Use the thread spool as a guide when collecting these objects: find one about half its size, one about twice its diameter, and one about three or four times its diameter).

Approximate Budget

$3.

Timetable

20 minutes.

Step-by-Step Instructions

1. Measure and note the diameters of the two equal-size cylinders in a data chart.
2. Set up a wheel and axle control by placing the dowel into the two cylinders of the same size: the wheel and axle. Tape the spools together so they move as one unit. Set the dowel on a table with the wheel and axle hanging just over the edge, then tape the dowel

firmly to the table at the far end and several points along the dowel. The wheel is the outside cylinder.

3. Label the cups "A" and "B." Punch two holes in each of the cups on opposite sides near the open upper rim. Cut two pieces of string slightly larger than the diameter of the cup. Tie each end of the string to a hole on the outside of the cup so that it is slightly loose.

4. Pull down 20 inches (51 centimeters) of thread from the axle and attach cup A to the thread. Use several inches of the thread from the wheel to attach cup B. (Note: If you are not using thread spools or the thread is weak, then tape a piece of string to the center of the cylinder.)

5. Wrap the thread around the wheel until cup B is sitting just below the thread.

Data chart for Experiment 1.

6. Place eight washers in cup A.

	diameter		load	force
	wheel	axle		
control				
wheel 1				
wheel 2				
wheel 3				

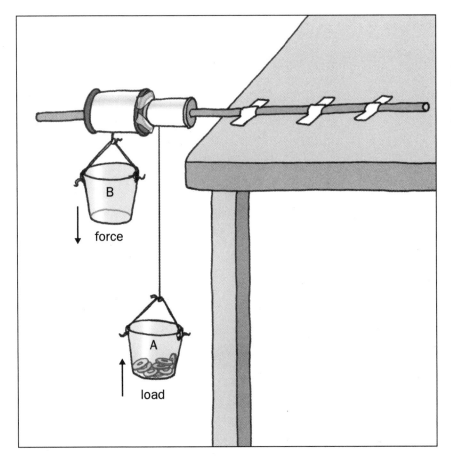

7. Apply force by placing washers in cup B, one at a time, until cup A has been raised and is sitting just below the axle. Note the force needed by counting the amount of washers. Record your results.

8. Remove the wheel; cup A will fall back in its starting point.

9. Measure the diameter of a second spool. Slide this wheel on the dowel and firmly attach it to the axle. Pull down the string (or ribbon) and reattach cup B to the new spool, making sure it is at the same starting point just below the spool.

10. Again, apply force by placing washers in cup B, one at a time, until cup A is sitting below the axle. Note the results.

11. Repeat Steps 7 through 10 for the next two wheels.

Summary of Results

Examine your chart. Compare the ratio of the diameters between the wheel and axle, and the ratio between the load and force for each

wheel. How do they relate to each other, and how do they relate to the control? What size wheel made the work of lifting the load the easiest? In your wheel and axle, look at what other type of machine is in use? How does changing the direction of the force provide an additional mechanical advantage?

Change the Variables

To change the variable in this experiment, you can alter the diameter of the axle instead of the wheel. You can also use more or less weights as the load.

Experiment 2
Lever Lifting: How does the distance from the fulcrum affect work?

Purpose/Hypothesis

A lever is a bar that pivots on a fulcrum. The mass placed on a lever is called the load. In a first-class lever, the fulcrum sits in between the two loads. The load presses down on the lever with a force or effort. In this experiment, you will vary the distances between the applied force, or effort, and the fulcrum to determine how to make the load easier to lift. You will use a ruler as the lever, metal washers as the load, and a small narrow object as the fulcrum.

What Are the Variables?

Variables are anything that might affect the results of an experiment. Here are the main variables in this experiment:

- the mass of the load
- the distance from load to fulcrum

In other words, the variables in this experiment are everything that might affect the work of the lever. If you change more than one variable at the same time, you will not be able to tell which variable had the most effect on the work.

Before you begin, make an educated guess about the outcome of this experiment based on your knowledge of levers and machines. This educated guess, or prediction, is your **hypothesis.** A hypothesis should explain these things:

- the topic of the experiment
- the **variable** you will change
- the variable you will measure
- what you expect to happen

A hypothesis should be brief, specific, and measurable. It must be something you can test through further investigation. Your experiment will prove or disprove whether your hypothesis is correct. Here is one possible hypothesis for this experiment: "More force is needed when it is applied closer to the fulcrum than farther from the fulcrum."

In this case, the variable you will change is the distance from the fulcrum. The variable you will measure is the force needed to lift the load.

Level of Difficulty

Easy.

Materials Needed

- 12-inch (30-centimeter) flat ruler
- ten metal washers of the same size
- narrow flat object, such as a pencil or domino

Step 5: Place the washers closer to the fulcrum to determine how many it takes to lift the load.

Approximate Budget
$2.

Timetable
20 minutes.

Step-by-Step Instructions

1. Make a lever by placing the narrow object that serves as a fulcrum, such as a domino, under a ruler at the 6-inch mark.
2. Place four washers at one end of the ruler. Add washers on the opposite end of the ruler until the load is lifted and the lever is balanced. Note the number of washers and the distance.
3. Remove the washers on the 12-inch mark so that the opposite side lies on the table.
4. Place washers one at a time on the 10-inch (25.4-centimeter) mark, until the lever is balanced. Note the number of washers and the distance.

How to Experiment Safely
There are no safety hazards in this experiment.

5. Remove the washers on the 10-inch mark and repeat, placing the washers on the 8-inch (20.3-centimeter) mark.

Summary of Results
Examine your results and compare the different loads required to accomplish the same amount of work: lifting the load. For each trial, complete the equation work equals force times distance, where force is the number of washers needed to push down one side, and distance is the distance from the fulcrum. Predict how many washers you would need at several different points along the ruler.

Change the Variables
To change the variable in this experiment you could alter the position of the fulcrum. Keep the number of washers on one side the same, move the fulcrum, and then determine how much force is needed to lift the load.

 # Design Your Own Experiment

How to Select a Topic Relating to this Concept
To choose a topic related to simple machines and mechanics you can look at the objects that you use every day. Select several items and identify the type(s) of simple machines that it utilizes. You can use these tools to model the design of your machines. Check the For More Information section and talk with your science teacher to learn more about machines and mechanics.

Steps in the Scientific Method

To conduct an original experiment, you need to plan carefully and think things through. Otherwise, you might not be sure what question you are answering, what you are or should be measuring, or what your findings prove or disprove.

Here are the steps in designing an experiment:

- State the purpose of—and the underlying question behind—the experiment you propose to do.
- Recognize the variables involved and select one that will help you answer the question at hand.
- State your hypothesis, an educated guess about the answer to your question.
- Decide how to change the variable you selected.
- Decide how to measure your results.

Recording Data and Summarizing the Results

Your data should include charts and drawings such as the one you did for these experiments. They should be clearly labeled and easy to read. You may also want to include photographs and drawings of your experimental setup and results, which will help other people visualize the steps in the experiment.

Did you know that your jaw is a simple machine? The jaw acts as a first-class lever when you are chewing food. (Copyright © Kelly A. Quin. Reproduced by permission of Kelly A. Quin.)

If you are preparing an exhibit, you may want to display your results, such as any experimental setup you designed. You may also want to include specimens, in a closed container, so that others can observe what you studied. If you have completed a non-experimental project, explain clearly what your research question was and illustrate your findings.

Related Projects

Because simple machines are all around, finding materials and ideas related to simple machines is relatively simple. As machines are linked with force, you can investigate the principles behind force that are at work in a machine. A project idea can be to take one simple machine and use the same force in many different setups. You can take apart common household simple machines (with an adult's permission, of course) and compare the differences and similarities between machines that use the same principles. Compare one type of simple machine, such as a screwdriver, to its different types. Look at what features each machine has to make its work easier. You can also build or take apart complex machines, and sketch the simple machines that it uses. For a research project, you can investigate the history of simple machines and how they have impacted people's lives.

For More Information

"Exploring Leonardo." *Science Learning Network.* http://www.mos.org/sln/Leonardo/LeoHomePage.html (accessed on August 26, 2003). ❖ Exhibit on Leonardo da Vinci's work with machines.

James, Elizabeth, and Carol Barkin. *The Simple Facts of Simple Machines.* New York City: Lothrop, Lee & Shepard Co, 1975. ❖ Simple illustrations and text help to explain the basic simple machines with activity suggestions.

Lafferty, Peter. *Force & Motion.* New York: EyeWitness Books, Dorling Kindersley, 2000. ❖ With photographs and many graphics, this book describes the science of force and motion and their applications in simple machines.

Macaulay, David, and Peter Lafferty. *The Way things Work.* Boston: Houghton Mifflin, 1988. ❖ Clear text with many illustrations describes the principles behind numerous inventions and tools.

"Simple and Complex Machines." *University of Utah.* http://sunshine.chpc.utah.edu/javalabs/java12/machine/index.htm (accessed on August 26, 2003). ❖ Explanations of various machines.

"Simple Machines." *BrainPOP.* http://www.brainpop.com/tech/simplemachines/ (accessed on August 26, 2003). ❖ Animations, activities, and explanations of simple machines.

"Simple Machines." *Canada Science and Technology Museum.* http://www.sciencetech.technomuses.ca/english/schoolzone/Info_Simple_Machines.cfm (accessed on August 26, 2003). ❖ Informative site explaining various simple machines, including levers, pulleys, and more.

chapter 22

Soil

Commonly called dirt, soil is a central ingredient for life on Earth. **Soil** is the thin, outer layer of material on the surface of Earth, ranging from a fraction of an inch to several feet thick.

Plants depend on soil for their nutrients and growth. These plants are then consumed and used by animals, including people. Soils provide shelter and a home for insects and small animals. Microscopic organisms flourish in soil, breaking down dead matter, which returns nutrients into the soil for new life. People use soils directly as a material to build on and grow crops in. Soils also reveal a historical record of an area's past life and geography. Understanding the properties of a soil is a key to determining how the soil will function for a particular use.

The specific makeup of soil depends on its location, yet all soils share the same basic composition: **minerals,** water, air, and **organic** matter, meaning matter that contains carbon and comes from living organisms. Minerals are naturally occurring inorganic or nonliving substances that come from Earth's crust. Different types and combinations of these components form multiple types of soil. In the United States alone, researchers have identified over seventy thousand different soils. Soils are characterized by many features, including their structure, texture, living organisms, and acidity.

The scoop on dirt

Soil is a dynamic material that Earth is constantly manufacturing. The highest percent of any given soil is made of minerals, which all come from the same material: rocks. Nature churns rocks into new

Words to Know

Alkaline:
A substance that is capable of neutralizing an acid, or basic. In soil, soil with a pH of more than 7.0, which is neutral.

Bedrock:
Solid layer of rock lying beneath the soil and other loose material.

Clay:
Type of soil comprising the smallest soil particles.

Basic composition of soil.

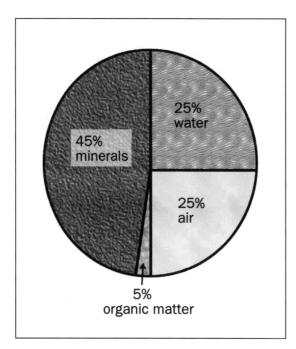

25% water

45% minerals

25% air

5% organic matter

soil regularly and slowly. A **rock** is a mixture of minerals that stays together under normal conditions. Rocks can be hard, relatively soft, small, or large. Over time, rocks get **weathered** or worn down naturally by their environment.

Several factors contribute to how fast the rock weathers. The rock's composition, climate,

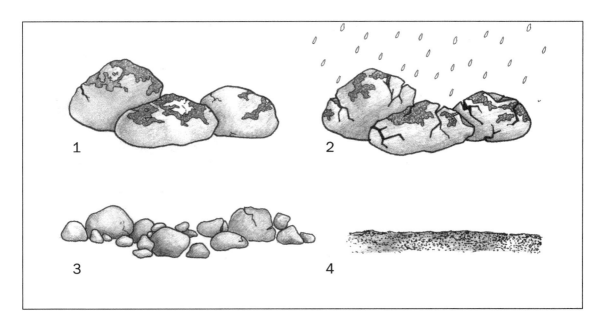

surrounding organisms, and location are all key factors. Weathering also needs time. It can take one hundred years to more than six hundred years to form one inch of topsoil.

The rocks that form soil are called the **parent material.** When some rocks weather, their minerals react with other elements to form different chemicals from the original parent material. Other rocks

TOP:
Climate and location are two factors that cause rocks to break down and form soil.

BOTTOM:
Nature churns rocks into new soil regularly and slowly. (CORBIS. Reproduced by permission.)

retain the same composition of the parent material. The makeup of the parent material determines many properties of the resulting soil.

The mineral content of the parent material can be acidic, neutral, or **alkaline.** The acidity of soil is measured on a pH scale from 0 to 14. On this scale, a pH of 7 is neutral, above 7 is alkaline, and below 7 is acidic. The acidity of the soil is a key factor in determining the types of plants and other organisms that thrive there. Iron, for example, is an acidic mineral in which azaleas and blueberries grow well. Elm, yucca, and sycamore grow in nonacidic soils. Soil life also depends upon minerals for essential nutrients, which come from the specific mineral content in the parent material. Calcium, phosphorus, and potassium are examples of familiar minerals soil life needs.

Winds, rain, sunshine, and temperature shifts all play a part in weathering. Water slips into the cracks of a rock. Varying temperatures freeze and thaw the water repeatedly, expanding the cracks and fragmenting the rock. Rain pounds against a rock, wearing it down into increasingly smaller particles. Winds beat against the rock's surface, tearing away its outer layers. In general, a moist, warm climate causes rocks to break down more quickly than a cool, dry climate.

The surface features of an area also impact soil formation and its erosion. Water that flows over land can carry soil with it and expose new rocks to weathering. Soils on slopes and hills have a high rate of water flow. Here, soils are carried by the water flow at a faster rate than soils on flat surfaces, which have more time to form.

Along with the weather, a warm climate also hastens the weathering process because it provides a comfortable environment for life. Organisms that live in and on the soil affect soil's formation in several ways. Plant roots stretch into the soil and break up small fragments. Burrowing animals wriggle through soil and move rock fragments to cause crumbling. Animals stomp on the soil and split up rock pieces. Some microscopic organisms that produce acid, such as fungi and lichens, break up the minerals within rocks.

Size matters

Soils are generally made up of one of three mineral particles: sand, silt, or clay. The type of particles is another major factor in determining the life in and on the soil. Water and air, needed by both plants and animals, sit in the spaces between the particles. Almost all soils have

Words to Know

Control experiment:
A setup that is identical to the experiment, but is not affected by the variables that affects the experimental group.

Humus:
Fragrant, spongy, nutrient-rich decayed plant or animal matter.

Hypothesis:
An idea in the form of a statement that can be tested by observation and/or experiment.

Leach:
The movement of dissolved minerals or chemicals with water as it percolates, or oozes, downward through the soil.

Mineral:
An nonorganic substance found in nature with a definite chemical composition and structure.

Organic:
Made of, or coming from, living matter.

experiment
CENTRAL

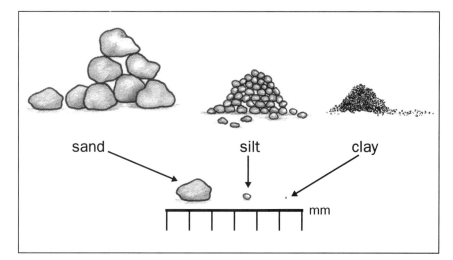

Soils are generally made up of one of three mineral particles: sand, silt, or clay.

some combination of these particles, and it is the relative percentage of one over the other that determines its category.

Sand particles are relatively large, ranging in size from 0.002 inches to 0.08 inches (0.05 millimeters to 2 millimeters) in diameter. Sandy particles feel gritty to the touch. The particles have large air spaces between them, causing water to run through easily. Because they do not retain moisture, sand is loose and crumbly. Water that runs through sand can cause minerals necessary for growth to drain or **leach** out of the soil. Leaching is the movement of dissolved particles downward through the soil.

Silt is the next largest soil particle, ranging in size from 0.00008 inches to 0.002 inches (0.002 millimeters to 0.05 millimeters) in diameter. Silt particles are fine and hold in some water. Silt particles feel soft and can hold together well when moist. When they are dry they are easily blown away by wind.

Clay particles are the smallest type of soil. Clay particles have little air space between them. They hold the highest amount of water and keep other soil particles together. Moist clay packs tightly together and can be molded. When clay particles are dry they harden, which can slow the growth of plant roots.

Dirty layers

As the weathering process continues over time, it causes soil to develop into layers that have distinct characteristics. A vertical slice of two or more of these layers is known as a **soil profile.** The layers are

(W)ords to Know

Parent material:
The underlying rock from which soil forms.

Rock:
Naturally occurring solid mixture of minerals.

Sand:
Granular portion of soil composed of the largest soil particles.

Silt:
Medium-sized soil particles.

Soil:
The upper layer of Earth that contains nutrients for plants and organisms; a mixture of mineral matter, organic matter, air, and water.

Soil horizon:
An identifiable soil layer due to color, structure, and/or texture.

Soil profile:
Combined soil horizons or layers.

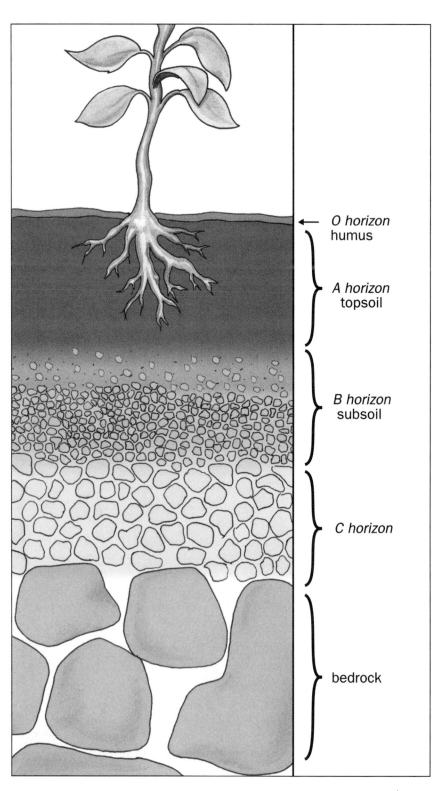

In a soil horizon the soil particles get gradually larger.

O horizon
humus

A horizon
topsoil

B horizon
subsoil

C horizon

bedrock

known as **soil horizons** and are named O, A, B, and C. How thick each horizon is depends upon its location. Soil horizon properties differ in their color, texture, consistency, life, and acidity.

The uppermost soil layer, the O layer, is filled with organic matter. As this matter gets decomposed from soil-dwelling creatures it forms a dark-brown, organic material called **humus.** Most humus comes from plant materials, such as dead leaves, twigs, and stems that fall to the ground. Dead animals in the soil and above it also contribute to humus. Humus retains water and contains nutrients for life to grow.

Sitting right below this layer is the A layer, called **topsoil.** Topsoil contains decaying plant and animal remains, along with a wealth of microscopic organisms such as bacteria. With all of its humus and organic matter, topsoil is usually the darkest and most fertile layer in the soil. Soil animals, such as earthworms and ants, live comfortably in this layer, using the plant and animal remains for food. Plant roots stretch out in this region to suck up the water and nutrients.

Subsoil is the middle, or B, soil layer. It is usually lighter in color than topsoil because it does not contain as much humus, making it less fertile. Denser and with less nutrients than topsoil, relatively few animals and plants are found here. Some plants with long roots reach down into the subsoil to get at the water stored between the particles.

The C layer, or horizon, contains partially disintegrated parent material and its minerals. It is far less altered and weathered than the layers above it and has none of the organic matter life needs to grow. Beneath this layer is the bottom region below the soil called **bedrock.** This layer contains bits of rock similar to the parent material.

Earthworms tunnel through the soil, creating air pockets and turning over the soil. (© Sally A. Morgan; Ecoscene/ CORBIS. Reproduced by permission.)

Life in the dirt lane

Soils are teeming with life, from the microscopic bacteria and fungi to the visible small animals and plants. Live organisms promote growth and new life in soil. Once dead, organisms contribute to the amount of decayed organic matter in soil, which influences its characteristics.

Pick up a handful of soil and you are holding billions of microscopic organisms. These microbes decompose organic matter and return vital nutrients into the environment. Plant roots hold soil particles together and prevent them from blowing away. Animals that burrow into the soil, such as squirrels and moles, create holes that allow air and water to enter. Insects such as beetles, ants, spiders, and snails eat organic matter and begin the decaying process. Worms tunnel through the soil, creating air pockets and turning over the soil.

Experiment 1
Soil Profile: What are the different properties of the soil horizons?

Purpose/Hypothesis

Soil is composed of three main categories of particles: sand, silt, and clay. Each of these particles has distinct properties including its feel, texture, color, nutrients, and size. While these three particles can form many different combinations in a soil , the proportion of each changes in each horizon.

In this experiment, you will take a soil profile and determine the properties of three different horizons. Because the depth of each soil horizon depends on location, the depth suggested to dig is a guide. You may need to dig farther down than suggested to find three unique horizons, or you may not have to dig as deep.

Once you have the three samples you will examine their characteristics in several ways. Using a kit, you will test each sample for nutrients. By feeling the soil and pressing it together you can determine its texture and feel. You will then estimate the relative proportions of sand, silt, and clay by measuring the point at which each layer settles in water. Larger particles will settle first; the smallest particles will settle last. Another varying characteristic among the horizons is the amount of microorganisms, which decompose organic matter and

experiment
CENTRAL

What Are the Variables?

Variables are anything that might affect the results of an experiment. Here are the main variables in this experiment:

- the patch of soil you choose

- the depth you dig

- the amount the jar is shaken

- the type of organic matter present

In other words, the variables in this experiment are everything that might affect the soil horizons. If you change more than one variable at the same time, you will not be able to tell which variable had the most effect on the properties of each horizon.

create the humus. An optional part to this experiment is to determine the amount of microorganisms in each horizon by placing chopped organic matter in each sample and examining the results.

Before you begin, make an educated guess about the outcome of this experiment based on your knowledge of soil horizons and soil particles. This educated guess, or prediction, is your **hypothesis.** A hypothesis should explain these things:

- the topic of the experiment
- the **variable** you will change
- the variable you will measure
- what you expect to happen

A hypothesis should be brief, specific, and measurable. It must be something you can test through further investigation. Your experiment will prove or disprove whether your hypothesis is correct. Here is one possible hypothesis for this experiment: "The soil horizons at lower depths will contain more sand, be grittier, lighter, and have less minerals and organic matter than the soil of the top horizon."

In this case, the variable you will change is the depth of the soil. The variable you will measure is the soil's properties, including its particle makeup, organic matter, color, and mineral content.

Level of Difficulty

Difficult (because of the digging and the multiple parts).

Materials Needed

- area with soil that you can dig (another option is to find an area already dug; see also Change the Variables)
- shovel
- plastic container that can hold about 2 cups (500 milliliters)
- grasses, flowers, leaves (optional part)
- yardstick
- ruler
- three self-sealing bags
- three 1-quart (about 1-liter) straight jars with lids
- water
- marking pen
- nutrient testing kit (available from garden or hardware stores)

Approximate Budget

$18.

Timetable

Varies because of digging; 3 hours experiment time; 24 hours waiting. Optional part will take 3 weeks; 15 minutes per week.

Step-by-Step Instructions

1. Find a clear area of soil and dig to a depth of about 30 inches (76 centimeters). Place the ruler in the hole to measure depth.
2. Label the self-sealing bags "Soil A," "Soil B," and "Soil C."
3. Use the plastic containers to collect three samples at different depths. (Examine the soil profile for differences in color and texture and use this as your collection indicators. The following measurements are guidelines.) Collect the first soil sample by placing the top of the container at 2 inches (5 centimeters) down and

How to Experiment Safely

This is a messy experiment; be sure to wash your hands thoroughly after collecting the soil. Watch out for any insects in the soil.

Step 3: Collect soil samples from three horizons.

Data chart for Experiment 1.

	Depth	Color	Texture		% Sand, Silt, Clay	Nutrients
			Feel	Ribbon		
soil A						
soil B						
soil C						

scooping dirt inside the container. When filled, place the soil in Soil A bag and note the depth on a data chart. Collect the next soil sample at roughly 15 inches (38 centimeters). Place the soil in Soil B bag and note the depth. Collect the third soil sample at 30 inches (76 centimeters). Place the soil in Soil C bag and note the depth. Remove any visible insects from the soil samples.

4. Note the color(s) of each sample on your data chart.

5. Determine the texture of each layer: Collect a small ball of soil in your hand from Soil A and spray it with water so that it is damp. (If it is already damp leave as is.) Rub the soil between your fingers and feel if the texture is floury (silt), sticky (clay), or gritty (sand).

6. Use that same ball to determine if the soil sticks together. Press the soil between your thumb and forefinger to make a ribbon. Note whether the soil forms a ribbon without breaking, forms a ribbon with breaking, or does not form a ribbon.

7. Repeat Steps 5 and 6 for Soil B and Soil C.

8. Estimate the relative percentage of clay, sand, and silt particles: Place 1 cup of Soil A in a labeled jar and add water until the jar is almost full. Repeat with the other two soils, adding the same amount of water in each jar and making sure the jars are labeled. Cover the jars and shake for at least 2 minutes.

Steps 9 to 11: Measure each layer of particle.

silt
sand→
clay

9. After 1 minute, make a mark on the jar at the level the particles have settled to the bottom. This is the sand. Measure up to the mark with the ruler.

10. Let the jars sit undisturbed. After 2 to 3 hours, mark and measure the thickness of the next layer. This is the silt.

11. Wait at least 24 hours to measure the last level, which is the clay.

experiment
CENTRAL

Troubleshooter's Guide

Below are some problems that may arise during this experiment, some possible causes, and some ways to remedy the problem.

Problem: The soil horizons were very similar.

Possible cause: You may not have dug down deep enough when you collected the samples. There should be a change in texture and color marking the different horizons. Repeat the experiment, digging down another 12 inches (30 centimeters) or more.

Problem: The organic matter did not decompose.

Possible cause: You may not have allowed enough time for the microorganisms in the soil to decompose it. It is also possible that you have few microorganisms in any of your soils. Repeat with another sample from the same location, and use a soil as a control that is a rich, dark brown color from the top layer of the soil.

12. Divide the thickness of each layer by the total height of all three layers. Multiply that number by 100 for a rough percentage of each type of particle. Note the results.

13. Test for nutrients: Follow the directions on the nutrient kit to determine the level of nutrients in each soil sample.

14. (Optional) Determine the relative amount of microorganisms in each sample: Leave 1 cup (about 240 milliliters) of each soil sample in the bag and add enough water to moisten (the rest of the soil can be returned to ground). Seal the bag and poke small holes in the top.

15. Chop up organic matter, such as leaves, grass, and/or flowers. Add 2 tablespoons (30 milliliters) of the chopped organic matter to each bag. Spray each soil so each is the same moistness and place bags in a dark environment, such as a drawer. Every 5 to 7 days add another tablespoon of water (15 milliliters) to each of the soils. Every week for 2 to 3 weeks, note the decomposition of the organic matter and any visible life, such as fungi.

Summary of Results

Examine your chart of the three soils. What is the most striking difference in soil properties between them? How did Soil A compare to Soil C in texture and color? How do the differences in the estimated soil particles relate to the soils color and whether it sticks together? Determine if any of your soils showed the property of only one type of soil particle? Hypothesize would happen if you grew the same plant in each soil. Based on your results, how does each soil hold water? Write a brief summary of the experiment and your analysis.

Change the Variables

The main way to change the variable in this experiment is to alter the type of soil. If digging is not possible in your area, you can purchase different soil types in a garden shop and repeat the same steps for each soil. To change the variable in the microorganisms part, you can use the same type soil and alter the kind of organic matter.

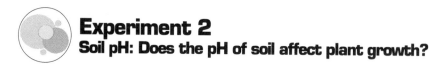

Experiment 2
Soil pH: Does the pH of soil affect plant growth?

Purpose/Hypothesis

A soil's pH is a measure of how acidic or basic it is. A soil that is basic is called alkaline. Alkaline soils are often referred to as sweet; acidic soils are referred to as sour. Soil pH is measured on a pH scale. The pH scale ranges from 1 to 14, with 7 being neutral, neither acid nor alkaline. Water, for example has a pH of 7. Acidic soils have a pH less than 7; the lower the number, the more acidic the soil. Alkaline soils have a pH above 7; the higher the number, the more alkaline the soil.

Most plants prefer a neutral to slightly acidic soil, with a pH between 6 and 7, yet some plants prefer acidity whereas others grow best in alkaline soil. Potatoes, gardenias, and blueberries grow best in acidic soils. Geraniums, asparagus, and mint grow best at higher pH levels. The pH of the soil also affects how available the nutrients are for plants to absorb. For example, nitrogen, potassium, and phosphorous are key nutrients that plants needs to grow. In soil that is highly acidic or alkaline, plants cannot get phosphorus. Potassium is most available in soils with high pH and unavailable at low pH. Nitrogen becomes available to plants with a pH of roughly 5.5 or above.

experiment
CENTRAL

To ensure proper growth of crops or other plants, it is important to know the pH level of the soil before planting. (Reproduced by permission of Field Mark Publications.)

In this experiment, you will test how acidity affects plant growth by growing the same type of plant in both an acidic and an alkaline soil. To make soil more alkaline, gardeners add calcium carbonate (limestone). This is referred to as liming. For a quick way to make soil more alkaline you can add baking soda, which is also alkaline. To increase the acidity of the soil you will add vinegar (gardeners use sulfur or aluminum sulfate). To determine the soil pH's effect, you can measure height, number of leaves, how fast the plants grow, leaf color, and number of flowers.

Before you begin, make an educated guess about the outcome of this experiment based on your knowledge of soil and acidity. This educated guess, or prediction, is your **hypothesis.** A hypothesis should explain these things:

- the topic of the experiment
- the **variable** you will change
- the variable you will measure
- what you expect to happen

A hypothesis should be brief, specific, and measurable. It must be something you can test through further investigation. Your experiment will prove or disprove whether your hypothesis is correct. Here is one possible hypothesis for this experiment: "The plant will grow best in one type of soil pH; plants grown in the other two pH soils will not be as healthy."

What Are the Variables?

Variables are anything that might affect the results of an experiment. Here are the main variables in this experiment:

- the type of soil
- the nutrients in the soil
- the type of plant
- the pH of the soil

In other words, the variables in this experiment are everything that might affect the growth of the plant. If you change more than one variable at the same time, you will not be able to tell which variable had the most effect on the plant's growth.

In this case, the variable you will change is the pH of the soil. The variable you will measure is the health of the plant.

Conducting a **control experiment** will help you isolate each variable and measure the changes in the dependent variable. Only one variable will change between the control and the experimental setup, and that is the soil pH. For the control, you will use a neutral potting soil, between pH of 6 and 7. At the end of the experiment you can compare the results of the control to the experimental trial.

Level of Difficulty

Moderate.

Materials Needed

- fifteen seeds of one plant type
- three plant pots, such as plastic containers
- potting soil
- white vinegar
- baking soda
- cheesecloth
- small bucket that cheesecloth can fit over
- rubber band or string (to fit around container)
- ruler

- container that holds 8 cups (about 2 liters), such as a soda bottle
- pH test kit or strips (available at garden or hardware store)
- measuring spoons
- measuring cup
- marking pen

Approximate Budget
$10.

Timetable
Varies depending on the plant selected and soil; an estimated 1 hour for setup, then 10 minutes every 5 days for 6 weeks.

Step-by-Step Instructions
1. Measure the pH of the Control soil and note the results. It should be somewhere between 6 and 7.
2. Prepare acidic soil: The soil should be dry to moist. Make a solution of 1 tablespoon (15 milliliters) vinegar with 8 cups (about 2 liters) of water in the bottle or container and shake it.
3. Secure the cheesecloth over the top of the small bucket with a rubber band or string. Put the soil on top of the cheesecloth. One cup at a time, pour the vinegar-water solution over the soil until it is saturated, then test the pH. Have the soil reach a pH of roughly 5.0. Depending on the soil, you may need to add more of the vinegar solution. If more acidity is needed, wait until the soil becomes dry to moist (try putting it in the Sun), then again pour the vinegar-water solution over the soil. Retest the pH of soil. When the pH is at the right level for the experiment, note the pH on a chart.
4. Prepare alkaline soil: The soil should be dry to moist. Make up a solution of 1 tablespoon baking soda with 4 cups (about 1 liter) of water and shake it.
5. Repeat Step 3, replacing the vinegar-water solution with the baking soda-water solution. Have the soil reach a pH of roughly 8.0.

How to Experiment Safely
There are no safety hazards in this experiment.

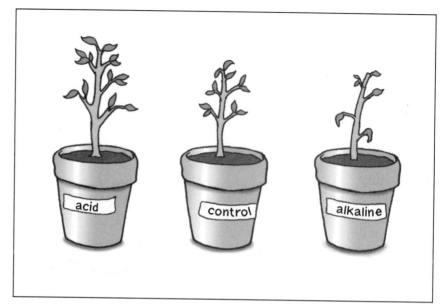

Steps 7 and 8: Measure how pH affects the plants' health.

Depending on the soil, you may need to make the soil more alkaline. Wait until the soil becomes dry to moist, then pour more of the baking soda-water solution over the soil. Retest the pH of soil and when it is alkaline enough note the number.

6. Label each of the containers: "Alkaline," "Acidic," and "Control."

7. Plant five seeds in each container, using the indicated soil, and care for as indicated.

8. Every five days (this may vary depending on your plant) measure the height of the plant, number of leaves, flowers/buds, or any other characteristic of your plant.

Summary of Results

When the control plants have reached full height, examine your results. Was your hypothesis correct? How did each of the other plants compare to the control? Are there specific characteristics of the plant that were especially different than the control? Once you have determined the best pH of your plant, research what nutrients are available to your plant in that soil. What nutrients are lacking?

Change the Variables

There are a few ways that you can change the variables in this experiment. You can alter the type of plant you grow, or you may want to grow several different types at once. (Some plants display interesting differences in a range of soil pHs, such as hydrangeas, which have a

Troubleshooter's Guide

Below is a problem that may arise during this experiment, a possible cause, and a way to remedy the problem.

Problem: The soil did not turn very acidic or alkaline.

Possible cause: The soil may not have been dry enough for it to soak up the vinegar or baking soda. Make sure you wait long enough so that when you press the soil together it falls apart, then add the solution.

visible petal-color change.) You can also choose a soil with a low amount of nutrients, then add different nutrients to the soil to determine each one's effect on plant growth. Nutrient-testing kits are available at garden or hardware stores.

 Design Your Own Experiment

How to Select a Topic Relating to this Concept

Whether it is bought or dug, soil offers many possible project ideas. Check the For More Information section and talk with your science teacher to learn more about soil. You may want to visit a garden store or greenhouse to look at the different varieties of soils available. Look around at the types of soils in your area and the kinds of plants that grow in them.

Steps in the Scientific Method

To conduct an original experiment, you need to plan carefully and think things through. Otherwise, you might not be sure what question you are answering, what you are or should be measuring, or what your findings prove or disprove.

Here are the steps in designing an experiment:

- State the purpose of—and the underlying question behind—the experiment you propose to do.

- Recognize the variables involved and select one that will help you answer the question at hand.
- State your hypothesis, an educated guess about the answer to your question.
- Decide how to change the variable you selected.
- Decide how to measure your results.

Recording Data and Summarizing the Results

Your data could include charts and graphs to display your data. If included, they should be clearly labeled and easy to read. You may also want to include photographs and drawings of your experimental setup and results, which will help other people visualize the steps in the experiment.

If you are preparing an exhibit, you may want to bring samples of any soil samples you used, and display your results, such as any experimental setup you designed. If you have completed a nonexperimental project, explain clearly what your research question was and illustrate your findings.

Related Projects

Soils' diversity and significance offer a range of project ideas. You could further compare the properties of soil particles by measuring how different types of soils hold water. The amount of water soils hold relates to pesticides and fertilizers that people put in the soil. A project could explore what happens to these products when they are placed in soils of various types. This could lead to a project on leaching and nutrient deficiencies in the soil.

You could also explore the properties of parent materials and the process of weathering. A project could look at why certain parts of the world have distinct soils, such as deserts. You may be able to collect or purchase rock samples and compare their characteristics with one another. How does the soil composition in certain geographic areas impact their economy, environment, and agriculture? You could also look at the methods scientists have developed to replenish the soil of minerals, nutrients, and other vital properties.

For More Information

Bial, Raymond. *A Handful of Dirt.* New York: Walker and Company, 2000. ❖ Explains what soil is made of and what lives in it.

"Soil Science Education Home Page." *NASA Laboratory for Terrestrial Physics.* http://ltpwww.gsfc.nasa.gov/globe/index.htm (accessed on August 26, 2003). ❖ Basic information and learning activities about soil, with good graphics.

"Soils and their Conservation." *University of Adelaide.* http://www.waite.adelaide. edu.au/school/Soil/ (accessed on August 26, 2003). ❖ Basic soil information with activities.

Stell, Elizabeth P. *Secrets to Great Soil.* Pownal, VT: Storey Publishing Book, 1998. ❖ Comprehensive book on soil properties and how to create fertile soil.

"Utah Soils." *Utah Office of Education.* http://www.uen.org/utahlink/lp_res/ TRB020.html (accessed on August 26, 2003). ❖ Clear descriptions of soils and soil components.

chapter 23

Space Observations

People's fascination with space goes back hundreds of years to simple stargazing and trying to understand the heavens. Today's astronomers use a wealth of tools to study space. Most astronomers are involved in measuring things, such as the speed, distance, and mass of objects in the universe. Knowing these facts can lead to further knowledge, such as the object's origin or composition. To measure things astronomers use observations and laws of the universe.

Just about everything known about space originates from the study of light given off by objects in space. The change from observing objects with the naked eye to powerful instruments was one of the major advances in astronomy. **Telescopes** are one of the main tools astronomers use to gather light. Understanding the physical laws of how light and objects move also fueled astronomers' knowledge of the universe. Merging the visual data with calculations has led to awesome findings on stars, planets, galaxies, and solar systems that are far, far away.

Mountains on the Moon

Peer through the right telescope on Earth and it is possible to view something in space that is a billion light years away—just one light year is about 5,865,696,000,000 miles (9,460,800,000,000 kilometers)! The telescope was the first groundbreaking tool used in astronomy. With the telescope, astronomers could study the motions of celestial objects that were previously undetectable.

The telescope was invented in the Netherlands in the early 1600s. Soon afterwards, Italian scientist Galileo Galilei (1564–1642) became

Words to Know

Blueshift:
The shortening of the frequency of light waves toward the blue end of the visible light spectrum as they travel towards an observer; most commonly used to describe movement of stars towards Earth.

Concave lens:
A lens that is thinner in the middle than at the edges.

Control experiment:
A setup that is identical to the experiment, but is not affected by the variable that acts on the experimental group.

Did You Know?

- The largest optical telescope in the world is the W. M. Keck telescope in Hawaii. It measures 33 feet (10 meters) in diameter. It is located at an elevation of 2.7 miles (4.3 kilometers) above sea level on top of Mount Mauna Kea, an extinct volcano.

- With an amateur telescope, you can see light from objects in space that are 40 million to 500 million light years away.

- Doppler radar uses the principles of the Doppler effect to forecast weather. In Doppler radar, an antenna sends out radio waves that are reflected back by particles in the air, such as dust, raindrops, hailstones, and snowflakes. As these particles move toward or away from the antenna, the returning radar pulse will change in frequency, allowing meteorologists to track a storm's speed and distance.

- In 2003, astronomers detected the most distant galaxy ever using a telescope that filtered out light outside of a specific wavelength. The galaxy is 12.8 billion light years away—that's about 75 trillion miles (121 trillion kilometers).

- When telescopes came into use and millions of stars appeared, astronomers changed their system of naming stars from names to numbers. In modern day, the International Astronomical Union (IAU), agreed upon by sixty-six countries, regulates the naming of all celestial objects.

Words to Know

Convex lens:
A lens that is thicker in the middle than at the edges.

Crest:
The highest point reached by a wave.

Doppler effect:
The change in wavelength and frequency (number of vibrations per second) of either light or sound as the source is moving either towards or away from the observer.

Focal length:
The distance from the lens to the point where the light rays come together to a focus.

Frequency:
The rate at which vibrations take place (number of times per second the motion is repeated), given in cycles per second or in hertz (Hz). Also, the number of waves that pass a given point in a given period of time.

the first person to use this new instrument to study the sky. He made a series of remarkable discoveries. Among his observations was that the Moon had mountains and craters on it and was not smooth as previously believed. He observed four bright objects orbiting or revolving around Jupiter, what is now known as Jupiter's moons. He also saw that the Sun had spots, which rotated. His observations led him to conclude that objects rotated and that they revolved around other objects.

The largest optical telescope in the world is the W. M. Keck telescope in Hawaii. It measures 33 feet (10 meters) in diameter. (© Roger Ressmeyer/CORBIS. Reproduced by permission.)

The Hubble Space Telescope was launched into space in 1990 and has transmitted up-close views of celestial objects that are billions of light years away. (UPI/Bettmann. Reproduced by permission.)

In modern day astronomers use telescopes of all shapes and sizes. Some are located on Earth and others sit in space. One of the most famous telescopes in space is the Hubble Space Telescope. The Hubble was launched into space in 1990 and has transmitted up-close views of celestial objects that are billions of light years away.

How they work

In the way that they collect and magnify the light, telescopes make objects appear larger than they are. There are two basic types of tele-

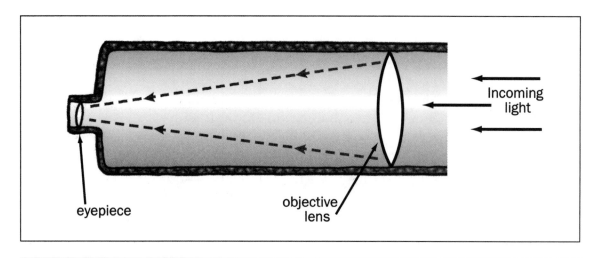

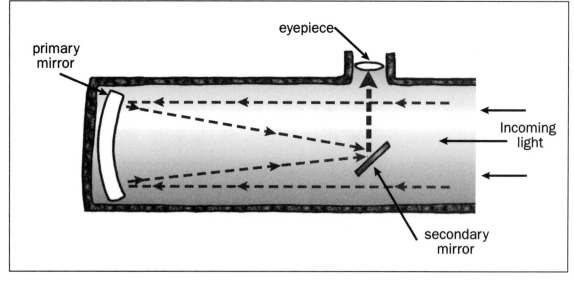

TOP:

A refractor telescope uses two types of lenses to gather and bend or refract the light.

BOTTOM:

A reflector telescope uses mirrors instead of lenses to collect light.

scopes: refractor telescopes and reflector telescopes. Each goes about enlarging an image in different ways. The amount of light a telescope can collect relates to the size of the lens or mirror used to gather light. Telescopes that have a larger lens or mirror will generally collect more light, and so will detect much fainter objects.

The Galileo-style of telescope is a **refractor telescope** and it uses two types of lenses to gather and bend or refract the light. The lens in the front of the telescope, the **objective lens,** gathers the light from the object. In a refracting telescope the objectives lens is a **convex lens,** a lens that is thicker in the middle and curves outward. Convex lenses make objects appear larger but blurry. This is the type of lens used in a magnifying glass.

In one type of refractor telescope the second lens, called the eyepiece lens, uses a smaller **concave lens.** A concave lens caves or curves inward in the middle. This focuses the light from the objective lens and magnifies it. A long tube, or series of tubes, holds the lenses in place at the correct distance from one another.

The **reflector telescope** uses mirrors instead of lenses to collect light. The primary mirror that collects and focuses the light is usually a concave mirror. The light reflects off the primary mirror to another mirror, which directs the light to the eyepiece. Each type of telescope has strengths and weaknesses. Most of the largest telescopes in the world are reflectors. Large mirrors cost less and are easier to support than lenses.

The deeper astronomers look into space, the farther back in time they are looking. It takes so long for light traveling through space to reach Earth that astronomers scanning the edges of the universe are seeing objects as they were billions of years ago.

Shifty light

Astronomers take observations gathered from telescopes and apply their knowledge of how light travels to theorize on the past, present, and future behavior of objects in space. The **Doppler effect** or **Doppler shift** is one way that astronomers make measurements on the light they observe. Astronomers use the Doppler effect to calculate the speed of an object and its movements.

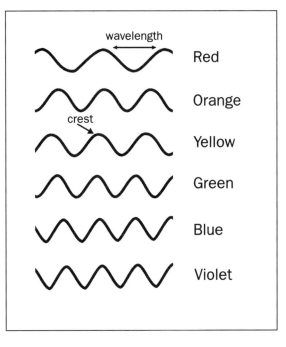

Light travels in waves; each color has its own wavelength.

Although they are not visible, light energy travels in **waves.** Water and sound energy also travel in waves. A wave is a vibrational disturbance that travels through a material or space. Light waves can travel through matter or a vacuum, such as space. Every wave has a high point called a **crest.** The distance from one crest to the next crest is called the **wavelength.**

Visible light is made up of seven basic colors—red, orange, yellow, green, blue, indigo, and violet. Each color has its own unique wavelength. For example, blue light waves are shorter than red light waves. The **frequency** is the number of waves that pass a point in space during any time interval. What a person sees as color is actually the frequency of the light. Because red has a longer wavelength, something red has a lower frequency than something blue.

The Doppler shift occurs because there is an apparent shift in the wavelength depending on whether an object is moving towards or away from the observer. As objects in space move away, or recede, from Earth, the wavelengths appear stretched or longer. This is called a **redshift,** because the light appears to have a lower frequency. If the object moves towards Earth, the wavelengths appear compressed or shorter. This makes the light appear to have a higher frequency and a **blueshift** occurs.

In a vacuum, such as space, all the wavelengths in light travel at one speed. If scientists know the amount and colors of light that an

When an object approaches a person, waves bunch together and there is a blueshift; when an object recedes, waves spread out and there is a redshift.

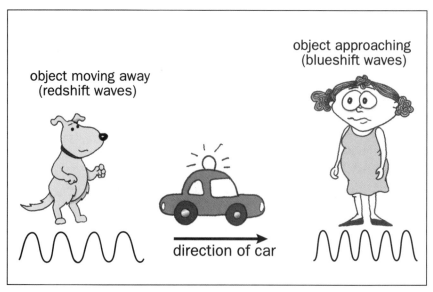

object moving away
(redshift waves)

object approaching
(blueshift waves)

direction of car

object gives off, they can measure the amount of color shift. Since the wavelength of each color is known, the color shift will determine the direction and speed of the object.

The Doppler effect can be used by astronomers to gather information about how fast stars, galaxies, and other astronomical objects move toward or away from Earth. Using the Doppler shift, astronomers calculated that the more distant galaxies are moving away from Earth more rapidly than the ones that are closer. This finding led to the theory that the universe is expanding, and to the origins of the solar system.

In the following two experiments you will explore the Doppler effect and telescopes.

Experiment 1
Telescopes: How do different combinations of lenses affect the image?

Purpose/Hypothesis

Telescopes take advantage of the properties of light to enlarge and focus images. The basic design of a telescope aligns two lenses a set distance from each other. In general, the objective lens is relatively large in diameter so that it can gather light; the eyepiece is smaller and stronger. For this experiment, you will test different combinations of convex (curving outward) and concave (curving inward) lenses. If possible, try to gather several different strengths and sizes of lenses; the listed sizes are only suggestions. Check the For More Information section for places to find lenses.

The objective lens will always be a convex lens. This lens should be larger in diameter and weaker than the eyepiece lens. The thinner a lens is in the center, the weaker it is. Use an eyepiece lens that is smaller and more powerful than the objective lens. You can determine a lens' power by its **focal length,** the distance required by the lens to bring the light to a focus. In general, as the focal length of a lens decreases, the power of the lens increases. You will use both a convex and a concave eyepiece lens. Cardboard, or construction paper, tubes that slide in and out from each other will hold the lenses. The distance between the two lenses should be about the sum of the focal lengths of the lenses.

Words to Know

Hypothesis:
An idea in the form of a statement that can be tested by observation and/or experiment.

Objective lens:
In a refracting telescope, the lens farthest away from the eye that collects the light.

Redshift:
The lengthening of the frequency of light waves toward the red end of the visible light spectrum as they travel away from an observer; most commonly used to describe movement of stars away from Earth.

Reflector telescope:
A telescope that directs light from an opening at one end to a concave mirror at the far end, which reflects the light back to a smaller mirror that directs it to an eyepiece on the side of the tube.

Powerful telescopes allow scientists to observe parts of space that the human eye never could, such as this cluster of thousands of stars. (Reproduced by permission of Space Telescope Science Institute.)

ⓦords to Know

Refractor telescope:
A telescope that directs light through a glass lens, which bends the light waves and brings them to a focus at an eyepiece that acts as a magnifying glass.

Telescope:
A tube with lenses or mirrors that collect, transmit, and focus light.

Variable:
Something that can affect the results of an experiment.

Using a convex and a concave lens will produce a right-side-up image. Using two convex lenses will produce an upside-down image. (When viewing celestial objects, astronomers do not care that much whether the object is upside down or not.)

You can also calculate the magnification power of your telescope if you know the focal lengths of your lenses. The magnification power equals the focal length of the objective lens divided by the focal length of the eyepiece lens. For example, if the focal length of the objective lens is 50 centimeters, and the focal length of the eyepiece is 5 centimeters, your telescope will magnify the object ten times the actual size of the object. If the focal length of that same telescope had a focal length of 1 centimeter, the telescope would magnify the object 50 times its actual size.

Before you begin, make an educated guess about the outcome of this experiment based on your knowledge of telescopes. This educated guess, or prediction, is your **hypothesis.** A hypothesis should explain these things:

What Are the Variables?

Variables are anything that might affect the results of an experiment. Here are the main variables in this experiment:

- the thickness of the lens
- the size of the lens
- the curvature of the lens
- the distance between the lenses

In other words, the variables in this experiment are everything that might affect the magnified image. If you change more than one variable at the same time, you will not be able to tell which variable had the most effect on seeing the image.

- the topic of the experiment
- the **variable** you will change
- the variable you will measure
- what you expect to happen

A hypothesis should be brief, specific, and measurable. It must be something you can test through further investigation. Your experiment will prove or disprove whether your hypothesis is correct. Here is one possible hypothesis for this experiment: "Two convex lenses will produce a larger but blurrier image than a convex and a concave lens combination."

In this case, the variable you will change is the type of eyepiece lens. The variable you will measure is the size and sharpness of the image produced.

Level of Difficulty

Moderate.

Materials Needed

- one convex lens for the objective lens (can be about 2 to 4 inches [5 to 10 centimeters] in diameter, and over 500-millimeters in focal length). (Lenses are available from scientific supply houses and hobby stores. You could also try to find lenses around the house, such as from magnifying glasses or old eyeglasses, as well as

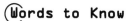

Words to Know

Wave:
A motion in which energy and momentum are carried away from some source; a wave repeats itself in space and time with little or no change.

Wavelength:
The distance between the crest of a wave of light, heat, or energy and the next corresponding crest.

experiment
CENTRAL

asking an eyeglass store if they have any lenses they are going to discard.)

- one convex lens for the eyepiece, smaller in diameter than the objective lens (can be 1 to 1.5 inches [2.5 to 3.5 centimeters] in diameter, focal length of less than 20 to 50 millimeters)
- one concave lens for the eyepiece, (can be 1 to 1.5 inches [2.5 to 3.5 centimeters] in diameter, focal length of less than 20 to 50 millimeters)
- sturdy tape, such as masking tape
- scissors
- ruler
- two cardboard tubes, one that slides inside the other: The tubes should be about the same size as the lenses. If you do not have tubes, you can roll up thick construction paper and tape to make them.
- helper
- picture or news article to view
- other concave and convex lenses of different sizes (optional)

Approximate Budget
$15.

Timetable
1 hour.

Step-by-Step Instructions
1. Tape the picture or printed piece of paper on a wall.
2. Begin with the smaller, stronger convex lens to use as the eyepiece, and the larger, less powerful convex lens for the objective lens. Hold the objective lens towards the picture at arms length.
3. Hold the eyepiece near your eye, in front of the objective lens.
4. Move the eyepiece closer and farther away to the objective lens while focusing on the picture.
5. When the object is in focus, have your helper measure the distance between the two lenses. (If you know the focal length of your lenses, the distance of the tubes should about equal the sum of the focal lengths of the lenses.)
6. Place the smaller tube inside the larger tube. The tubes should fit snugly inside each other, with the inner tube able to slide. Extend the tubes and cut them so the combined length of the tubes is slightly greater than the distance between the lenses. If you are rolling tubes out of thick construction paper, make sure you roll

How to Experiment Safely
If you use the telescope outside, never look directly at the Sun. The Sun's rays are so powerful they can cause permanent eye damage.

the paper into tubes where the openings are roughly equal to the size of the lenses.

7. Tape the objective lens to the far end of the telescope, and the eyepiece lens to the near side.

8. Look at the picture through the telescope, sliding the tubes until the object comes into focus.

9. Note whether the image is right side up or inverted, and the relative size of the image.

10. Remove the eyepiece lens and repeat Steps 2 through 7 using the concave lens as the eyepiece.

11. If you have other lenses of differing sizes and thickness, repeat the process to compare the results. Old glasses and magnifying glasses are a couple inexpensive sources for lenses. Record whether the lens is thicker or thinner than the one you already used when you note the results. If you know the focal lengths of the lenses, calculate the magnification power.

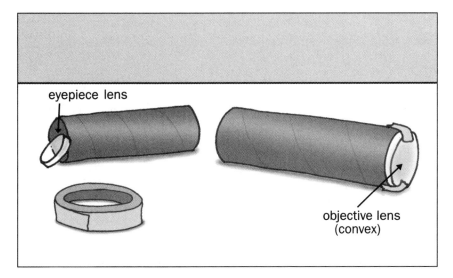

Step 7: Tape the objective lens to the far end of the telescope, and the eyepiece lens to the near side.

eyepiece lens

objective lens
(convex)

Troubleshooter's Guide
Below is a problem that may arise during this experiment, some possible causes, and some ways to remedy the problem.

Problem: The picture is blurry.

Possible cause: The distance between the two lenses may be too short or long. The distance should be equal to the sum of the focal lengths of the two lenses. Building a telescope involves some trial and error to get the correct distance and focus. Take careful measurements when holding the lenses up and try to gather several different lenses to investigate telescopes thoroughly.

Summary of Results

Was your hypothesis correct? What does sliding the inner tube in and out do to the image? If you tried using other lenses, how did these compare to the first set? Think about what change the eyepiece made in the appearance of the image once you placed it in front of the objective lens. If you want to continue the project to view celestial objects, go outside at night. Pick one particular light in the night sky and compare the image using each of the telescopes.

Change the Variables

To change the variables in this experiment you can change the type of lens you use, the thickness of the lens, or the length between the lenses.

Experiment 2
Doppler Effect: How can waves measure the distance and speed of objects?

Purpose/Hypothesis

Astronomers use the Doppler effect to determine whether an object in space is moving towards or away from Earth and how fast it is moving. However, the Doppler effect was first discovered using sound waves, not light waves. The perception of both light and sound is

experiment
CENTRAL

from the waves emitted. Waves coming from an object moving away from an observer have a lower frequency than those from an object moving toward the observer.

In sound, pitch is determined by how many waves per second reach the ear. The more sound waves a person hears, the higher the pitch. When an object moves toward a person, it takes less and less time for each wave to reach the person. The waves crowd together. The person gets more waves per second and it results in an increase in pitch. When the sound moves away from a person, the waves spread out. A person gets fewer waves per second and the person hears a decrease in pitch.

In this experiment, you will determine how the Doppler effect relates to sound waves. You will record the sound of an alarm clock or noise-making device that is approaching and moving past you at varying speeds. You can then draw conclusions about the relative distance and speed of the object from listening to the increase and decrease in pitch.

Before you begin, make an educated guess about the outcome of this experiment based on your knowledge of the Doppler effect and waves. This educated guess, or prediction, is your **hypothesis.** A hypothesis should explain these things:

- the topic of the experiment
- the **variable** you will change
- the variable you will measure
- what you expect to happen

A hypothesis should be brief, specific, and measurable. It must be something you can test through further investigation. Your experiment will prove or disprove whether your hypothesis is correct. Here is one possible hypothesis for this experiment: "The object moving at the fastest speed will emit a pitch that quickly increases, then decreases, as it passes a stationary person."

In this case, the variable you will change is the speed of the moving object. The variable you will measure is the pitch of the sound.

Conducting a **control experiment** will help you isolate each variable and measure the changes in the dependent variable. Only one variable will change between the control and the experimental setup, and that is the movement of a noisy object. For the control in this experiment you will record the sound of an unmoving object, which will release its sound waves at a steady pitch.

What Are the Variables?

Variables are anything that might affect the results of an experiment. Here are the main variables in this experiment:

- the sound

- the speed of the object (in this case, the bicycle)

- the direction the object is moving—either towards or away from the person holding the microphone

In other words, the variables in this experiment are everything that might affect the sound of the noise maker. If you change more than one variable at the same time, you will not be able to tell which variable had the most effect on the distance and speed of the object.

Level of Difficulty

Easy.

Materials Needed

- an assistant to help perform experiment
- bicycle
- wind-up alarm clock with continuous sound or other portable noise-making appliance, such as a kitchen timer
- tape recorder with microphone
- helper

Approximate Budget

$0 (assuming that you have the tape recorder and bike).

Timetable

20 minutes.

Step-by-Step Instructions

1. For the control: Stand at the side of a low-traffic area with the tape recorder. Start the alarm clock or buzzer and record the noise as you hold it for about 5 to 10 seconds. When finished record-

How to Experiment Safely

Be careful when biking. Find an empty area with little or no traffic before you begin.

ing, say the word "control" into the microphone to identify what is happening on the tape.

2. One person will hold the tape recorder and one will ride the bike. Have your helper (or you) walk a set distance away with the tape recorder; when the biker is ready to ride, he or she should turn the alarm clock or buzzer on.

3. The person at the side of the road begins tape recording, as the biker slowly rides the bike past the tape recorder. The biker should keep at a steady, slow pace, by counting the rotations of each pedal.

4. Say the word "Slow" into the microphone after the bike stops.

5. Repeat the bike ride, returning to the set distance, this time riding at a steady quick pace past the tape recorder with the alarm clock on.

6. Say the word "Fast" into the microphone after the bike stops.

7. Turn off the noise and listen to the tape recordings.

Step 3: Tape record the sound of the alarm clock as it approaches and moves past you.

Troubleshooter's Guide

Below is a problem that may arise during this experiment, a possible cause, and a way to remedy the problem.

Problem: There was no difference between the "Slow" tone and the "Fast" tone.

Possible cause: The biker may not have been riding at a significantly slower speed than the fast speed. Try biking at two different speeds as you steadily count, matching your counting to each pedal rotation. Practice for the slow and fast speeds, then repeat the experiment.

Summary of Results

Write a brief description of each recording. How did the control sound compare to the fast sound? Did you hear the sound increasing in pitch? By using the data on both the fast and slow sounds, and the set distance, what conclusions can you draw on the relative speed at which each object was traveling? How does this help you draw conclusions on the relative distance the object was from you? Write a summary of the experimental results and how these results relate to astronomical measurements.

Change the Variables

You can change the variable in this experiment by changing the speed of the moving object. You can physically throw the sound maker, or move it around in a ball or a string. You can also see what happens when the person with the microphone runs alongside the bike at the same speed.

 Design Your Own Experiment

How to Select a Topic Relating to this Concept

There are many types of tools and theories astronomers use for space measurements. You can further experiment with the telescope and the Doppler effect, or explore other tools.

Check the For More Information section and talk with your science or physics teacher to learn more about space measurements. You may also want to visit a planetarium or science museum to get some ideas. There are also many amateur astronomy groups and organizations you could join.

Steps in the Scientific Method

To conduct an original experiment, you need to plan carefully and think things through. Otherwise, you might not be sure what question you are answering, what you are or should be measuring, or what your findings prove or disprove.

Here are the steps in designing an experiment:

- State the purpose of—and the underlying question behind—the experiment you propose to do.
- Recognize the variables involved and select one that will help you answer the question at hand.
- State your hypothesis, an educated guess about the answer to your question.
- Decide how to change the variable you selected.
- Decide how to measure your results.

Recording Data and Summarizing the Results

Your data could include charts and graphs to display your data. If included, they should be clearly labeled and easy to read. You may also want to include photographs and drawings of your experimental setup and results, which will help other people visualize the steps in the experiment.

If you are preparing an exhibit, you may want to display your results, such as any experimental setup you designed. If you have completed a nonexperimental project, explain clearly what your research question was and illustrate your findings.

Related Projects

Space observations and calculations is a broad topic with many related projects. Every day, astronomers are learning new information produced from tools on Earth and in space. There are many different types of telescopes with varying combinations of lenses and mirrors. You can explore the strengths and weaknesses of the different types. Once you have built a standard telescope, you can experiment with building telescopes of varying powers and materials.

You could explore the data from telescopes and how humans' view of space has changed over the past several centuries. A project related to space measurement could involve identifying stars with a telescope that you have constructed. You could also look at how computer calculations have influenced people's knowledge of space. The Doppler effect also has many commonplace usages that you could examine.

For More Information

Bad Astronomy. http://www.badastronomy.com/ (accessed on August 26, 2003). ❖ Straightforward answers to astronomy questions and common misconceptions.

Freudenrich, Craig. "How Light Works." *How Stuff Works.* http://www.howstuff works.com/light2.htm (accessed on August 26, 2003). ❖ Simple explanation of light.

Freudenrich, Craig. "How Telescopes Work." *How Stuff Works.* http://science.how stuffworks.com/telescope1.htm (accessed on August 26, 2003). ❖ Simple explanation of telescopes.

"Galileo's Biography." *The Galileo Project.* http://es.rice.edu:80/ES/humsoc/Galileo/Bio/index.html (accessed on August 26, 2003). ❖ Details of Galileo's life and work.

"How Telescopes Work." *Yes Mag.* http://www.yesmag.bc.ca/how_work/telescope. html (accessed on August 26, 2003). ❖ Brief, clear explanation of how telescopes work, with references.

Kerrod, Robin. *The Night Sky.* Austin, TX: Raintree Steck-Vaughn Publishers, 2002. ❖ A look at the history of the exploration of the sky, with graphics and illustrations.

"Telescopes." *Astro-Tom.com.* http://www.astro-tom.com/telescopes/telescopes.htm (accessed on August 26, 2003). ❖ Explanation of telescopes along with lots of other astronomy information.

Thompson, Rod. "Hawaii scientists find star, dust disk." *Starbulletin.com.* http://starbulletin.com/2002/01/08/news/story5.html (accessed on August 26, 2003). ❖ News story of a discovery by scientists at the observatory on Mauna Kea, Hawaii.

Science Supply House

American Science & Surplus. http://sciplus.com (accessed on August 26, 2003). ❖ Lab supplies, such as packets of lenses, at discount prices.

experiment
CENTRAL

chapter 24

Spoilage

When food has spoiled it is usually noticeable to your senses of smell and sight. **Spoilage** is when food has taken on an undesirable color, odor, or texture. Eating spoiled food can result in food poisoning, which can cause vomiting, nausea, and more severe symptoms. There are two main causes of natural food spoilage: microscopic organisms and chemical changes.

Attack of the microbes

Leave food out on the kitchen countertop and within seconds it can become the home of microorganisms that are floating by in the air. When these microbes land on a suitable environment, they settle down and begin to grow. Many foods present an ideal environment.

The three main types of microbes that cause food spoilage are yeasts, molds, and **bacteria.** (See chapters on Bacteria and Fungi.) Bacteria are single-celled organisms that grow under a wide range of conditions. Yeasts and molds are both types of **fungi,** a large grouping of organisms that have both plant and animal characteristics. These microorganisms cause beverages to sour, fuzz to grow, slime to form, and the color and smell of foods to change.

Microorganisms are everywhere: in the air, water, soil, homes, and people. The majority of microorganisms are harmless or helpful to humans and all life on Earth. When they start living on food items though, they can quickly cause the food to spoil. The amount and rate of food spoilage increases as the number of microorganisms rise. And microorganisms grow, meaning they reproduce, at a speedy rate.

Words to Know

Additive:
A chemical compound that is added to foods to give them some desirable quality, such as preventing them from spoiling.

Antioxidants:
Used as a food additive, these substances can prevent food spoilage by reducing the food's exposure to air.

Bacteria:
Single-celled microorganisms that live in soil, water, plants, and animals that play a key role in the decay of organic matter and the cycling of nutrients. Some are agents of disease.

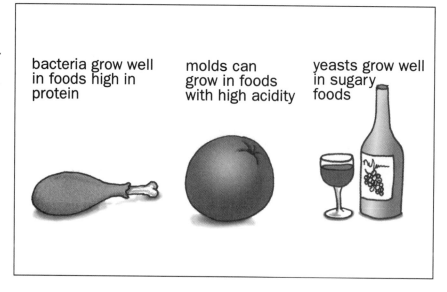

Each type of microorganism has its own unique requirements for growth.

bacteria grow well in foods high in protein

molds can grow in foods with high acidity

yeasts grow well in sugary foods

Bacteria, for example, can reproduce once every twenty minutes under ideal conditions. That means, if there are no limitations, a food product that starts off with one bacterium will multiply to over five billion in about ten hours. If bacteria grew at this rate in real life they would soon overtake the planet. Fortunately, once too many bacteria live in one area, their food runs out and eventually they start dying.

The leftover that became a home

Each type of microorganism has its own unique requirements for growth, but there are general conditions that most food-munching microbes need.

- Food: Each type—and species—of microbe thrives on different nutrients. Many bacteria thrive on proteins, such as meat; the fungi mold commonly grows on sugars and bread; and yeasts like simple sugars.

- Moisture or water: Yeasts, molds, and bacteria all need water; some need more than others. Molds, for example, grow at lower levels of water than most bacteria.

- Suitable temperature: Many microbes grow well at warm temperatures roughly equal to the inside of the human body.

- Exposure to air: Yeasts and molds need air to grow. Most bacteria that cause food spoilage also need air to grow. One exception is the *Clostridium* bacterium, which is a common cause of canned food spoilage because it does not need air to live.

- Suitable acidity level: Bacteria generally prefer mid- to low-acid foods such as vegetables and meat. Certain yeasts and molds grow in fruits that can tolerate a high-acid environment.
- Time to grow: Even though bacteria can reproduce quickly, they still need time to grow. If food is consumed immediately after it is prepared, the bacteria won't have time to cause spoilage.

Slowing spoilage

Long before people knew about microorganisms, ancient civilizations developed methods to prevent their food from spoiling. These techniques prevented microorganisms from living on the food in some way—either by making living conditions unpleasant or deadly, or by preventing the microorganisms from ever settling down on the food.

Any substance added to food to give it a desired quality is called an **additive. Preservatives** are a type of additive that causes food to last longer without spoiling. There are both synthetic and natural preservatives. Natural preservatives were one of the earliest methods used to prevent spoilage. Spices are natural preservatives people have long valued. When Italian explorer Christopher Columbus (1451–1506) set sail for the New World, one of the items he was searching for was spices. Other natural preservatives include vinegar, salt, and Vitamin C. Some foods contain a high concentration of these items, giving them a natural resistance to microbial growth.

Antioxidants are substances that prevent spoilage by reducing the food's exposure to air. Vitamin C and Vitamin E are natural antioxidants.

Dehydration involves removing the water from food. When food is dehydrated, microorgan-

Dried snacks, such as fruits and raisins, are common dehydrated foods. (Copyright © Kelly A. Quin. Reproduced by permission of Kelly A. Quin.)

Jars of home-canned vegetables. (© Craig Lovell/CORBIS. Reproduced by permission.)

Words to Know

Pasteurization:
The process of slow heating that kills bacteria and other microorganisms.

Preservative:
An additive used to keep food from spoiling.

Rancidity:
Having the condition when food has a disagreeable odor or taste from decomposing oils or fats.

Spoilage:
The condition when food has taken on an undesirable color, odor, or texture.

Spore:
A small, usually one-celled, reproductive body that is capable of growing into a new organism.

Variable:
Something that can affect the results of an experiment.

isms no longer have the moisture they need to live. Ancient peoples dried strips of meat and other foods out in the sun. Dried snacks, such as fruits and raisins, are common dehydrated foods.

Salting is another ancient method of preventing spoilage that combines the techniques of adding preservatives and dehydrating. Salt lowers the amount of water in the food and also removes water from the microbial cells, making it a harsh environment for organisms to live. Using salt to preserve food remains widespread in modern day. Pickles, meat, and fish are commonly salted. While salting can make food last longer, it also increases the sodium in food.

Canning was another major breakthrough in food preservation. In the 1700s French leader Napoleon Bonaparte was searching for a method that would preserve foods for his troops. He offered a large cash prize to anyone who could develop a preservation method. In response a French candy maker came up with the idea of sealing foods in cans. Although the technique has changed over time, the basic process remains the same. The food is placed in a can, heated, and the can is quickly sealed. Modern canning techniques suck the air from the can before it is sealed.

Chilling/heating: Microorganisms do not like it too hot or too cold. Temperatures that are outside the microorganisms' living requirements will cause their growth to slow. Extreme hot and cold temperatures will kill the microbes. Before the refrigerator was invented, people wrapped foods in snow and ice. Refrigerators and freezers will slow or stop the growth, yet the low temperatures will not kill the microorganisms. When the food item is returned to a suitable environment the microorganisms will again start to grow. There are even bacteria that grow well in the cool refrigerator air. Boiling is another method of destroying microorganisms, yet boiling can change the taste and nutritional value of the food. Cooking food thoroughly also destroys microorganisms.

French chemist Louis Pasteur (1822–1895) was the first person to demonstrate that microorganisms in the air produce food decay. In 1865, he developed a gentle heating method to destroy microorganisms in liquids and cause little change in the taste. After heating the liquid to 131°F (55° Celsius), he placed the liquid in an airtight container. This process is known as **pasteurization** and in modern day, it uses slightly higher temperatures. Pasteurization destroys almost all the microorganisms without altering the composition, flavor, or nutritional value of the liquid. Most milk is treated this way.

All by themselves
Spoilage also can occur from natural chemical changes within the food without any help from microorganisms. **Rancidity** occurs when fats in the food break down, producing undesirable flavors and smells. For

Pasteurization is a preservation technique that destroys most microbes by heating a liquid, then placing it in an airtight container.

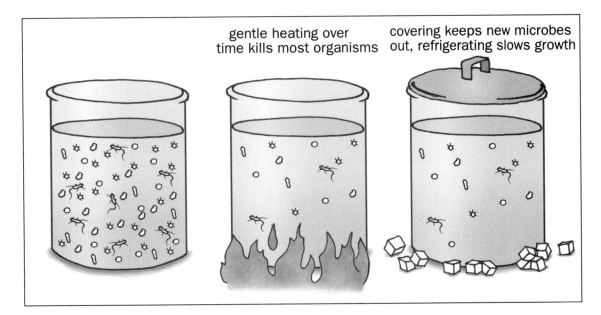

gentle heating over time kills most organisms

covering keeps new microbes out, refrigerating slows growth

example, rancidity gives butter a strong, bitter taste. Salt in butter helps prevent the butter from turning rancid. Food can also decay on its own from natural proteins that begin to decompose or break down the food.

Experiment 1
Preservatives: How do different substances affect the growth of mold?

Purpose/Hypothesis

Mold is a type of fungi that reproduces via **spores.** Spores are similar to plant seeds except they are microscopic. They move about in the air and when they land on a food source with a comfortable environment, they begin to grow. Once spores begin to grow, the mold releases more spores and the cycle continues. There are thousands of different kinds of molds.

In this experiment you will examine how additives can act as preservatives for the bread. You will use different types of possible preservatives: vinegar, salt, Vitamin C, and lemon juice. Molds grow well in a moist environment. You will spray the liquid preservatives on the bread to dampen the bread. For the salt, you will dampen the bread with water before you apply the salt.

Bread that is not refrigerated or exposed to air for a period of time can get moldy very quickly. (Copyright © Kelly A. Quin. Reproduced by permission of Kelly A. Quin.)

What Are the Variables?

Variables are anything that might affect the results of an experiment. Here are the main variables in this experiment:

- the type of bread
- the temperature
- the amount of light
- the additive
- the amount of the additive
- the quantity of the preservative in the additive

In other words, the variables in this experiment are everything that might affect the mold's growth. If you change more than one variable at the same time, you will not be able to tell which variable had the most effect on inhibiting mold growth.

Before you begin, make an educated guess about the outcome of this experiment based on your knowledge of molds and spoilage. This educated guess, or prediction, is your **hypothesis.** A hypothesis should explain these things:

- the topic of the experiment
- the **variable** you will change
- the variable you will measure
- what you expect to happen

A hypothesis should be brief, specific, and measurable. It must be something you can test through further investigation. Your experiment will prove or disprove whether your hypothesis is correct. Here is one possible hypothesis for this experiment: "All the preservatives will inhibit the growth of fungi to some degree; salt will inhibit it the most."

In this case, the variable you will change is the substance sprayed on the bread. The variable you will measure is the amount of mold growth.

Conducting a **control experiment** will help you isolate each variable and measure the changes in the dependent variable. Only one variable will change between the control and your experiment. For your control in this experiment you will spray plain water on the bread. At the end of the experiment you can compare the control and the experimental results.

Level of Difficulty
Moderate.

Materials Needed
- water
- five slices of nonpreservative white bread
- spray bottle, such as one used to water plants
- five plastic bags
- graph paper marked in 0.05-inch or 1.0-millimeter increments
- transparent paper
- preservatives: white vinegar, lemon juice, table salt, nonpulp orange juice high in Vitamin C (you can also select other, or additional, items to test)
- marking pen
- microscope or magnifying glass (optional)

Approximate Budget
$10.

Timetable
1 hour, 20 minutes setup; about 15 minutes daily for about 6 to 9 days.

Step-by-Step Instructions
1. Lay out five slices of bread.
2. Label each of the bags with the name of one preservative; label one bag "Control."
3. Prepare the preservatives by making sure each of the liquids flows easily through the spray bottle. If not, try to get a bottle with wider holes or dilute the liquid.
4. Pour a small amount of vinegar in the spray bottle. Spray the vinegar on a piece of bread to dampen it, counting the number of sprays it takes to dampen. Do not soak it.
5. Rinse the spray bottle thoroughly with water and repeat the process for the lemon juice and orange juice, rinsing the bottle out in between. Use the same number of sprays for each.

How to Experiment Safely

When conducting experiments with microorganisms, treat them all as if they could cause disease. Do not touch the mold or try to smell the bread. Never taste or ingest any of the bread.

6. Rinse out the sprayer and fill with water.
7. Spray the same number of sprays on the two remaining pieces of bread.
8. On one piece of bread sprinkle salt lightly over the damp bread.
9. Allow the breads to sit on the counter for one hour.
10. Place each piece of bread in the appropriate bag; put the water bread in the "Control" bag. Seal the bags.

Step 10: Place each damp slice of bread in its labeled bag and seal.

Surface Area Growth

Bread	1 day	2 days	3 days	4 days	5 days	6 days
control						
vinegar						
orange juice						
salt						
lemon						

Data chart for Experiment 1.

11. Set the bags in a dim area, such as in a drawer.
12. Either trace or copy the graph paper on a clear piece of transparency.
13. Every day at roughly the same time, examine each piece of bread for mold. Do not remove the bread from the bag. If there is any mold, lightly place the transparent graph over the bread and determine the surface area of the mold by counting the number of squares. Note the results on a chart.
14. Continue examining each of the breads until mold has covered at least one of the slices.
15. If you have a magnifying glass or microscope, examine the mold(s) up close and note their descriptions.
16. After you have completed the summary, throw away the breads in their bags.

Summary of Results

Graph your data, labeling "Days" on the x-axis and "Surface Area" on the y-axis. Use a different color pen or type of line for each of the substances on the bread, and mark the graph clearly. What was the substance that prevented mold growth for the greatest number of days? Once mold did begin to grow, how did the rate of growth compare to the first few days when there was no growth? If the growth rate increased rapidly, theorize why you think this occurred. Describe the

Troubleshooter's Guide

Below are some problems that may arise during this experiment, some possible causes, and some ways to remedy the problems.

Problem: Mold did not grow on any of the breads.

Possible cause: Make sure the bread you purchased has no preservatives in it. You may want to buy fresh bread from a bakery. Once you have bread that has no preservatives, repeat the experiment.

Possible cause: You may have saturated the bread, not giving the fungi an environment that promotes growth. Repeat the experiment, lowering the number of sprays for each of the liquids to make sure the bread is only dampened.

Problem: Mold grew at the same rate on the Control slice as on one of the slices with the preservative.

Possible cause: There may not have been enough of the preservative in the additive, such as if you used a juice that did not have a high percentage of Vitamin C or an imitation lemon juice. Make sure the additive contains the preservative you want to test, and repeat the experiment.

Possible cause: If you added water to the additive, you may have diluted the additive too much. Repeat the experiment, using another liquid additive or a spray bottle with wider holes as opposed to diluting the liquid.

mold or types of mold on the breads. Common types of molds that grow on bread are bluish-green or green molds; black or brown-black molds; and reddish or pink molds. By examining the molds and referring to a reference source you may be able to identify them.

Change the Variables

In this experiment you can change the variables in several ways.

• change the temperature, higher or lower

- change the type of bread, using bread with preservatives or comparing brands
- leave the breads out in both light and dark areas and compare growth
- use a different growth substance, such as a type of fruit instead of bread

Experiment 2
Spoiled Milk: How do different temperatures of liquid affect its rate of spoilage?

Purpose/Hypothesis

The two main groups of bacteria in milk are Lactic acids and Coliforms. Lactic acid is the natural bacteria present in milk and dairy products. Coliforms are the main reason for milk spoilage. Pasteurization kills almost all of the bacteria, but some of the bacteria that cause milk to spoil still remain. If these bacteria are given an environment that promotes growth, they will rapidly multiply.

In this experiment, you will be conducting two mini-trials in which you will determine how temperature affects the rate of milk spoilage. You will examine the environmental temperatures that affect milk by allowing glasses of milk to sit in cool, warm, and room-temperature environments. You will also determine how the temperature of the milk affects spoilage. One cup of milk will be boiled, then left in a room-temperature environment. After three days, you will examine each of the milks. When milk spoils it changes in consistency, appearance, and smell. Spoiled milk also undergoes a chemical change. As the milk spoils, the bacteria produce acid. It is the acid that causes the milk to clot. You can compare the acidity of the test milks by using indicator strips.

Before you begin, make an educated guess about the outcome of this experiment based on your knowledge of spoilage. This educated guess, or prediction, is your **hypothesis**. A hypothesis should explain these things:

- the topic of the experiment
- the **variable** you will change
- the variable you will measure

What Are the Variables?

Variables are anything that might affect the results of an experiment. Here are the main variables in this experiment:

- the temperature of the milk
- the milk's exposure to heat
- the amount of light
- the type (wholeness) of the milk
- the type of milk

In other words, the variables in this experiment are everything that might affect the growth of bacteria. If you change more than one variable at the same time, you will not be able to tell which variable had the most effect on the spoilage of the milk.

- what you expect to happen

A hypothesis should be brief, specific, and measurable. It must be something you can test through further investigation. Your experiment will prove or disprove whether your hypothesis is correct. Here is one possible hypothesis for this experiment: "The milk in the warm area will spoil the quickest; the milk that was boiled will take the greatest amount of time to spoil."

In this case, the variable you will change is the temperature of the milk. The variable you will measure is the relative amount of spoilage of each milk.

Conducting a **control experiment** will help you isolate each variable and measure the changes in the dependent variable. Only one variable will change between the control and your experiment. For the control for the boiled milk at room temperature, use the unboiled milk at room temperature. To compare milk spoilage among the test milks choose a standard among them, such as the milk at room temperature. Use the data from this standard to gauge the spoilage of the other test milks.

Level of Difficulty

Easy to Moderate.

experiment
CENTRAL

 ## How to Experiment Safely
When conducting experiments with microorganisms, treat them all as if they could cause disease. Do not touch the milk and, if you do, wash your hands thoroughly. Do not taste or ingest any of the milk. Be careful when working at the stove.

Materials Needed
- whole milk
- refrigerator
- heat lamp, such as one used for plants
- four tall heat-resistant glasses
- plastic wrap
- four rubber bands
- pot
- spoon
- hot plate or stove
- measuring cup
- acid/base indicator strips
- masking tape
- marking pen

Approximate Budget
$3 (not including lamp).

Timetable
20 minutes setup; about 10 minutes daily for 4 to 5 days.

Step-by-Step Instructions
1. Label each of the cups: "Cold," "Warm," "Room Temp/Control," and "Boiled."
2. Measure out 1 cup of milk and pour it in the glass labeled "Cold." Pour another cup in the glass labeled "Warm," and another cup in the "Room Temp/Control."
3. Pour 1 cup in the pot and bring the milk to a low boil.
4. Stir continuously while letting the milk boil for 1 minute.
5. Pour the hot milk in the glass labeled "Boiled."
6. Immediately, place plastic wrap over each of the glasses.

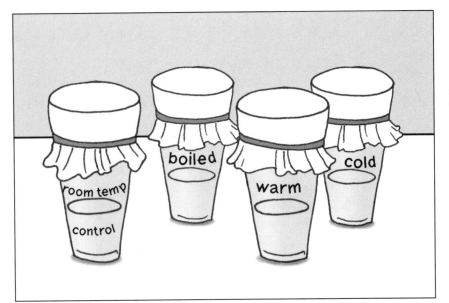

Steps 6 and 7: Place a rubber band around the plastic wrap and then place in its designated environment.

7. Wrap a rubber band around the plastic wrap to secure it to the glass.

8. Set the "Cold" glass in the refrigerator; the "Warm" glass near the heat lamp; and the remaining two glasses in an undisturbed area at room temperature.

9. Describe how each glass of milk appears each day for 4 to 5 days. Do not remove the plastic wrap or shake the glass.

10. At the end of the experiment, when at least one of the milks has separated, place an indicator strip in each glass and note the results—acid, base, or neutral—by comparing the color of the wet strips with the chart provided with the indicator strips.

Summary of Results

Examine your results and note the acidity level of the milk(s) that spoiled at the fastest rate. How did the control milk compare to the boiled milk? Compare the appearance of the milk at the warm environment to the cool environment. How did the spoiled milk's appearance change daily? When acid causes milk to curdle it forms solids called curds, and a liquid, called whey. Which of the test milks formed curds and whey? In an analysis of this experiment summarize what conclusions you can draw about the environment(s) that promote bacterial spoilage.

After you keep the milk clot for a while, the clot shrinks and a yellow fluid (whey) is released. You can make this happen more quickly by squeezing a little lemon juice (acid) into a small amount of milk.

Troubleshooter's Guide

Below is a problem that may arise during this experiment, a possible cause, and a way to remedy the problem.

Problem: After several days, the milk at room temperature appeared to have the same amount of spoilage as the milk in the refrigerator.

Possible cause: The room may be at a cool temperature and the bacteria could need longer to grow. Continue the experiment for several more days.

The curds are the white caseins, or milk proteins, and they are sticky (people once used them as glue). If you touch them, remember to wash your hands immediately..

Change the Variables

In this experiment you can change the variables in several ways. You can change the fat content of the milk by comparing skim milk, whole milk, 2 percent milk, and other types. You can add a substance to the milk, such as sugar or chocolate, that may alter the speed of bacteria growth. Another way to change the experiment is to vary how much light the milk is exposed to by leaving the same type of milk out in a bright and dark area. You could also alter the food substance by using different beverages or solid foods instead of milk.

 Design Your Own Experiment

How to Select a Topic Relating to this Concept

Food spoilage is a common problem, with many possible project ideas. You could examine spoilage among different types of foods. You can also examine the steps taken to prevent spoilage, both in terms of additives and food handling. Check the For More Information section and talk with your science teacher to learn more about spoilage. You could also talk with a microbiologist for details on the microorganisms involved in spoilage.

When experimenting with food, do not taste or ingest any of the food items, and make sure to mark the item clearly to keep others away. Aside from causing food poisoning, some microorganisms that are attracted to food can cause diseases that are potentially deadly. If you conduct an experiment with food in the home, make sure you tell an adult.

Steps in the Scientific Method

To conduct an original experiment, you need to plan carefully and think things through. Otherwise, you might not be sure what question you are answering, what you are or should be measuring, or what your findings prove or disprove.

Here are the steps in designing an experiment:

- State the purpose of—and the underlying question behind—the experiment you propose to do.
- Recognize the variables involved and select one that will help you answer the question at hand.
- State your hypothesis, an educated guess about the answer to your question.
- Decide how to change the variable you selected.
- Decide how to measure your results.

Recording Data and Summarizing the Results

Your data should include charts and graphs such as the one you did for these experiments. They should be clearly labeled and easy to read. You may also want to include photographs and drawings of your experimental setup and results, which will help other people visualize the steps in the experiment.

If you are preparing an exhibit, you may want to display your results, such as any experimental setup you designed. If you have completed a nonexperimental project, explain clearly what your research question was and illustrate your findings.

Related Projects

Projects related to spoilage are numerous, inexpensive, and waiting in the kitchen. You could conduct a project examining the uses of synthesized versus natural preservatives. Foods spoil at different rates and under different environments. You could test different foods, all with the same main ingredient, for variables that affect the rate of spoilage.

You could also examine how spoilage poses a serious health threat by examining potential diseases and illnesses from spoiled food.

You could group certain foods together and determine if the rate of spoilage changes, depending on what the food is near. You could also examine expiration dates and conduct an experiment that tests how accurate the date is to when it begins to spoil. When working with food, make sure not to taste or ingest any of the food, and to always label it clearly as an experiment. Spoiled food contains microorganisms, some of which could be extremely harmful.

For More Information

Blumenthal, Dale. "The Canning Process." *U.S. Food and Drug Administration.* http://www.fda.gov/bbs/topics/CONSUMER/CON00043.html (accessed on August 26, 2003). ❖ A history of canning as a way of preserving food.

Dalton, Louisa. " What's that Stuff?: Food Preservatives." *Chemical & Engineering News,* November 11, 2002. http://pubs.acs.org/cen/science/8045/8045sci2.html (accessed on August 26, 2003). ❖ Information on various food preservatives.

Schuler, George; William Hurst; Estes Reynolds; and James Christian. "Food Spoilage and You." *University of Georgia College of Agricultural and Environmental Sciences Cooperative Extension Service.* http://www.ces.uga.edu/pubcd/b906-w.html (accessed on August 26, 2003). ❖ An overview of food spoilage.

chapter 25

Storms

Right now, at least one area of the world is experiencing some type of powerful **storm.** Storms are periods of extreme bad weather that can bring powerful winds and torrential rains. Storms can rip buildings apart, toss cars through the air, cause deaths, and spark forest fires. Every day there are as many as fifty thousand storms occurring throughout the world. They can stretch for hundreds of miles, or remain isolated to a few hundred yards. Either way, storms can cause enormous devastation. Some of the more common types of storms are thunderstorms and tornadoes.

How air works

Storms all begin by the movement of **air.** Air is made up of a mixture of different gases, mainly oxygen and nitrogen with about four times as much nitrogen. Air is constantly moving around as it changes temperatures. The movement of air causes wind. (For more details on how air works, see Air chapter.)

When air gets warmer its particles start to move about quickly and expand. The warm air particles take up more room in a given space. This makes the warm air rise because it is lighter than the air around it. Cooler air particles move closer together and take up less room. That makes cooler air heavier than the air around it and causes it to sink. As the Sun heats the air around Earth's surface, this warm air moves upwards and the cooler air sinks. The faster that air is warmed and rises, the faster the winds.

Clouds a brewing

Thunderstorms need three basic ingredients to form. The first is moisture in the air or **water vapor,** which forms clouds and rain. The

Words to Know

Air:
Gaseous mixture that envelopes Earth, composed mainly of nitrogen (about 78 percent) and oxygen (about 21 percent) with lesser amounts of argon, carbon dioxide, and other gases.

Condense:
When a gas or vapor changes to a liquid.

Control experiment:
A setup that is identical to the experiment, but is not affected by the variable that acts on the experimental group.

Did You Know?

- In a typical year about one thousand tornadoes strike the United States. Central United States is nicknamed "tornado alley" because more tornadoes strike there than any other place in the world.

- Some thunderclouds are as tall as 11 miles (18 kilometers) from top to bottom

- About one hundred bolts of lightning strike Earth every second.

- Storm chasers captured the highest winds ever recorded on Earth in a 1999 Oklahoma tornado—speeds over 300 miles per hour (480 kilometers per hour).

- The deadliest and longest tornado in the United States sliced across Missouri, Illinois, and Indiana in 1925. It traveled 219 miles (350 kilometers) and killed almost 689 people.

- Scientists have observed lightning on other planets including Jupiter, Saturn, and Venus.

- On average, the odds are about 280,000 to 1 that a person will be struck by lightning in a given year: That works out to about 4,000 to 1 over a person's lifetime.

Words to Know

Cumulonimbus cloud:
The parent cloud of a thunderstorm; a tall, vertically developed cloud capable of producing heavy rain, high winds, and lightning.

Funnel cloud:
A fully developed tornado vortex before it has touched the ground.

Hypothesis:
An idea in the form of a statement that can be tested by observation and/or experiment.

Storm:
An extreme atmospheric disturbance, associated with strong damaging winds, and often with thunder and lightning.

Storm chasers:
People who track and seek out storms, often tornadoes.

Tornado:
A violently rotating, narrow column of air in contact with the ground and usually extending from a cumulonimbus cloud.

second is a column of unstable air, which provides relatively warm, moist air on the bottom layers with cold, dry air high above it. And lastly, a thunderstorm needs some kind of force to lift the air upwards.

When the moist, warm air rises it eventually meets colder air and begins to cool. That forms the beginning of a cloud. Inside a cloud, currents of air move up and down quickly. This air is filled with tiny particles of dust. Water vapor is pushed upwards by the warm air. When it comes into contact with cooler air, the water vapor **condenses.** Condensation is when a gas (or vapor) changes into a liquid. The condensed drops of water will then surround a dust particle. Clouds form where millions of water-dust droplets gather together. Each of the particles in a cloud has a positive and a negative electrical charge.

experiment
CENTRAL

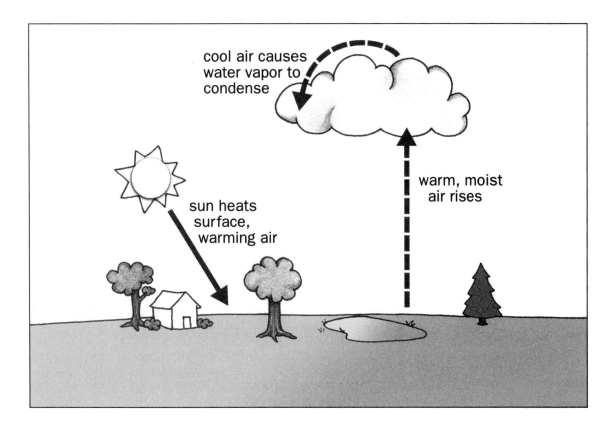

The process of cloud formation.

These small, puffy clouds grow increasingly larger as more warm air rises from the ground. If the cloud gets large enough, it may continue to rise into the ever-colder air. Strong winds can blow the top of the cloud downwind, and this gives the top of the cloud an anvil shape. This thunderstorm cloud is called a **cumulonimbus cloud** and it can extend upwards for miles.

Shocking sights, loud noises

To be called a thunderstorm there must be thunder. Thunder is caused by lightning, and lightning begins in the cumulonimbus clouds. Lightning is an intense discharge of electricity. Scientists estimate that about a hundred lightning flashes occur each second around the world. The electricity flowing within a lightning bolt is so powerful that it can kill instantly, split trees, and spark fires. The average flash of lightning could turn on a 100-watt light bulb for more than three months.

As a storm advances, strong winds blow the particles of dust and water in the cloud and cause them to hit each other. Each particle

Lightning forms when the negative charges in the cloud are attracted to the positive charges on the ground.

contains positive and negative charges, which are attracted to each other under normal conditions, but collisions cause the positive and negative charges to separate. Positive charges tend to move towards the top of a cloud and negative charges move towards the bottom. Both types of charges hold energy. Charges that are alike repel each other and charges that are opposites pull together. When enough charges and time build up, the negative charge in the cloud reach out towards the positive charges on the ground. The result is a burst of electricity, or a lightning bolt.

Every lightning flash produces thunder. In just a fraction of a second a lightning flash can heat up the air to 50,000°F (28,000°C)—a temperature hotter that the surface of the Sun. The burst of heat causes the air molecules around it to expand quickly away from the lightning's flash. As this hot air cools, it contracts. This quick expansion and contraction of air causes the air molecules to shake or vibrate, making sound waves that create the sound of thunder.

Thunder and lightning occur simultaneously, yet people will always see lightning before they hear thunder because light and sound travel at different speeds. Light travels at about 186,000 miles per second (299,800 kilometers per second). The speed of sound is only about 0.2 miles per second (0.3 kilometers per second). That means a person will see lightning almost instantly, but won't hear the thunder

Words to Know

Updraft:
Warm, moist air that moves away from the ground.

Variable:
Something that can affect the results of an experiment.

Vortex:
A rotating column of a fluid such as air or water.

Water vapor:
The change of water from a liquid to a gas.

experiment
CENTRAL

Thunder and lightning occur simultaneously, yet people will always see lightning before they hear thunder because light and sound travel at different speeds. (Reproduced by permission of FMA Productions.)

experiment
CENTRAL

for several seconds. Knowing this allows any storm watcher to calculate the distance of the lightning strike. Count the number of seconds between the lightning and the thunder, and divide the number of seconds by five to calculate the miles distance; divide the number of seconds by three to calculate the kilometers distance.

Twisting about

Tornadoes are swirling columns of air that have enormous power. They have a short life span, from a few minutes to over an hour, yet are one of the most ferocious storms. They develop on land and come from the energy released in a thunderstorm. This energy is concentrated in a small area, such as the size of a football field, and moves across the ground at speeds of 20 to 40 miles per hour (32 to 64 kilometers per hour). On average, the United States gets about a thousand tornadoes each year. The most violent tornadoes can reach wind

Developed by Dr. T. Theodore Fujita in 1971, the Fujita Tornado Scale, or F-Scale, classifies tornadoes according to the damage caused.

Fujita Tornado Scale

F-Scale	Winds	Type of Damage
F0	40-72 mph 64-116 km/h	MINIMAL DAMAGE: Some damage to chimneys, TV antennas, roof shingles, trees and windows.
F1	73-112 mph 117-180 km/h	MODERATE DAMAGE: Automobiles overturned, carports destroyed, trees uprooted.
F2	113-157 mph 181-253 km h	MAJOR DAMAGE: Roofs blown off homes, sheds and outbuildings demolished, mobile homes overturned.
F3	158-206 mph 254-332 km/h	SEVERE DAMAGE: Exterior walls and roofs blown off homes. Metal buildings collapsed or are severely damaged. Forests and farmland flattened.
F4	207-260 mph 333-418 km/h	DEVASTATING DAMAGE: Few walls, if any, standing in well-built homes. Large steel and concrete missiles thrown far distances.
F5	261-318 mph 419-512 km/h	INCREDIBLE DAMAGE: Homes leveled with all debris removed. Schools, motels, and other larger structures have considerable damage with exterior walls and roofs gone.

experiment
CENTRAL

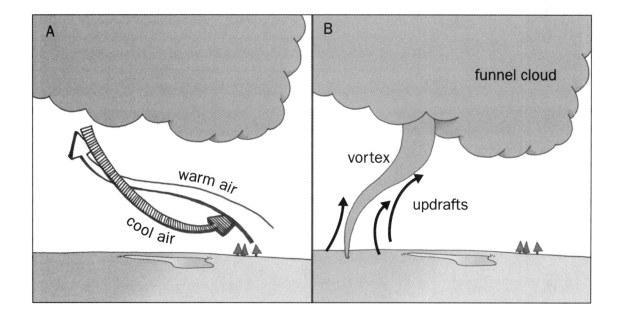

speves of over 250 miles per hour (400 kilometers per hour) and can slice a path of destruction more than 1 mile (1.6 kilometers) wide and 50 miles (80 kilometers) long.

The formation of a tornado. (A) formation of vortex; (B) when the funnel cloud touches the ground it becomes a tornado.

Tornadoes are often called "twisters" because of their rapidly spinning, funnel-shaped clouds. Only a small percentage of thunderstorms will turn into a tornado, and scientists have different theories on what exactly causes a tornado to form. One widespread theory says tornadoes form mainly due to wind. When winds at two different heights move at two different speeds this can create a horizontal spinning column of air.

Thunderstorms supply the rising warm air or **updrafts** that a tornado needs to form. The updraft tilts the spinning air from the horizontal to the vertical direction. This whirling air is called a **vortex** and it causes the funnel cloud to form. When the warm air gets pulled up and meets the cold air, the moisture in the air condenses. Water droplets get swept into the mass of whirling air, starting at the top of the vortex where the temperature is lowest. This begins to form the tornado's visible **funnel cloud.**

Strong updrafts will cause the funnel cloud to narrow, which causes it to spin faster. This principle works much as an ice skater spinning. When an ice skater brings his or her arms closer to the body, the skater will spin faster.

Using special equipment, storm chasers gather data on tornadoes to help scientists learn more about this powerful, destructive form of storm. (© CORBIS SYGMA. Reproduced by permission.)

The funnel extends downwards from the cloud to the land as a tornado forms. A funnel cloud that touches land becomes a tornado. Some funnel clouds are hard to spot until they strike. As they pick up dirt and other materials from the ground these materials swirl about and cause the funnel cloud to darken and become more visible.

Scientists are still working to answer several questions on tornadoes. One of the key questions is why updrafts in some thunderstorms become twisting funnel clouds, while those in similar thunderstorms do not. Some of the people who are helping to answer questions on tornadoes and other storms are **storm chasers.** Storm chasers seek out storms for study or adventure. They often use special equipment and can capture the spectacular sights and sounds of these violent storms.

Experiment 1
Lightning Sparks: Explore how separating charges causes an attraction between objects

Purpose/Hypothesis

Lightning that is produced during a storm is simply a massive electric spark, which is called static electricity. Friction causes the particles to separate into positive and negative charges. These opposite charges attract one another, and when the electric charges are separat-

What Are the Variables?

Variables are anything that might affect the results of an experiment. Here are the main variables in this experiment:

- the object that is charged
- the degree of friction
- the material that produces the friction
- the distance from the balloon to the objects

In other words, the variables in this experiment are everything that might affect the charge of the balloon. If you change more than one variable at the same time, you will not be able to tell which variable had the most effect on the action of the charged particles.

ed they look for a way to get back together. In a storm, the jump of numerous negative charges reaching out towards the positive charges produces a bolt of lighting. A miniature version of static electricity will produce sparks and an attraction between charged objects.

In this experiment you will explore what happens when you cause charges to separate. You will use friction to create electrical charges on a balloon, and observe how three different objects react to these charges. The three objects you will use are: salt and pepper, water, and another balloon.

Before you begin, make an educated guess about the outcome of this experiment based on your knowledge of lightning and charges. This educated guess, or prediction, is your **hypothesis.** A hypothesis should explain these things:

- the topic of the experiment
- the **variable** you will change
- the variable you will measure
- what you expect to happen

A hypothesis should be brief, specific, and measurable. It must be something you can test through further investigation. Your experiment

experiment
CENTRAL

will prove or disprove whether your hypothesis is correct. Here is one possible hypothesis for this experiment: "If enough charges are separated, the balloon will attract different objects and create electricity."

In this case, the variable you will change is the separation of the negative and positive charges on the balloon. The variable you will measure is how the balloon's charges are attracted to other objects.

Having a control experiment will help you isolate each variable and measure the changes in the dependent variable. Only one variable will change between the control and the experimental setup, and that is the amount of charged particles. At the end of the experiment you will compare the charged balloon with the neutrally charged balloon.

Level of Difficulty
Easy.

Materials Needed
- two balloons
- salt and pepper
- access to sink
- small plate
- wool cloth or nylon (optional)

Approximate Budget
$2.

Timetable
30 minutes.

Step-by-Step Instructions
1. Sprinkle some salt and pepper on a plate.
2. Inflate both balloons. For the control, do not rub one balloon. Place the balloon about 1 inch (2.5 centimeters) above the salt and

How to Experiment Safely
This project poses little hazards, but remember you are experimenting with electricity, however small. Do not conduct this experiment if there are any flammable vapors in the air, such as gasoline from an open container.

Step 5: Hold the balloon close to, but not touching, the stream of water.

pepper. Then place the balloon about 1 inch (2.5 centimeters) away from a trickle of water from the faucet. Note the results.

3. Rub the second balloon briskly against a piece of wool or your hair.

4. Hold this balloon about 1 inch (2.5 centimeters) above the salt and paper. Note what you see and hear.

5. Hold the balloon about 1 inch (2.5 centimeters) from a trickle of water. Note the results.

6. Darken the room. Rub both balloons against a cloth or your hair, and place them together. Note what you see and hear.

7. Place your hand gently over the section of the balloon that you rubbed. Again place the two balloons together and note the results.

Summary of Results

Create a data chart that describes the results of each trial. Compare the results to the control experiment. What did placing your hand over the balloon do to the charges in the balloon? Write a paragraph explaining your conclusions. Include how powerful bolts of lightning relate to this experiment.

Change the Variables

You can change the variables in this experiment in several ways. You can use different types of material to create friction, and determine if

experiment
CENTRAL

Troubleshooter's Guide

Below is a problem that may arise during this experiment, a possible cause, and a way to remedy the problem.

Problem: There was no difference between the control and the experimental balloon.

Possible cause: You may not have created enough friction, in which case not enough charges would separate. Try rubbing the balloon vigorously against your hair, and repeat the experiment.

this produces less or more attraction. You can also create charges on different objects, such as a comb. Try creating sparks or picking up different objects.

Experiment 2
Tornadoes: Making a violent vortex

Purpose/Hypothesis

Tornadoes occur when air masses clash and result in a spinning vortex. The air in the vortex becomes stretched and narrower with time. As the shape of the funnel gradually narrows, it creates an increase in the rotation speed, resulting in a twist similar to that of a spinning skater.

In this experiment you will observe the relationship between the intensity of a vortex and its shape. You will create a vortex using water; a vortex of fluids behaves similar to that of air. A whirlpool and the water in a draining bathtub are examples of a vortex in liquids. The vortex forms when spinning water, or air, is pulled downwards, in this case by gravity. The funnel of water narrows as it is pulled down.

You will fill two bottles with water, create a vortex, and observe the water movement from one bottle to another. You will control the narrowness of the vortex by placing two different size holes between the two bottles. Observing small colored materials placed in the water will provide a way to measure the speed of the water's rotation.

experiment
CENTRAL

Before you begin, make an educated guess about the outcome of this experiment based on your knowledge of tornadoes and vortexes. This educated guess, or prediction, is your **hypothesis.** A hypothesis should explain these things:

A tornado rips across the countryside in Jarrell, Texas, in May 1997. (Reproduced by permission of AP/Wide World.)

- the topic of the experiment
- the **variable** you will change
- the variable you will measure
- what you expect to happen

A hypothesis should be brief, specific, and measurable. It must be something you can test through further investigation. Your experiment will prove or disprove whether your hypothesis is correct. Here is one possible hypothesis for this experiment: "The speed of the water will increase as the vortex becomes increasingly narrow."

experiment
CENTRAL

What Are the Variables?

Variables are anything that might affect the results of an experiment. Here are the main variables in this experiment:

- the size of the hole
- the shape of the bottles
- the size of the bottles
- the temperature of the liquid
- the type of liquid

In other words, the variables in this experiment are everything that might affect the vortex. If you change more than one variable at the same time, you will not be able to tell which variable had the most effect on the water's speed.

In this case, the variable you will change is the size of the vortex hole, and the variable you will measure is the speed of the water.

Conducting a control experiment will help you isolate each variable and measure the changes in the dependent variable. Only one variable will change between the control and each of your vortexes. For the control, you will observe the water's speed without narrowing the hole. At the end of the experiment you will compare the intensity of the control with each of the experimental vortexes.

Level of Difficulty

Easy.

Materials Needed

- two identical 2-liter clear plastic soda bottles
- scissors
- duct tape or electrical tape
- water
- sparkles or any other small visible material that does not dissolve in water, such as oregano
- two washers the same outside diameter as the mouth of the bottles, one with a small center hole and one with a larger center hole
- marking pen

How to Experiment Safely

There are no safety hazards in this experiment.

Approximate Budget

$5.

Timetable

30 minutes.

Step-by-Step Instructions

1. Label one bottle "A" and the other "B."
2. For your control: Fill Bottle A about two-thirds full of water.
3. Sprinkle in some of the sparkles or other visible material.
4. Place bottle B upside down on top of bottle A.

Step 5: Line up the two bottles exactly and tape together.

5. Tape the mouths of the two bottles tightly together with the tape, aligning the openings up exactly. Test for leakage by carefully tilting the bottles. (See illustration on page 479.)

6. Turn the bottles over so that bottle A (with the water in it) is on top of bottle B, and quickly swirl the bottles several times, just like you would spin a hula-hoop. Set the bottles down and observe the water, noting the shape and speed of the swirling water.

7. Untape the bottles and tape the washer with the larger hole to the mouth of bottle A. Do not cover the washer hole with tape.

8. Again, tape the two bottles tightly together, lining the mouths up exactly. Quickly turn the bottles over and swirl. Note the description of the shape and speed of the vortex.

9. Repeat Steps 7 and 8, taping the washer with the smaller hole to bottle A. Note the results.

Summary of Results

Evaluate your results. Was your hypothesis correct? How does the water relate to the actions of a tornado? Compare the results of the two experimental trials with the control experiment. Write a summary

Troubleshooter's Guide

Below are problems that may arise during this experiment, some possible causes, and some ways to remedy the problems.

Problem: There was no vortex.

Possible cause: You may not have lined up the washer exactly with the mouths of the bottles, or the tape may have covered some of the circular opening. Repeat the experiment, making sure the opening is clear.

Problem: It was difficult to gauge the speed of the vortex.

Possible cause: Determining the speed of the water is an estimate based on how quickly the sparkles are swirling. You may need to place less sparkles in the bottle. Select the same point on the bottle for every experiment to focus on the swirl.

of the experiment that explains your results. You may want to include drawings of the shape and speed of each vortex.

Change the Variables

To alter this experiment you can change several of the variables, one at a time, and again observe the flow pattern of the water. You can use bottles of different shapes and sizes. You can also try changing the type of liquid you use and the temperature of the liquid. Would the experiment give the same results with a thick liquid substance as opposed to one that has greater flow? Different swirling techniques may also provide interesting results.

 # Design Your Own Experiment

How to Select a Topic Relating to this Concept

To select a related project, you can create models of weather phenomena and collect information from observing. An experiment with storms could include observing collecting data before and during a thunderstorm. You can also use the information meteorologists and storm chasers have gathered on tornadoes. The tools used to measure storms opens up another branch of related projects.

Check the For More Information section and talk with your science teacher to learn more about storms. You may also want to contact a local weatherperson in your area to talk about his or her work and possible project ideas.

Steps in the Scientific Method

To conduct an original experiment, you need to plan carefully and think things through. Otherwise, you might not be sure what question you are answering, what you are or should be measuring, or what your findings prove or disprove.

Here are the steps in designing an experiment:

- State the purpose of—and the underlying question behind—the experiment you propose to do.
- Recognize the variables involved and select one that will help you answer the question at hand.

- State your hypothesis, an educated guess about the answer to your question.
- Decide how to change the variable you selected.
- Decide how to measure your results.

Recording Data and Summarizing the Results

If appropriate, your data should include charts and graphs. They should be clearly labeled and easy to read. You may also want to include photographs and drawings of your experimental setup and results, which will help others visualize the steps in the experiment. If you are observing or reporting on a weather phenomena, you may want to include a series of drawings or photographs taken over a set period of time. Make sure you note the time each picture occurred.

If you are preparing an exhibit, you may want to display your results, such as any experimental setup you designed. If you have completed a nonexperimental project, explain clearly what your research question was and illustrate your findings.

Related Projects

You can design your own experiments on storms. Investigate methods that meteorologists use to measure storms and how these tools have changed over history. How far in advance can meteorologists predict a storm and how accurate are these predictions? You can also conduct a project related to storm safety and how people should behave in a storm. Scientists have broken down each storm into stages. You could create models of each of the stages and provide explanations for each one.

There still remain many questions about how tornadoes form. You can look at differing theories of what causes a tornado and evaluate the evidence for these theories. Where are tornadoes most likely to form and why? With lightning, there are theories on how lightning is attracted to some types of trees more than others. You can investigate what lightning hits and the cause of attraction of each object.

For More Information

"The Disaster Area." *FEMA for Kids.* http://www.fema.gov/kids/dizarea.htm (accessed on August 26, 2003). ❖ Simple instructions and explanations of storms by the Federal Emergency Management Agency.

Grazulis, Thomas P. *Significant Tornadoes 1680–1991.* St. Johnsbury, VT: Environmental Films, 1993. ❖ Comprehensive listing of significant tornadoes and their effects.

experiment
CENTRAL

"Hazardous Weather." *USA Today.com.* http://www.usatoday.com/weather/resources/basics/wsevere0.htm (accessed on August 26, 2003). ❖ Graphics and clear text on hazardous weather phenomena.

Kahl, Jonathan, D. *Thunderbolt: Learning about Lightning.* Minneapolis, MN: Lerner Publishing Group, 1993. ❖ Simple explanations, photographs, and charts related to lightning.

Kramer, Stephen. P. *Lightning.* Minneapolis, MN: Lerner Publishing Group, 1993. ❖ Lots of illustrations and color to explain this phenomena.

Powell, Corey S. "Turn! Turn! Turn! Scientists unravel the twisted ways of tornadoes." *Scientific American,* May 20, 1996. http://www.sciam.com/article.cfm?articleID=00007AD9-70C1-1C76-9B81809EC588EF21 (accessed on August 26, 2003). ❖ A look at the information scientists know about tornadoes.

"Thunderstorms." *Met Office.* http://www.met-office.gov.uk/education/curriculum/leaflets/thunderstorms.html (accessed on August 26, 2003). ❖ Thunderstorms leaflet includes illustrations.

"Tornadoes: The Most Ferocious Storm." *The Why Files.* http://whyfiles.org/013tornado/tornado_main1.html (accessed on August 26, 2003). ❖ Clear, basic information on the formation and effects of a tornado, with the tornado scale.

"Weather Resources." *Weather.com.* http://www.weather.com/education/student/index.html (accessed on August 26, 2003). ❖ Articles on various weather-related phenomena, including an encyclopedia and information on weather careers.

chapter 26

Time

Anyone who has ever raced to finish an activity knows the importance of time. In modern day, people monitor time by the minute. Yet thousands of years ago, keeping track of time was not important. People went about their work and play when the Sun was in the sky and they slept when the Sun was down. Over the years, people began to notice patterns in the Sun's rising and falling. Eventually these patterns led to a system of keeping time that was accepted throughout the world.

The natural rhythms of the Sun and Moon established the time concepts of year, month, and day. Other timekeeping classifications—weeks, hours, minutes, and seconds—are manmade inventions. The concept of time has intrigued some of the most prominent scientists. It has also led to the development of several major discoveries.

Breaking up time

Ancient Egyptians noticed that the Sun rose at different positions on the horizon depending on the season. In the warmer season when the crops grew, the Sun rose farther to the north. In the cooler season after the last harvest, the Sun rose farther to the south. They noted the position of the sunrise on a particular morning and tracked this position through the seasons. They found it took 365 sunrises before the Sun returned to the same position. Today people know that 365 days is the time it takes Earth to orbit around the Sun. We call that length of time a year. Technically, a year is 365 days, 5 hours, 48 minutes, and 46 seconds.

The ancient Egyptians also noticed a full moon occurred once every 29½ days—which is what we now called a month, from the

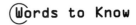

Words to Know

Control experiment:
A setup that is identical to the experiment, but is not affected by the variable that acts on the experimental group.

Gnomon:
The perpendicular piece of the sundial that casts the shadow.

Greenwich Mean Time (GMT):
The time at an imaginary line that runs north and south through Greenwich, England, used as the standard for time throughout the world.

Did You Know?

- On the planet Mercury a day lasts for 58.7 Earth days (the time it takes for Mercury to spin once on its axis). A year on the planet Pluto is about 248 Earth years.

- The abbreviations A.M. and P.M. come from the Romans, who described the hours before mid-day as *ante meridiem*, meaning "before noon," and the hours after midday as *post meridiem*, meaning "after noon."

- If you look at a star 240 trillion miles (384 trillion kilometers) away, the light you are seeing started out from the star 40 years ago.

- Water clocks were the first alarm clocks. They were made to set off an alarm to wake up monks in medieval monasteries for their prayers.

- Today is ever so slightly longer than yesterday. Earth's spin is slowing down, but it is so gradual that each day is 0.00000002 seconds longer than the one before. That means every 7,500 years a whole day will be lost.

Words to Know

Hypothesis:
An idea in the form of a statement that can be tested by observation and/or experiment.

Oscillation:
A repeated back-and-forth movement.

Pendulum:
A free-swinging weight, usually consisting of a heavy object attached to the end of a long rod or string, suspended from a fixed point.

Solar day:
Called a day, the time between each arrival of the Sun at its highest point.

Sidereal day:
The time it takes for a particular star to travel around and reach the same position in the sky; about four minutes shorter than the average solar day.

Sundial:
A device that uses the position of the Sun to indicate time.

Greek and Latin words for moon. The Egyptians chose to split up a month into groups of seven days. Historians theorize they could have selected the number seven because ancient peoples believed (wrongly) that seven heavenly bodies revolved around Earth.

As Earth revolves around the Sun, the planet also rotates. A day is the amount of time it takes for Earth to complete one rotation. As it spins, half of Earth faces the Sun and has light; the other half faces away from the Sun and is dark. When a day exactly begins depends upon one's point of view. Ancient Egyptians began their day at dawn; Babylonians, Jews, and Muslims began at dusk; and Romans began their day at midnight. A **solar day** is the time it takes the Sun to return to its highest point in the sky. While the average day in a year measures twenty-four hours, lengths of individual days vary. After Earth has completed one rotation it must spin for about an extra four minutes around the Sun for the Sun to reach the same point in the

sky. Astronomers measure a day by the length of time it takes for Earth to make a complete turn with respect to the stars, which is constant throughout the year. This is called a **sidereal day** and it lasts 23 hours 56 minutes and 4.1 seconds of average solar time.

It takes 365 days—one year—for Earth to orbit around the Sun. (Reproduced by permission of NASA.)

Hours came about when Egyptians studied the movement of the stars at night. They noted a regular motion of the stars and divided the night into twelve equal parts, based on the rising of a particular star or stars in the night sky. They then decided to divide the day into the same number of parts, known as hours.

To measure daylight's hours, they used a **sundial** to track a shadow as the Sun moved across the sky (actually as Earth revolved beneath the Sun). A sundial has an upright part in the center called a **gnomon.** The gnomon casts a shadow across a surface that is divided into twelve equal parts. As the Sun moves across the sky, the tip of the gnomon's shadow creeps across the twelve sections. The sundials in

Egypt were probably fairly accurate because this area is relatively close to the equator. Near the equator the position of the Sun is always high overhead throughout the year, and the length of time the sun is up each day is almost constant. Farther north or south from the equator, the time the sun is up can be very long or very short depending on the season. For example, in northern Alaska the Sun never sets in mid-summer and never rises during mid-winter. Under those conditions, sundials would not be of much value in keeping time.

The **water clock** was another type of time measurement that ancient people used. The water clock did not depend on an area's location or the changing rhythms of the Sun. In a water clock, a bowl with a small hole in the bottom was filled with water. Lines were marked on the inside of the bowl to symbolize the hours. As the water dripped slowly out the bottom, the water level sank, revealing the lines in the bowl. A water clock worked steadily at all times of the night and day, but someone had to refill the supply of water when it was empty.

Swing time

A revolution in science that began in the sixteenth century had a significant impact on time. First, Polish mathematician Nicolas Copernicus (1473–1543) found that Earth rotates around the Sun, not the

LEFT:
Sundials tell time by the position of the sun. (Corbis-Bettmann. Reproduced by permission.)

RIGHT:
The water clock was a type of time measurement that ancient peoples used.

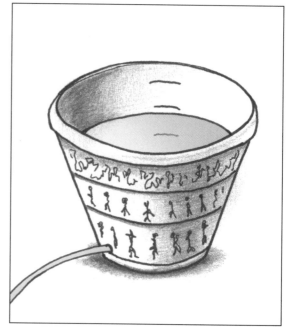

other way around as was previously believed. His work caused a great deal of controversy because it was generally accepted at the time that Earth was the center of the universe. Eventually, the Copernican theory became accepted, and people could know Earth's location when they calculated time.

Then in 1581 Italian teenager Galileo Galilei (1564–1642) made a significant finding. The story goes that while Galileo was attending a church service, he began to watch a heavy lamp swinging from a chain attached to the ceiling. He used his pulse as a timepiece to note how long it took for each swing or **oscillation.** Whether the length of the swings was long or short, each swing always took the same amount of time.

In the late 1500s, Galileo Galilei was the first to begin experimenting with the concepts of a pendulum and oscillation. (Courtesy of the Library of Congress.)

Galileo began experimenting with a **pendulum,** a free-swinging weight, usually consisting of a heavy object attached to the end of a long rod or string, suspended from a fixed point. He found that the amount of time it takes a pendulum to complete one full swing had nothing to do with the weight of the pendulum or how far the pendulum swings. The length of time it takes for the pendulum to go back and forth depends only on the length of the pendulum. Galileo designed a simple pendulum timepiece, but he never built it.

In 1656 Dutch scientist Christian Huygens (1629-1695) used Galileo's ideas of oscillation to build the first pendulum clock. Inside this clock the regular movements of the pendulum turned wheels that controlled the hands of the clock. It was accurate to within one minute a day.

A mess of times

Until the late 1800s, the world was a jumble of times. Countries, cities, and even neighboring towns were using their own local time,

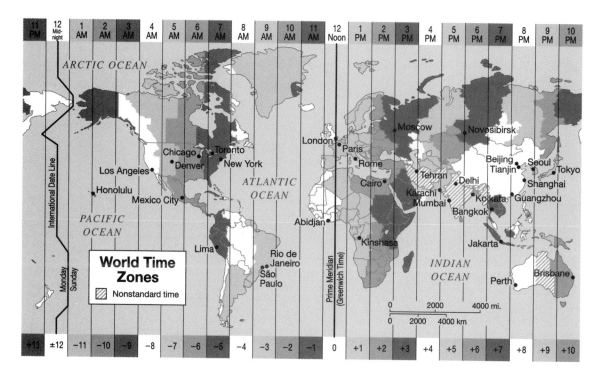

setting their clocks to noon when the Sun was directly overhead. Four o'clock in one city could be seven minutes past four in a town a short distance away. As travel, industry, and communication began to grow, it was decided there should be a standard time throughout the world.

In 1884 the world was officially divided into twenty-four time zones, like twenty-four segments of an orange. There was one zone for each hour of the day, and the time within each zone was the same. The starting point for the time zones was an imaginary north-south line that ran through Greenwich, England. The east-west distance around the world from this imaginary line determined each area's time zone. This system of time is called **Greenwich Mean Time** (GMT).

Space-time: It's all relative

Moving into the past and future has long been a favorite theme of science fiction authors, but the subject of moving in time has also fascinated scientists. For years people thought that time was an absolute: It could not be stretched or condensed. In 1887 two scientists found that the speed of light—how fast light travels in a vacuum—appeared unchanged by the movement of its source or that of the observer. The speed of light is rounded off to 186,000 miles per second (297,600 kilometers per second).

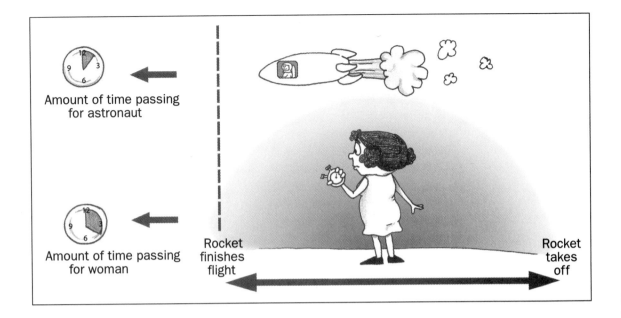

Amount of time passing
for astronaut

Amount of time passing
for woman

Rocket
finishes
flight

Rocket
takes
off

Then in the early 1900s physicist Albert Einstein (1879–1955) changed people's view of time and space. Where something is located is its place in space. Einstein said that time combines with space to form space-time, and that it is not absolute: How fast time moves depends on how fast the person measuring time is moving in space. Einstein's theory showed that time is relative, and so his theory is called the **Theory of Special Relativity.** The faster an object travels, the more slowly time passes for that object. This would only be noticeable at speeds approaching the speed of light.

The Theory of Special Relativity says that time is relative: Less time will pass for the person in the fast-moving rocket than for a person moving relatively slowly.

A simple theoretical example would be how you would perceive time if you were looking at a clock while moving away from it on a rocket traveling at the speed of light. When you first look back at the clock, you see that it reads 2 hours, 20 minutes, and 11 seconds. This image of the clock is being carried to you through space on a beam of light traveling at the speed of light—the same speed as your rocket. When you look back at the clock 5 seconds later, you discover that the clock still reads the same time as it did before because the beam of light is just barely able to keep up with your rocket, so the image you see does not change. Therefore time does not change for you either.

Atomic time

Over the years scientists have broken up time into increasingly smaller bits. In the early 2000s, a scientist can measure a millionth of a billionth of a billionth of a second. To divide time with such precision, researchers again turned to something found in nature—a vibrating atom. The negative charges in atoms oscillate at a regular and nonchanging rhythm. Atomic clocks tell time by measuring the frequency of oscillations of one particular atom, cesium. One second is now defined as the time it takes a cesium atom to make 9,192,631,770 oscillations.

The first atomic clock was developed in the 1940s and its accuracy was improved upon in the early 1990s. This clock is so accurate that it loses or gains just one second every 1.6 million years.

Experiment 1
Pendulums: How do the length, weight, and swing angle of a pendulum affect its oscillation time?

Purpose/Hypothesis
The swing of a pendulum led to one of the first accurate timepieces ever developed. There are three main factors in a pendulum: the weight hanging on the pendulum, the length of the pendulum from the point of suspension to the weight, and the distance or angle of the pendulum's swing. In this experiment, you will predict what factors affect the amount of time it takes a pendulum to complete one full back-and-forth motion, or oscillation.

Before you begin, make an educated guess about the outcome of this experiment based on your knowledge of pendulums. This educated guess, or prediction, is your **hypothesis.** A hypothesis should explain these things:

- the topic of the experiment
- the **variable** you will change
- the variable you will measure
- what you expect to happen

A hypothesis should be brief, specific, and measurable. It must be something you can test through further investigation. Your experiment will prove or disprove whether your hypothesis is correct. Here is one possible hypothesis for this experiment: "The time it takes a pendulum to complete an oscillation is only affected by

What Are the Variables?

Variables are anything that might affect the results of an experiment. Here are the main variables in this experiment:

- the weight of the substance on the pendulum
- the length of the string or twine
- the angle of the pendulum's swing

In other words, the variables in this experiment are everything that might affect the pendulum's oscillation. If you change more than one variable at the same time, you will not be able to tell which variable had the most effect on the time it takes to make one oscillation.

the length of the pendulum: the shorter the length, the less time it takes."

In this case, the variables you will change, one at a time, are the weight you hang on the pendulum, the length of the pendulum, and the angle of its swing. The variable you will measure is the time it takes for the pendulum to complete an oscillation.

Conducting a **control experiment** will help you isolate each variable and measure the changes in the dependent variable. Only one variable will change between the control experiment and each of your pendulum trials. To change only one variable at a time, it is important to always begin the pendulum's swing at the same point, and to use the same weight and string length. Then you will change one variable. The pendulum in your control experiment will always have a length of 16 inches (40 centimeters), start at a 45-degree angle, and have a weight of two washers.

You will complete three tests in this experiment. You will measure how a pendulum's oscillation is affected by the pendulum's swing angle, weight, and length. For each variable you will use a stopwatch to note the exact time it takes for the pendulum to complete one back-and-forth swing, or oscillation. To lessen the effect of human error, you will conduct three trials of each test, then average the times.

experiment
CENTRAL

Level of Difficulty

Easy to Moderate (because of the number of trials needed).

Materials Needed

- stopwatch
- six metal washers
- a 16-inch (40-centimeter) piece of string or twine
- a 24-inch (60-centimeter) piece of string or twine
- a paperclip
- pendulum support: any stable object at least 3 feet (91 centimeters) high, such as a table
- pencil
- protractor
- masking tape

Approximate Budget

$5 (not counting stopwatch. If you do not have a stopwatch, try using a precise timer that you can start and stop).

Timetable

45 minutes.

Step-by-Step Instructions

1. Tape the pencil onto the table so that half the pencil hangs over the edge of the table (or other pendulum support).
2. Pull a paperclip slightly apart to make a hook and tie the end of the 16-inch (40-centimeter) long piece of string tightly to the closed end of the paperclip. Tie the other end of the string to the pencil. Place two washers on the paperclip hook.
3. Create a chart with a column listing the control, the varying weights, angles, and lengths. List the time it takes for one oscillation across the top row for three trials and the average time.

How to Experiment Safely

Make sure the pendulum stand you are using will not tip over.

Time

	Trial 1	Trial 2	Trial 3	Average
Angle				
45°				
60°				
75°				
Weight				
2 washers				
4 washers				
6 washers				
Length				
8 inches				
16 inches				
24 inches				

4. Tape the protractor to the edge of the table, directly in back of the pendulum so that the 0° mark lines up with the string.

5. Control Swing: Pull the pendulum back to the 45° mark. Using your stopwatch, time how long it takes for the pendulum to complete one full swing. Repeat two more times, noting the times for each swing in the control row for each variable.

6. Swing Angle: Repeat Step 5, pulling the pendulum back to 60° and 75°. Write down the time it takes for each trial.

7. Weight: Add two more washers so there are a total of four washers on the paperclip. Pull the pendulum back to the 45° mark and time one complete swing. When you have completed the three trials, add another two washers and repeat.

8. Length: Remove the string from the pencil and cut the string in half. Tie the 8-inch (20-centimeter) string to the pencil. Return to the standard weight, two washers, and pull back to the standard 45° angle. Time one full swing for the three trials.

Step 5: Pull the pendulum back to the 45° mark.

9. Construct the standard pendulum except with the 24-inch (60 centimeter) piece of string: Attach the paperclip with two washers and tie to the pencil. Pull the weight back to 45° and time one full swing. Repeat two more trials. Note the results in a chart.

Summary of Results

Either with a calculator or by hand, average the three times for each trial and note them on your chart. (In this case, you add up the three times and divide the total by three to get the average.) Compare the data from the nine different tests. Determine which of the variables affected the time of the pendulum's swing—the swing angle, the weight, or the length. How did this variable affect the time? Check your findings against the predictions you made in your hypothesis. You can create three separate graphs of the data, each conveying the results of one variable, and compare them to each other. The y-axis can represent the change in the variable and the x-axis can represent the amount of time it takes to complete an oscillation.

Change the Variables

Using the same materials and methods, you can change the variables by combining the different variables you tested. Does using a heavy weight and a short angle cause the time of a pendulum's swing to dif-

Troubleshooter's Guide

Below are some problems that may arise during this experiment, some possible causes, and some ways to remedy the problems.

Problem: One of my trials came out with a much different time than the other two trials.

Possible Cause: This experiment requires careful attention to detail. This could be due to human error. Make sure you always reset the stopwatch after every trial. Redo the three trials again. If you have trouble accurately measuring the time of one swing, measure the time of two swings and divide the time you measured by 2 before recording it on your chart.

Problem: The pendulum is swinging erratically and not moving in a smooth, flat arc.

Possible Cause: Make sure the pendulum stand is on a flat surface and the pencil is flat on that surface. There could also be outside factors effecting the swing, such as wind, the jostling of the pendulum stand, or brushing the string with your hand while swinging.

Problem: The washers are falling off the paperclip.

Possible Cause: Try using either smaller, flatter washers or a larger paperclip. The washers should be of equal size and weight for all trials, but what they weigh will not affect the experiment.

fer between a light weight and a long angle? Would an oscillation of a short cord and a heavy weight take more, less, or the same amount of time than an oscillation of a long cord and a light weight? Make sure you change only one variable at a time so that you can determine which variable is causing the change. For example, if you are looking at the heavy weight/short angle versus the light weight/long angle, conduct an experiment first timing the oscillation of a heavy weight/short angle, a heavy weight/long angle, a light weight/short angle, and a light weight/long angle.

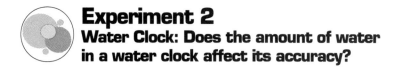

Experiment 2
Water Clock: Does the amount of water in a water clock affect its accuracy?

Purpose/Hypothesis

Unlike sundials, water clocks do not depend on the daylight hours or a sunny day. This fact made water clocks useful timekeeping devices among ancient cultures. There are many different versions of water clocks. Ancient water clocks used one container with markings on it. A later water clock design has water drip at a constant rate from one container into another container below it. The height of the water in the bottom container indicates the amount of time that has passed since the clock was started.

One challenge in designing an accurate water clock relates to the rate at which the water flows or drips out of the container. The quantity of water in a container is one factor that can affect the drip rate of the water. In a container of water, all the water pushes downwards, causing pressure on the water at the bottom. A greater quantity of water will cause a greater quantity of pressure pushing downwards; less water will result in less pressure.

In this experiment you will investigate how the amount of water can affect a water clock's accuracy. You will first make a simple water clock and measure a specific period of time with the water always remaining at a constant level. This will be your control. You will then use three different levels of water that will each drip into the container: a quarter, half, and three-quarters filled.

Before you begin, make an educated guess about the outcome of this experiment based on your knowledge of water clocks and time-keeping. This educated guess, or prediction, is your **hypothesis.** A hypothesis should explain these things:

- the topic of the experiment
- the **variable** you will change
- the variable you will measure
- what you expect to happen

A hypothesis should be brief, specific, and measurable. It must be something you can test through further investigation. Your experiment will prove or disprove whether your hypothesis is correct. Here is one

What Are the Variables?

Variables are anything that might affect the results of an experiment. Here are the main variables in this experiment:

- The temperature of the water
- The size of the containers
- The size of the hole in the container
- The number of containers the water flows through
- The amount of water used

In other words, the variables in this experiment are everything that might affect the drip rate of the water. If you change more than one variable at the same time, you will not be able to tell which variable had the most effect on the water clock's accuracy.

possible hypothesis for this experiment: "As the amount of water in a water clock decreases, the accuracy of the water clock will also decrease."

In this case, the variable you will change is the amount of water in the water clock. The variable you will measure is the clock's ability to measure time. At the end of the experiment you will examine the water's ability to keep time compared to the control.

Having a control experiment will help you isolate each variable and measure the changes in the dependent variable. Only one variable will change between the control experiment and the experimental water clocks, and that is the amount of water in the container. For the control experiment you will use a full container that will have level water pressure and time one minute. At the end of the experiment you will compare the one-minute markings with the markings of the experimental clocks.

Level of Difficulty

Moderate.

Materials Needed

- thumbtack or pin

- watch with second hand
- ruler
- water
- rectangular plastic container (roughly 1 gallon or 3.7 liters)
- cylindrical tall glass jar
- two chairs, with flat seats
- masking tape
- cup
- marking pen

Approximate Budget
$10.

Timetable
45 minutes.

Step-by-Step Instructions
1. Measure the height of the rectangular plastic container and draw a mark at the one-quarter, one-half, and three-quarters points.
2. Use the thumbtack to punch a small hole in the bottom of the plastic container in the center. Position the container so that each side rests on a chair, with the middle open.
3. Place the cylindrical glass on the floor directly beneath the hole.
4. Hold your finger tightly over the hole in the plastic container and completely fill the container with water. Have a cup of water nearby to keep the container full as the water drips out.
5. Take your finger off the hole and let the water drip out into the glass on the floor for 1 minute. While the water is dripping, refill the container with water so that it remains completely full.
6. After 1 minute place your finger over the hole and empty the container in a sink. Place a piece of masking tape lengthwise along the

How to Experiment Safely
This project poses very few hazards. Be careful with the thumbtack. If you are concerned about spilling water, place old newspapers on the floor under the area where you are conducting the experiment.

Setup of Experiment 2: Making a water clock.

cylindrical glass and draw a small line on the tape at the water level.

7. Use the ruler to precisely measure the height of the water in the glass. This measurement equals 1 minute. From the 1-minute mark measure four more 1-minute marks. You should have five evenly spaced lines along the masking tape, one for each minute.

8. Return the plastic container to its position on the chairs. Hold your finger over the hole and fill the water level to the one-quarter

Troubleshooter's Guide

Below is a problem that may arise during this experiment, a possible cause, and a way to remedy the problem.

Problem: The water ran out before it completes the five minutes.

Solution: The pinhole may be too large or your plastic container may not be large enough. Repeat the experiment, using a smaller pin or thumbtack. You could also shorten your time measurement, but the experiment works best if timed for at least three minutes.

mark. Remove your finger and time how long the water takes to reach each of the marks on the tape. Do not put more water in the container. Note your results in a chart.

9.   Repeat the process with the starting water level at the one-half point and the three-quarters point. Note your results.

Summary of Results

Examine your chart of the times. Was your hypothesis correct? How did the starting water level at the one-quarter mark compare to the control minute? How did the times change as a result of the water level? Plot your results with the time on one axis and the starting water level on the other axis. Can you think of ways to make your water clock remain accurate? Write a summary of your results and conclusions.

 # Design Your Own Experiment

How to Select a Topic Relating to this Concept

The topic of time has many angles that you can explore. You could examine areas related to the mechanical property of time, such as in a watch or grandfather clock. Other topics you could explore include cultural differences in keeping time, the inventions of keeping time and how they have impacted everyday life; and the theory of time travel.

Check the For More Information section and talk with your science or physics teacher to learn more about time. If you want to build something for an experiment, such as a timekeeping device, make sure to check with an adult before using any tools.

Steps in the Scientific Method

To do an original experiment, you need to plan carefully and think things through. Otherwise you might not be sure what question you are answering, what you are or should be measuring, or what your findings prove or disprove.

Here are the steps in designing an experiment:

•   State the purpose of—and the underlying question behind—the experiment you propose to do.
•   Recognize the variables involved and select one that will help you answer the question at hand.

- State your hypothesis, an educated guess about the answer to your question.
- Decide how to change the variable you selected.
- Decide how to measure your results.

Recording Data and Summarizing the Results

In any experiment you conduct, you should look for ways to clearly convey your data. You can do this by including charts and graphs for the experiments. They should be clearly labeled and easy to read. You may also want to include photographs and drawings of your experimental setup and results, which will help others visualize the steps in the experiment. You might decide to conduct an experiment that lasts several months. In this case, include pictures or drawings of the results taken at regular intervals.

If you are preparing an exhibit, you may want to display your results, such as any experimental setup you designed. If you have completed a nonexperimental project, explain clearly what your research question was and illustrate your findings.

Related Projects

The subject of time is a broad one and can include many projects. You could examine how different timekeeping devices work, such as a watch and a solar watch, by carefully taking them apart. You could also investigate solar time by building a sundial. There are many different types of sundials. You can build a sundial with the goal to tell time to within minutes or build a sundial to examine how keeping time with it changes over the seasons. Other timekeeping devices you could explore include a shadow clock, a sand clock, and different types of water clocks.

You could also examine the idea of time and relativity. There are scientists who hypothesize that moving backwards or forwards in time is theoretically possible, and there are other scientists who disagree. You could explore this debate and make your own conclusions.

For More Information

"Albert Einstein: Person of the Century." *Time.com*. http://www.time.com/time/time100/poc/home.html (accessed August 26, 2003). ❖ Albert Einstein was named *Time* magazine's Person of the Century; site includes articles, links, and the runners up.

The Children's Museum of Indianapolis. http://www.childrensmuseum.org/generalinfo/waterclock.htm (accessed August 26, 2003). ❖ The largest water clock in North America: 26.5 feet tall.

Ganeri, Anita. *The Story of Time and Clocks.* New York: Oxford University Press, 1996. ❖ Explores the development of recording and measuring time.

Local Times Around the World. http://www.hilink.com.au/times (accessed August 26, 2003). ❖ See what time it is in places around the world.

MacRobert, Alan M. "Time and the Amateur Astronomer." *Sky & Telescope.* http://skyandtelescope.com/howto/basics/article_259_1.asp (accessed August 26, 2003). ❖ Summary of the different time systems used from ancient to modern day.

Skurzynski, Gloria. *From Seasons to Split Seconds.* Washington D.C.: National Geographic Society, 2000. ❖ The history and science of time and timekeeping.

Snedden, Robert. *Time.* New York: Chelsea House, 1996. ❖ Looks at scientists involved with time and time's role in the universe.

experiment
CENTRAL

chapter 27

Vitamins and Minerals

Vitamins and **minerals** are substances that are essential for people to grow, develop, and remain healthy. Vitamins are **organic,** meaning that they contain carbon and come from living organisms. Minerals are **inorganic,** meaning that they do not contain carbon or come from living organisms. Except for two vitamins, humans cannot make any of their own vitamins and minerals. People must get these nutrients from foods. Diseases characterized by lack of nutrients are called **deficiency diseases.**

There are hundreds of vital functions that require proper vitamins and minerals. Maintaining strong bones and muscles, ensuring good vision, healing wounds, providing energy, and fighting infections are a few examples of how the body uses these substances. For years researchers focused their work on determining the amount of each vitamin and mineral needed to avoid any health problems. The **Recommended Daily Allowance (RDA)** are guidelines formulated by the U.S. government for the amount of each substance a person needs every day. Researchers also are exploring how vitamins and minerals can prevent and treat disease.

An alphabet of vitamins

The discovery of vitamins is a story of many people working to understand disease symptoms. In England during the 1700s, it was common for sailors traveling on long voyages to develop bleeding gums, loose teeth, and bruised skin. Some symptoms were more severe and caused many sailors to die. A Scottish naval doctor found that citrus fruits cured the sick sailors, and prevented others from getting ill. The

Words to Know

Control experiment:
A setup that is identical to the experiment, but is not affected by the variable that acts on the experimental group.

Deficiency disease:
A disease marked by a lack of an essential nutrient in the diet.

Fat-soluble vitamins:
Vitamins such as A, D, E, and K that can be dissolved in the fatof plants and animals.

Fortified:
The addition of nutrients, such as vitamins or minerals, to food.

Did You Know?

- British sailors were nicknamed Limeys because they always carried limes in their cargo to prevent scurvy.

- Cats, dogs, and most other animals can make their own Vitamin C.

- Ancient Egyptians knew that night blindness could be cured by eating liver—a food source later found to be rich in vitamin A.

- Researchers can reveal the mineral content of a person's body by analyzing the person's hair. In 2001, a clip of pianist Ludwig van Beethoven's (1770-1827) hair was found to contain a high amount of lead—leading researchers to theorize Beethoven suffered from lead poisoning.

Vitamins and minerals perform many functions in the body and are essential for good health.

Vitamin A for healthy vision

Fluorine gives strong enamel, which prevents cavities

Vitamin K clots blood when cut

A combination of vitamins and minerals gives strong bones and muscles

substance in these fruits was unknown at the time. The disease, called **scurvy,** is now known to be caused by a lack of Vitamin C, also called ascorbic acid.

Other physicians around the world were recognizing how the changes in a person's—or animal's—diet affected health. For the deadly disease beriberi, it was a study of chickens that furthered vitamin research. When a group of chickens started coming down with beriberi-like symptoms, it was discovered they had been fed white rice instead of their usual brown rice. Upon switching them back to the brown rice, the chickens recovered. This led to the theory that patients were not falling ill from something they took in, but from something they were missing from their diet.

In 1913, scientists isolated the first vitamin, Vitamin A, and named it after the first letter of the alphabet. Vitamin B_1, or thiamine, was the first B vitamin found and is the vitamin in brown rice that prevents beriberi, a deficiency disease involving the nervous system. As more vitamins were isolated, scientists continued to name them with letters.

The human body needs thirteen different vitamins. These vitamins serve many functions vital to good health (see chart on page 508). For example, one of Vitamin A's main roles is in the production of **retinal.** Eyes need retinal to sense light, and it is manufactured with the help of

(see chart on page 508)

Words to Know

Hypothesis:
An idea in the form of a statement that can be tested by observation and/or experiment.

Inorganic:
Made of or coming from nonliving matter.

Macrominerals:
Minerals needed in relatively large quantities.

Minerals:
Inorganic substances that originate in the ground; many are essential nutrients.

Organic:
Made of, or coming from, living matter.

Scurvy:
A disease caused by a deficiency of vitamin C, which causes a weakening of connective tissue in bone and muscle.

Supplements:
A substance intended to enhance the diet.

Vitamins	Major functions	Major sources
A (fat soluble)	helps night vision and color vision, growth, healthy skin, fights sickness	apricots, nectarines, carrots, liver, eggs, milk, broccoli, pumpkin
B_1 - thiamine (water soluble)	strong muscles, growth	brown breads, beans, grain, cereals, nuts, peas
B_2 - riboflavin (water soluble)	helps eyesight; heals cuts, bruises; involved in making red blood cells	milk, cheese, eggs, leafy vegetables, meat, brown breads
C - absorbic acid (water soluble)	repairs broken bones, strong gums and teeth, fights infections	green vegetables, berries, tomatoes, oranges, lemons, grapefruit, and citrus juices
D (fat soluble)	strong bones, teeth	body makes this with sun; tunafish, eggs; added to milk
E (fat soluble)	protects eyes, skin, liver; protects lungs from pollution; helps store Vitamin A	vegetable oils, leafy green vegetables, peanuts
K (fat soluble)	clots blood when wounded	leafy green vegetables, cabbage, cheese, broccoli
Minerals		
Calcium	strong teeth, bone; crucial roles in nerve and muscle cells	milk, yogurt, cheeses, fortified in some juices
Iron (trace mineral)	transports oxygen in red blood cells	red meat, poultry, fish, dried beans, apricots, raisins
Zinc (trace mineral)	heals cuts, helps body grow	seafood, liver, eggs, peanuts, grain food, dark meat of chicken
Fluorine (trace mineral)	strong tooth enamel	sardines, salmon, apples, eggs; added to water
Magnesium (macromineral)	strong bones, controls body temperature	milk, eggs, cheese, yogurt, meats, seafood, molasses
Potassium (macromineral)	keeps the heart strong	bananas, potatoes, raisins, melons, broccoli, beef

experiment
CENTRAL

Vitamin A. Even today, Vitamin A deficiency causes blindness in millions around the world, and is a major cause of childhood blindness. Vitamin B_{12} maintains healthy nerve cells and red blood cells, and is also needed to make DNA, the genetic material in all cells.

People's bodies can only make two vitamins—Vitamin K and Vitamin D. The sunlight reacts with a chemical in the skin to produce Vitamin D, which is necessary for hard bones. About half of the Vitamin K a person needs is made in the intestines, from the bacteria that live there. Vitamin K helps make blood clot when there is a cut, preventing too much blood from flowing out of the body. People need to get the rest of the required Vitamin K, and all the other vitamins, through foods.

Fats and water

Vitamins are also divided into two categories: fat-soluble and water-soluble. The **fat-soluble vitamins** dissolve in fats. These vitamins are stored in the body's fat tissues and liver until the body needs them. Fat-soluble vitamins can remain in storage from a few days to a year. Vitamins A, D, E, and K are all fat-soluble vitamins.

Water-soluble vitamins dissolve in water and travel through the bloodstream. They move quickly through the blood and need to be replenished often. As the vitamins stream through the body, organs and tissues pick up the vitamins they need. Whatever the body does not use comes out in urine. Water-soluble vitamins include Vitamin C and the B vitamins.

Mind your minerals

Minerals originate in the ground and are taken in by plants and animals. Water in the ground soaks up such minerals as calcium (Ca), magnesium (Mg), and iron (Fe). This natural, mineral-rich water is called **hard water.** Animals get their minerals when they eat the plants. Plants absorb minerals from the water in the soil (see Soil chapter). People ingest the majority of minerals directly from foods. They either eat plants directly or consume the animals that have eaten the plants.

People need a smaller amount of minerals than vitamins. These minerals play a number of crucial roles. They are needed to build strong bones and teeth, transmit nerve signals, maintain a regular heartbeat, metabolize food, and many other functions.

OPPOSITE PAGE:
A selection of the roles some vitamins and minerals play and their sources.

Vitamins are categorized into two types: water soluble and fat soluble.

water soluble
vitamins travel
in bloodstream

fat soluble
vitamins stored
in liver and fat
until needed

excess vitamins
eliminated

Minerals are categorized into two types based on how much of the mineral a person requires to remain healthy. The two groups are **macrominerals** and **trace minerals.** The body needs a larger amount of macrominerals than trace minerals, although both types are essential. The macromineral group is made up of calcium, phosphorous, magnesium, sodium, potassium, and chloride. Trace minerals include iron, manganese, copper, iodine, zinc, chromium, fluoride, and selenium.

Food sources

Vitamins and minerals are found in a variety of foods. Each type of food contains a certain amount of vitamins and minerals. Some foods are a rich source of these nutrients, such as broccoli, and others, such as soda, are not a significant source. For most people, eating a well-balanced diet with a wide variety of foods supplies the necessary amounts of vitamins and minerals. People who are ill or do not get their nutrients through food take **supplements,** or additional vitamins and minerals.

Minerals in the earth are taken in by plants, which are then ingested by animals. Humans can get their required minerals by eating plants and animals.

For most people, eating a well-balanced diet with a wide variety of foods supplies the necessary amounts of vitamins and minerals.(Copyright © Kelly A. Quin. Reproduced by permission of Kelly A. Quin.)

Many foods are **fortified** or enriched with essential vitamins and minerals. Water, for example, is fortified with additional mineral fluorine. Vitamin D is added to milk after it is heated to kill germs, which causes it to lose Vitamin D in the process. Many cereals and juices are also fortified with vitamins and minerals.

Packages list the RDA for the vitamins and minerals they contain. There are RDAs provided for children, teenagers, and adults. The

RDA listed on food packaging is the amount that an average, healthy adult should consume each day.

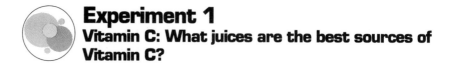

Experiment 1
Vitamin C: What juices are the best sources of Vitamin C?

Purpose/Hypothesis
Vitamin C is a water-soluble vitamin that is essential for human growth and health. In this experiment, you will explore the relative quantity of Vitamin C in different juices. To measure the amount of Vitamin C you will observe the chemical reaction of Vitamin C with iodine.

Iodine mixed with water forms ions, which are charged particles. When ions mix with starch they produce a compound that has a blue color. Ascorbic acid, or Vitamin C, breaks up the bond between the ions and the starch, reversing the color change. The more Vitamin C in a substance, the quicker the bonds will be broken, and the faster the liquid will turn clear.

You will test the Vitamin C content of orange, grapefruit, and apple juice. Make sure all the juices are fresh—not from concentrate. You can use your imagination and test a variety of other juices also, such as tomato, grape, and carrot. You will first create a bond between a starch solution and iodine. You will then slowly add juice to the solution to determine the amount it takes for the juice to break the bond, turning the solution clear.

Before you begin, make an educated guess about the outcome of this experiment based on your knowledge of Vitamin C. This educated guess, or prediction, is your **hypothesis.** A hypothesis should explain these things:

- the topic of the experiment
- the **variable** you will change
- the variable you will measure
- what you expect to happen

A hypothesis should be brief, specific, and measurable. It must be something you can test through further investigation. Your experiment will prove or disprove whether your hypothesis is correct. Here

What Are the Variables?

Variables are anything that might affect the results of an experiment. Here are the main variables in this experiment:

- the type of juice
- the freshness of the juice
- the temperature of the juice

In other words, the variables in this experiment are anything that might affect the speed at which the Vitamin C breaks up the bond. If you change more than one variable at the same time, you will not be able to tell which variable has the highest concentration of Vitamin C.

is one possible hypothesis for this experiment: "The orange juice will contain more Vitamin C than the other two juices."

In this case, the variable you will change is the type of juice. The variable you will measure is the relative amount of juice it takes to make the solution clear.

Conducting a **control experiment** will help you isolate each variable and measure the changes in the dependent variable. Only one variable will change between the control and your experiment. For your control in this experiment you will use a solution of pure Vitamin C. At the end of the experiment you can compare the results of the control with the experimental results.

Level of Difficulty
Moderate.

Materials Needed
- paper towel
- spoon
- 500-milligram Vitamin C tablet
- cornstarch
- four small clear glasses or jars, such as baby food jars
- iodine (available at drug stores)
- apple juice

- orange juice
- grapefruit juice
- other juices: tomato, carrot, or grape (optional)
- dropper
- measuring cup
- measuring spoons
- paper towel
- marking pen
- two mixing cups

Approximate Budget
$10.

Timetable
1 hour.

Step-by-Step Instructions
1. Write the name of the juice to be tested on each of the jars. Label one jar "Vitamin C."
2. To prepare the starch solution, mix 1/2 teaspoon (2.5 milliliters) of cornstarch in 1 cup (0.25 liters) warm water. Stir thoroughly until the cornstarch dissolves.
3. Crush the Vitamin C tablet in a folded paper towel.
4. Dissolve the crushed tablet in 2 cups (0.5 liters) of warm water. The Vitamin C solution is now 500 milligrams/milliliters, or 1 milligram/milliliter. Allow to cool to room temperature.
5. Put 2 tablespoons (30 milliliters) of the starch solution into each jar.
6. Add 1 drop of iodine to each jar. Cap the jar and swirl. The solution should turn blue-black.
7. Test the control solution: Add 1 drop of the Vitamin C solution to its jar and swirl. Add another drop, if needed, until the blue-black color has disappeared. Note the results in a chart.

How to Experiment Safely
Be careful when handling iodine: It is a poison and can stain your skin, clothing, and countertops.

experiment
CENTRAL

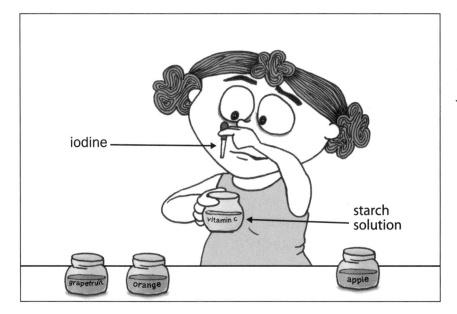

Step 6: Add 1 drop of iodine to each jar. Cap the jar and swirl.

iodine

starch solution

8. Test each juice: Add 1 drop of the orange juice to its jar and swirl. Continue to add drops, swirling after each drop, until the blue color clears completely. Note the number of drops in the chart.
9. Repeat with the apple and the grapefruit juices. Note your results.

Summary of Results

Examine how many drops it took for each juice to dissolve the bond and clear the color. Graph the results of your experiment. Which juice had the highest concentration of Vitamin C? How did this juice com-

Troubleshooter's Guide
Below is a problem that may arise during this experiment, a possible cause, and a way to remedy the problem.

Problem: The pure Vitamin C took as many drops as a juice to turn clear.

Possible cause: You may not have crushed and dissolved the Vitamin C thoroughly. Make sure the tablet is in a fine powder before you pour it in the water, then mix briskly and repeat the experiment.

pare to the test standard, pure Vitamin C? Hypothesize how the Vitamin C content of other types of beverages—vegetable juice, carrot juice, soda, and sports drinks—would compare the juices you tested.

Change the Variables

In this experiment you can change the variables in several ways. You can use the same type of juice, such as orange juice, and vary the brands. You could also test the Vitamin C content in different solid foods by blending a set quantity of each food with a set amount of water. Length of storage, heat, light, and oxygen can all affect the amount of Vitamin C in beverages and food. You could change each of these variables for one kind of food or beverage. With one type of juice you could also vary the freshness. For example, you could test one frozen concentrate orange juice, one store-bought refrigerated orange juice, and one freshly squeezed orange juice.

Experiment 2
Hard Water: Do different water sources have varying mineral content?

Purpose/Hypothesis

Water that contains minerals in it is called hard water. The hardness or level of the mineral content varies from location to location. In this experiment, you will examine the mineral content of various waters by mixing the water with soap.

Two common elements in hard water are magnesium and calcium. These minerals can lessen the cleaning ability of soap by preventing the lathering action. Hard-water minerals readily bind to the soap molecules, forming a large and heavy compound that sinks. The result is a soap scum that does not dissolve in water. (Water softeners remove the hard minerals.)

To determine the hardness of varying water sources, you will mix water with soap. You will use tap water, rainwater, and chalk-water. Chalk is a form of limestone, which is composed of calcium.

Before you begin, make an educated guess about the outcome of this experiment based on your knowledge of minerals and hard water. This educated guess, or prediction, is your **hypothesis.** A hypothesis should explain these things:

What Are the Variables?

Variables are anything that might affect the results of an experiment. Here are the main variables in this experiment:

- the water source
- the amount of soap
- the type of soap
- the mineral added

In other words, the variables in this experiment are everything that might affect the amount of soap scum the water produces. If you change more than one variable at the same time, you will not be able to tell which variable had the most effect on the soap scum.

- the topic of the experiment
- the **variable** you will change
- the variable you will measure
- what you expect to happen

A hypothesis should be brief, specific, and measurable. It must be something you can test through further investigation. Your experiment will prove or disprove whether your hypothesis is correct. Here is one possible hypothesis for this experiment: "The water highest in minerals will be the chalk water; the water least high in minerals will be the rainwater."

In this case, the variable you will change is the water source. The variable you will measure is the hardness of the water.

Conducting a **control experiment** will help you isolate each variable and measure the changes in the dependent variable. Only one variable will change between the control and your experiment. For your control you will use distilled water, water that has no minerals in it. At the end of the experiment you can compare the control and the experimental results.

Level of Difficulty

Easy to Moderate.

Materials Needed

- eyedropper
- liquid soap
- four small plastic bottles with caps
- measuring cup (with spout preferably)
- funnel (optional)
- piece of chalk (calcium)
- tap water
- rain water
- distilled water
- spoon
- cup or bowl to collect rain water
- marking pen

Approximate Budget

$5.

Timetable

45 minutes (not counting the time it takes to wait for rain).

Step-by-Step Instructions

1. On a day when rain is forecast, place a bowl outside to collect at least 1 cup of rainwater.
2. Over a measuring cup, scrape about 1 teaspoon (5 milliliters) of chalk into powder using the edge of a spoon.
3. Measure 1 cup (240 milliliters) of hot distilled water into the cup. Stir the ground chalk and water thoroughly. Cool to room temperature.
4. Label the bottles: "Calcium," "Tap," "Control," and "Rain."
5. Pour the chalk water into its designated bottle. (There may be some chunks left over on the bottom so pour slowly.) You may need to use a funnel for this. Rinse out the measuring cup.

How to Experiment Safely

If you are not using a disposable eyedropper, make sure to wash the dropper thoroughly to remove all traces of the soap. Be careful when handing the hot water.

Step 8: After placing two drops of liquid soap in each of the bottles, shake each bottle and examine the amount of soap scum.

6. Measure out 1 cup (240 milliliters) of tap water and carefully pour into its bottle. Rinse the cup and repeat with the distilled and rain water.
7. Using the eyedropper, place two drops of the liquid soap into each of the bottles.
8. Shake each of the bottles and examine the amount of soap scum. Note a description of the results.
9. Allow the bottles to sit for 15 minutes and, again, note the results.

Summary of Results

Examine the results of your experiment. Was your hypothesis correct? How does the rainwater compare to the control? The ability of soap and detergent to lather directly affects their ability to clean. Hypothesize why water softeners are popular in some areas of the country more than others. What would be the result of simply adding more soap or detergent? Write an analysis of the experiment, including an explanation of your results for each type of water.

Troubleshooter's Guide

Below are some problems that may arise during this experiment, some possible causes, and some ways to remedy the problems.

Problem: The chalk did not dissolve in the water.

Possible cause: You may not have scraped the chalk into a fine enough powder. Chalk will dissolve better in warmer water than cooler water. Repeat the experiment, making sure to use hot water and a fine powder.

Problem: There was no difference in the amount of scum between the calcium water and the tap water.

Possible cause: Try allowing the bottles to sit for another 15 minutes to determine if there is a difference as the soap bubbles disappear.

Change the Variables

In this experiment you can change the variable by altering the water source. You can focus on one type of water, such as tap water or mineral water. Different geographic locales will have varying amounts of mineral in the water. You can also try the experiment on different brands of mineral water. Another variable to change is the soap. What happens if you put water softener in the hard water?

Design Your Own Experiment

How to Select a Topic Relating to this Concept

There are many possible projects related to vitamins and minerals. As almost all foods contain some amounts of vitamins and minerals, you can work with food and beverages. You can also focus on where vitamins and minerals are derived from, and their effect on various life forms.

Check the For More Information section and talk with your science or nutrition teacher to learn more about vitamins and minerals.

You can also gather ideas from examining the vitamin and mineral contents listed on the packaging of the foods you eat.

In order to keep in top physical shape, athletes require the proper balance of vitamins and minerals. (Reproduced by permission of AP/Wide World.)

Steps in the Scientific Method

To conduct an original experiment, you need to plan carefully and think things through. Otherwise, you might not be sure what question you are answering, what you are or should be measuring, or what your findings prove or disprove.

Here are the steps in designing an experiment:

- State the purpose of—and the underlying question behind—the experiment you propose to do.
- Recognize the variables involved and select one that will help you answer the question at hand.
- State your hypothesis, an educated guess about the answer to your question.
- Decide how to change the variable you selected.
- Decide how to measure your results.

Recording Data and Summarizing the Results

Your data could include charts and drawings, such as the one you did for these experiments. They should be clearly labeled and easy to read. You may also want to include photographs and drawings of your experimental setup and results, which will help others visualize the steps in the experiment.

If you are preparing an exhibit, you may want to display your results, such as any experimental setup you designed. If you have completed a nonexperimental project, explain clearly what your research question was and illustrate your findings.

Related Projects

There are many possible project ideas related to vitamins and minerals. You can examine the vitamins and minerals that you and people you know take in by adding up the foods you eat and charting the results. Compare the numbers to the Recommended Daily Allowances (RDA). You can also experiment with removing the minerals from certain types of food.

You could also examine how other species, besides humans, use vitamins and minerals. Different animals produce certain vitamins that humans do not. You could look at what elements these animals produce and how vitamins and minerals impact an animal's health. Vitamin and mineral deficiency is also a serious health problem in many parts of the world. A project on deficiency diseases could include examining several of these diseases and possible foods people of that area could easily attain to stop or prevent the disease. You could also conduct a research project on the history of the discovery of vitamins and minerals, and the work of finding more of these elements.

For More Information

"All About What Vitamins and Minerals Do." *KidsHealth*. http://kidshealth.org/kid/stay_healthy/food/vitamin.html (accessed on August 26, 2003). ❖ Easy-to-read explanation of vitamins and minerals.

Kalbacken, Joan. *Vitamins and Minerals*. San Francisco, CA: Children's Press, 1998. ❖ Simple, basic information about vitamins and minerals.

"Scientists Discover New Vitamin." *MSNBC News*. http://www.msnbc.com/news/904817.asp?0si=- (accessed on August 26, 2003). ❖ News about a new vitamin discovered in 2003.

"Vitamins and Minerals." *Food & Nutrition Information Center*. http://www.nal.usda.gov/fnic/etext/000068.html (accessed on August 26, 2003). ❖ Provides general information, RDA guidelines, and details on vitamins and minerals.

"Vitamins and Minerals." *West Virginia Dietetic Association*. http://www.wvda.org/nutrient/ (accessed on August 26, 2003). ❖ List of all vitamins and minerals, their sources, and functions.

sources for science supplies

The following is a selected list of sources that stock science supplies. Your science teacher and local library are also good sources of information regarding how and where to locate supplies for a science project. Always consult with a parent or teacher before ordering supplies.

American Science and Surplus
P.O. Box 1030
Skokie, IL 60076
(847) 647-0011
Internet: http://sciplus.com

Anchor Optical Surplus
4124 Edscorp Bldg.
Barrington, NJ 08007
(856) 573-6865
Internet: http://www.anchoroptical.com

Carolina Biological Supply Co.
2700 York Road
Burlington, NC 27215-3398
(800) 334-5551
Internet: http://www.carolina.com/

Edvcotek
Box 34123
Bethesda, MD 20827-1232
(800) 338-6835
Internet: http://www.edvotek.com

sources for science supplies

Fisher Science Education
Internet: https://www1.fishersci.com/education/index.jsp

Flinn Scientific Inc.
P.O. Box 219
Batavia, IL 60510
(800) 452-1261
Internet: http://www.flinnsci.com

Sargent-Welch/VWR Scientific Products Science Education
P.O. Box 5229
Buffalo Grove, IL 60089-5229
(800) 727-4368
Internet: http://www.sargentwelch.com

The Science Fair
140 College Square
Newark, DE 19711-5447
(302) 453-1817
Internet: http://thesciencefair.com

Science Stuff
7801 N. Lamar Blvd. #E-190
Austin, TX 78752-1016
(800) 795-7315
Internet: http://www.sciencestuff.com

budget index

Chapter name in brackets, followed by experiment name; *italic* type indicates volume number, followed by page number; **boldface** volume numbers indicate main entries in *Experiment Central*, Volumes 5 and 6.

$5–$10

budget index

$16–$20

$21–$25

$26–$30

$31–$35

budget index

level of difficulty index

Easy

Easy means that the average student should easily be able to complete the tasks outlined in the project/experiment, and that the time spent on the project is not overly restrictive.

Chapter name in brackets, followed by experiment name; *italic* type indicates volume number, followed by page number; **boldface** volume numbers indicate main entries in *Experiment Central*, Volumes 5 and 6.

Easy/Moderate

Easy/Moderate means that the average student should have little trouble completing the tasks outlined in the project/experiment, and that the time spent on the project is not overly restrictive.

Moderate

Moderate means that the average student should find tasks outlined in the project/experiment challenging but not difficult, and that the time spent on the project/experiment may be more extensive.

**level of
difficulty
index**

Moderate/Difficult

Moderate/Difficult means that the average student should find tasks out-lined in the project/experiment challenging, and that the time spent on the project/experiment may be more extensive.

**level of
difficulty
index**

Difficult

*Difficult means that the average student will probably find the tasks out-
lined in the project/experiment mentally and/or physically challenging,
and that the time spent on the project/experiment will be more extensive.*

timetable index

Chapter name in brackets, followed by experiment name; *italic* type indicates volume number, followed by page number; **boldface** volume numbers indicate main entries in *Experiment Central*, Volumes 5 and 6.

1 hour

2 hours

3 hours

6 hours

1 day

2 days

3 days

6 days

experiment
CENTRAL

general subject index

This index cumulates entries from the six-volume *Experiment Central* series. *Italic* type indicates volume number; **boldface** type indicates entries in Volumes 5 and 6; (ill.) indicates illustration or photograph.

**general
subject
index**

**general
subject
index**

general
subject
index

general
subject
index

general subject index

general subject index